Steck-Vaughn

English ASAP™

Connecting English to the Workplace

SCANS Consultant

Shirley Brod
Spring Institute for International Studies
Boulder, Colorado

Program Consultants

Judith Dean-Griffin
ESL Teacher
Windham Independent School District
Texas Department of Criminal Justice
Huntsville, Texas

Marilyn K. Spence
Workforce Education Coordinator
Orange Technical Education Centers
Mid-Florida Tech
Orlando, Florida

Brigitte Marshall
English Language Training
for Employment Participation
Albany, California

Dennis Terdy
Director, Community Education
Township High School District 214
Arlington Heights, Illinois

Christine Kay Williams
ESL Specialist
Towson University
Baltimore, Maryland

STECK-VAUGHN
ELEMENTARY · SECONDARY · ADULT · LIBRARY
A Harcourt Company

www.steck-vaughn.com

Acknowledgments

Executive Editor:	Ellen Northcutt
Supervising Editor:	Tim Collins
Assistant Art Director:	Richard Balsam
Interior Design:	Richard Balsam, Jill Klinger, Paul Durick
Electronic Production:	Stephanie Stewart, Alan Klemp, David Hanshaw
Assets Manager:	Margie Foster

Editorial Development: Course Crafters, Inc., Newburyport, Massachusetts

Photo Credits

Alhadeff–p.15b, 15c, 27b, 34-35, 39a, 39b, 39c, 46-47, 51d, 58-59, 63a, 63c, 94-95, 106-107, 114, 118-119; Don Couch Photography–p.75a, 75c, 87a, 87b, 87d, 111d; Jack Demuth–p.3a, 3c, 15d, 27a, 27c, 51b, 52a, 52b, 87c, 99a, 99b, 116; Patrick Dunn–p.27d, 111c; Christine Galida-p.15a, 54, 57, 63b, 65, 111a, 111b, 113; David Omer–p.22-23, 82-83; Park Street–p.10-11, 30, 39d, 51a, 51c, 70-71, 75b, 75d, 99d; Ken Walker–p.3b, 3d, 52c, 73, 99c.

Illustration Credits

Cover: Tim Dove, D Childress

Cindy Aarvig–16, 19; Meg Aubrey (Represented by Cornell & McCarthy, LLC) p. 140; Karl Bailey–24, 28a, 28c-i, 35c, 35e, 91; Richard Balsam–6, 10-12, 14, 31, 33, 34, 35f, 37, 40b, 46, 49b, 95b, 96e-h, 97b, 104; Chris Celusniak–29, 42, 89, 90, 97a; David Griffin–17, 18, 25, 88, 98; Dennis Harms–36, 38; Laura Jackson–28b, 28j, 35a-b, 35d; Chuck Joseph–41, 64, 71, 76, 82-86, 100, 106-109, 112, 118-122, 137, 146; Linda Kelen–66, 96a-d; Michael Krone–5, 53, 68, 69, 92, 93, 135; John Scott–21, 94, 95a; kreativ-design/ Danielle Szabo–3, 15, 22, 23, 26, 27, 39, 40a, 43, 45, 47, 48, 49a, 50, 51, 58, 59, 61, 62, 63, 70, 72, 74, 75, 87, 99, 111; Victoria Vebell–77, 78, 101, 102.

ISBN 0-8172-7955-5

Contents

Units	SCANS Competencies	Workforce Skills
Communication	Serve customers Interpret and communicate information Understand technological systems	Take telephone messages Answer the telephone at work Make telephone calls Find telephone numbers
Your Workplace	Organize information Understand organizational systems Allocate materials	Get supplies Organize materials Maintain supplies and equipment Use filing systems
Technology	Monitor and correct performance Maintain and troubleshoot technology Select equipment and tools Apply technology to specific tasks	Complete a maintenance report Talk about problems with machines Read a user's manual
Time Management	Allocate time Interpret information Understand organizational systems	Understand schedules Interpret a holiday schedule Use calendars and planners
Customer Service	Serve customers Interpret and communicate information Participate as a member of a team Work with cultural diversity	Respond to requests Handle special requests Offer suggestions Understand customer service policies
Culture of Work	Understand social systems Interpret and communicate information Work on teams	Follow rules Make compromises Understand company goals Get along with others
Finances	Acquire and evaluate data Interpret and communicate information Allocate money Understand organizational systems	Understand a paycheck Report mistakes in your paycheck Understand Social Security Understand a W-2 form
Health and Safety	Interpret information Understand technological systems Apply technology to specific tasks Maintain and troubleshoot technologies Work on teams	Understand safety instructions Follow safety instructions Complete an accident report Report unsafe situations
Working with People	Allocate time Work on teams Acquire and evaluate data Interpret and communicate information Understand social systems Understand organizational systems	Understand an agenda Prepare for a meeting Ask questions in a meeting Make meetings work for you
Career Development	Organize and maintain information Interpret and communicate information Understand social systems Understand organizational systems Monitor and correct performance	Look for a job Interview for a job Understand hiring decisions Complete a job application

Each unit of *English ASAP* systematically presents one or more SCANS Competencies.
The SCANS Foundation Skills are integrated throughout the instruction.

Units	Grammar
Communication	Present tense of **be** (contractions) Simple present tense Present tense of **have** Object pronouns
Your Workplace	**There is/there are** (questions, short answers) **Some/any** Adverbials of location
Technology	Simple past tense (statements, negatives, questions, short answers) Irregular past tense (statements, negatives)
Time Management	**Have to** **Going to**
Customer Service	Simple past tense (**wh-** and **yes/no** questions, short answers) More irregular verbs in the simple past tense
Culture of Work	Comparative adjectives with **-er** and **more**
Finances	Polite requests with **could** Clauses with **so** and **because**
Health and Safety	**Should/shouldn't** Conditional sentences with **should**
Working with People	**Have to** (review) **(I)'d like to** Clauses with **so** and **because** (review)
Career Development	Simple past tense (review) Adverbs

English ASAP is a complete, communicative, SCANS-based, four-skill ESL program for teaching adult and young adult learners the skills they need to succeed at work.

FEATURES

♦ *English ASAP* **is SCANS-based.** *English ASAP*'s SCANS-based syllabus teaches skills learners need to succeed in the workplace. The syllabus is correlated with the SCANS competencies, a taxonomy of work skills recognized by the U.S. Department of Labor as essential to every job. Additionally, the syllabus is compatible with the work skills and competencies in the Comprehensive Adult Student Assessment System (CASAS) Competencies, the Mainstream English Language Training Project (MELT), the National Institute for Literacy's Equipped for the Future Framework for Adult Literacy, and state curriculums for adult ESL from Texas and California.

 The *On Your Job* symbol appears on the Student Book page and corresponding page in the Teacher's Edition each time learners apply a SCANS-based skill to their jobs or career interests.

♦ *English ASAP* **is about the world of work.** All of the conversations, reading selections, listening activities, and realia are drawn from authentic workplace situations. *English ASAP* presents settings and workers from major career clusters, including transportation, health care, service occupations, office occupations, construction, hospitality, and industrial occupations.

♦ *English ASAP* **teaches the skills required in all job descriptions.** Learners gain valuable experience working in teams; teaching others; serving customers; organizing, evaluating, and communicating information; understanding and using technology; negotiating; allocating resources; and completing projects.

♦ *English ASAP* **is communicative.** Numerous conversational models and communicative activities in the Student Books and Teacher's Editions—including problem-solving activities, surveys, and cooperative learning projects—get learners talking from the start.

♦ **English ASAP is appropriate for adults and young adults.** The language and situations presented in *English ASAP* are ones adults and young adults are likely to encounter. The abundance of attractive, true-to-life photographs, illustrations, and realia will interest and motivate adult and young adult learners.

- ◆ *English ASAP* **addresses all four language skills.** Each level of *English ASAP* addresses listening, speaking, reading, and writing. Starting in Level 1, a two-page grammar spread in each Student Book unit plus corresponding Workbook reinforcement and supplementary grammar Blackline Masters in the Teacher's Editions ensure that learners get appropriate grammar practice.

- ◆ *English ASAP* **starts at the true beginner level.** *English ASAP* begins at the Literacy Level, designed for learners who have no prior knowledge of English and have few or no literacy skills in their native language(s) or are literate in a language with a non-Roman alphabet. Learners master foundation literacy skills in tandem with listening and speaking skills. The next level, Level 1, is intended for learners with little or no prior knowledge of English. As learners continue through the program, they master progressively higher levels of language and work skills. The Placement Tests help teachers place learners in the appropriate level of the program. For information on placement, see page v of this Teacher's Edition.

- ◆ *English ASAP* **is appropriate for multilevel classes.** Because unit topics carry over from level to level with increasing sophistication, the series is ideal for use in multilevel classes. For example, a Literacy Level skill in the technology unit is naming machines. A Level 2 skill in the technology unit is completing machine maintenance reports. Units are situational and nonsequential, making *English ASAP* appropriate for open-entry/open-exit situations.

- ◆ *English ASAP* **meets the needs of individual workplaces and learners.** Because the demands of each workplace and each individual's job are unique, the abundance of *On Your Job* activities allows learners to relate their new skills to their workplaces and career interests. In addition, the Personal Dictionary feature in each unit beginning with Level 1 lets learners focus only on the vocabulary they need to do their jobs. Finally, with Steck-Vaughn's *Workforce Writing Dictionary,* learners can create a complete custom dictionary of all the vocabulary they need to know to succeed.

COMPONENTS

English ASAP consists of:

♦ Student Books

♦ Workbooks starting at Level 1

♦ Teacher's Editions

♦ Audiocassettes

♦ Steck-Vaughn *Workforce Writing Dictionary*

♦ Placement Tests, Form A and Form B

Student Books

Each four-color Student Book consists of ten 12-page units, providing learners with ample time on task to acquire the target SCANS competencies and language.

♦ **The Student Books follow a consistent format for easy teaching and learning.** Each unit is consistently organized and can be taught in approximately eight to twelve classroom sessions.

♦ **Complete front matter offers valuable teaching suggestions.** Ideas on how to teach each type of activity in the Student Book units and suggested teaching techniques give teachers valuable information on how to use *English ASAP* with maximum success.

♦ **Clear directions and abundant examples ensure that learners always know exactly what to do.** Examples for each activity make tasks apparent to learners and teachers. Clear exercise titles and directions tell teachers and learners exactly what learners are to do.

♦ **Performance Check pages provide a complete evaluation program.** Teachers can use these pages to evaluate learners' progress and to track the program's learner verification needs. Success is built in because work skills are always checked in familiar formats.

Workbooks

The Workbooks contain ten eight-page units plus a complete Answer Key. Each Workbook unit always contains at least one exercise for each section of the Student Book. To allow for additional reinforcement of grammar, there are multiple exercises for the Grammar section. The exercises for each section of the Student Book are indicated on the corresponding page of the Teacher's Edition and in a chart at the front of each Workbook. Because the Answer Keys are removable, the Workbooks can be used both in the classroom and for self-study.

Teacher's Editions

The complete Teacher's Editions help both new and experienced teachers organize their teaching, motivate their learners, and successfully use a variety of individual, partner, and teamwork activities.

♦ **Unit Overviews provide valuable information on how to motivate learners and organize teaching.** Each Overview contains a complete list of the SCANS and workplace skills in the unit to help teachers organize their teaching. The Unit Warm-Up in each Unit Overview beginning with Level 1 helps teachers build learners' interest and gets them ready for the unit. The Overviews also contain a list of materials—including pictures, flash cards, and realia—teachers can use to enliven instruction throughout the unit.

♦ **The Teacher's Editions contain complete suggested preparation and teaching procedures for each section of the Student Book.** Each section of a unit begins with a list of the workplace skills developed on the Student Book page(s). Teachers can use the list when planning lessons. The teaching notes give suggestions for a recommended three-part lesson format:

Preparation: Suggestions for preteaching the new language, SCANS skills, and concepts on the Student Book page(s) before learners open their books.

Presentation: Suggested procedures for working with the Student Book page(s) in class.

Follow-Up: An optional activity to provide reinforcement or to enrich and extend the new language and competencies. The Follow-Ups include a variety of interactive partner and team activities. Each activity has a suggested variant, marked with ♦, for use with learners who require activities at a slightly more sophisticated level. For teaching ease, the corresponding Workbook exercise(s) for each page or section of the Student Book are indicated on the Teacher's Edition page starting at Level 1.

♦ **The Teacher's Editions contain SCANS Notes, Teaching Notes, Culture Notes, and Language Notes.** Teachers can share this wealth of information with learners or use it in lesson planning.

♦ **Each Teacher's Edition unit contains an additional suggested Informal Workplace-Specific Assessment.** Teachers will find these suggestions invaluable in evaluating learners' success in relating their new skills to their workplaces or career interests. Designed to supplement the Performance Check pages in each unit of the Student

Books, these brief speaking activities include having learners state their workplace's customer service policies, their workplace's policies on lateness and absence, and the procedures they use at work to maintain equipment.

♦ **Blackline Masters.** In the Literacy Level, the Blackline Masters help teachers present or reinforce many basic literacy skills. Starting at Level 1, the Blackline Masters reinforce the grammar in each unit.

♦ **Additional features in the Teacher's Editions.** The Teacher's Editions contain Individual Competency Charts for each unit and a Class Cumulative Competency Chart for recording learners' progress and tracking the program's learner verification needs. A Certificate of Completion is included for teachers to copy and award to learners upon successful completion of that level of *English ASAP*. In addition, each unit of the Literacy Level Teacher's Edition contains an ASAP Project, an optional holistic cooperative learning project. Learners will find these to be valuable and stimulating culminating activities. Starting at Level 1, the ASAP Project appears directly on the Student Book pages.

Audiocassettes

 The Audiocassettes contain all the dialogs and listening activities marked with this cassette symbol. The Audiocassettes provide experience in listening to a variety of native speakers in the workplace. The Listening Transcript at the back of each Student Book and Teacher's Edition contains the scripts of all the listening selections not appearing directly on the pages of the Student Books.

Workforce Writing Dictionary

The Steck-Vaughn *Workforce Writing Dictionary* is a 96-page custom dictionary that lets learners create a personalized, alphabetical list of words and expressions related to their own workplaces and career interests. Each letter of the alphabet is allocated two to four pages and is illustrated with several workforce-related words. Learners can use the dictionary to record all of the relevant language they need to succeed on their jobs.

Placement Tests

The Placement Tests, Form A and Form B, help teachers place learners in the appropriate level of *English ASAP*. For more information see page v of this Teacher's Edition.

About SCANS

Each unit of *English ASAP* systematically presents one or more SCANS Competencies. The Foundation Skills are integrated through all the instruction.

WORKPLACE KNOW-HOW

The know-how identified by SCANS is made up of five competencies and a three-part foundation of skills and personal qualities needed for solid job performance. These include:

COMPETENCIES—effective workers can productively use:

- **Resources**—allocating time, money, materials, space, staff;

- **Interpersonal Skills**—working on teams, teaching others, serving customers, leading, negotiating, and working well with people from culturally diverse backgrounds;

- **Information**—acquiring and evaluating data, organizing and maintaining files, interpreting and communicating, and using computers to process information;

- **Systems**—understanding social, organizational, and technological systems, monitoring and correcting performance, and designing or improving systems;

- **Technology**—selecting equipment and tools, applying technology to specific tasks, and maintaining and troubleshooting technologies.

THE FOUNDATION—competence requires:

- **Basic Skills**—reading, writing, arithmetic and mathematics, speaking and listening;

- **Thinking Skills**—thinking creatively, making decisions, solving problems, seeing things in the mind's eye, knowing how to learn, and reasoning;

- **Personal Qualities**—individual responsibility, self-esteem, sociability, self-management, and integrity.

Reprinted from *What Work Requires of Schools—A SCANS Report for America 2000,* Secretary's Commission on Achieving Necessary Skills, U.S. Department of Labor.

For Additional Information

For more information on SCANS, CASAS, adult literacy, and the workforce, visit these websites.

For more information about Steck-Vaughn, visit our website.

www.steckvaughn.com

CASAS Information

www.casas.org

Center for Applied Linguistics

www.cal.org

Education Information

www.ed.gov

Literacy Link

www.pbs.org/learn/literacy

National Center for Adult Literacy

www.literacyonline.org/ncal/index.html

National Institute for Literacy

novel.nifl.gov

School-to-Work Information

www.stw.ed.gov

Workforce Information

www.doleta.gov

Steck-Vaughn

English ASAP™

Connecting English to the Workplace

SCANS Consultant

Shirley Brod
Spring Institute for International Studies
Boulder, Colorado

Program Consultants

Judith Dean-Griffin
ESL Teacher
Windham Independent School District
Texas Department of Criminal Justice
Huntsville, Texas

Marilyn K. Spence
Workforce Education Coordinator
Orange Technical Education Centers
Mid-Florida Tech
Orlando, Florida

Brigitte Marshall
English Language Training
for Employment Participation
Albany, California

Dennis Terdy
Director, Community Education
Township High School District 214
Arlington Heights, Illinois

Christine Kay Williams
ESL Specialist
Towson University
Baltimore, Maryland

STECK-VAUGHN
ELEMENTARY · SECONDARY · ADULT · LIBRARY

A Harcourt Company

www.steck-vaughn.com

About SCANS, the Workforce, and *English ASAP: Connecting English to the Workplace*

SCANS and the Workforce

The Secretary's Commission on Achieving Necessary Skills (SCANS) was established by the U.S. Department of Labor in 1990. Its mission was to study the demands of workplace environments and determine whether people entering the workforce are capable of meeting those demands. The commission identified skills for employment, suggested ways for assessing proficiency, and devised strategies to implement the identified skills. The commission's first report, entitled *What Work Requires of Schools—SCANS Report for America 2000,* was published in June 1991. The report is designed for use by educators (curriculum developers, job counselors, training directors, and teachers) to prepare the modern workforce for the workplace with viable, up-to-date skills.

The report identified two types of skills: Competencies and Foundations. There are five SCANS Competencies: (1) Resources, (2) Interpersonal, (3) Information, (4) Systems, and (5) Technology. There are three parts contained in SCANS Foundations: (1) Basic Skills (including reading, writing, arithmetic, mathematics, listening, and speaking); (2) Thinking Skills (including creative thinking, decision making, problem solving, seeing things in the mind's eye, knowing how to learn, and reasoning); and (3) Personal Qualities (including responsibility, self-esteem, sociability, self-management, and integrity/honesty).

Steck-Vaughn's *English ASAP: Connecting English to the Workplace*

English ASAP is a complete SCANS-based, four-skills program for teaching ESL and SCANS skills to adults and young adults. *English ASAP* follows a work skills-based syllabus that is compatible with the CASAS and MELT competencies. *English ASAP* has these components:

Student Books

The Student Books are designed to allow from 125 to 235 hours of instruction. Each Student Book contains 10 units of SCANS-based instruction. A Listening Transcript of material appearing on the Audiocassettes and a Vocabulary list, organized by unit, of core workforce-based words and phrases appear at the back of each Student Book. Because unit topics carry over from level to level, *English ASAP* is ideal for multilevel classes.

The *On Your Job* symbol appears on the Student Book page each time learners apply a work skill to their own jobs or career interests.

Tip An abundance of tips throughout each unit provides information and strategies that learners can use to be more effective workers and language learners.

Teacher's Editions

Teacher's Editions provide reduced Student Book pages with answers inserted and wraparound teacher notes that give detailed suggestions on how to present each page of the Student Book in class. Teacher's Editions 1 and 2 also provide Blackline Masters to reinforce the grammar in each unit. The Literacy Level Teacher's Edition contains blackline masters that provide practice with many basic literacy skills. The complete Listening Transcript, Vocabulary, charts for tracking individual and class success, and a Certificate of Completion appear at the back of each Teacher's Edition.

Workbooks

The Workbooks, starting at Level 1, provide reinforcement for each section of the Student Books.

Audiocassettes

The Audiocassettes contain all the dialogs and listening activities in the Student Books.

 This symbol appears on the Student Book page and corresponding Teacher's Edition page each time material for that page is recorded on the Audiocassettes. A Listening Transcript of all material recorded on the tapes but not appearing directly on the Student Book pages is at the back of each Student Book and Teacher's Edition.

Workforce Writing Dictionary

Steck-Vaughn's *Workforce Writing Dictionary* is a 96-page custom dictionary that allows learners to create a personalized, alphabetical list of the key words and phrases they need to know for their jobs. Each letter of the alphabet is allocated two to four pages for learners to record the language they need. In addition, each letter is illustrated with several workforce-related words.

Placement Tests

The Placement Tests, Form A and Form B, can be used as entry and exit tests and to assist in placing learners in the appropriate level of *English ASAP.*

Placement

In addition to the Placement Tests, the following table indicates placement based on the CASAS and new MELT student performance level standards.

Placement

New MELT SPL	CASAS Achievement Score	English ASAP
0–1	179 or under	Literacy
2–3	180–200	Level 1
4–5	201–220	Level 2
6	221–235	Level 3
7	236 and above	Level 4

About Student Book 2

Organization of a Unit

Each twelve-page unit contains these nine sections: Unit Opener, Getting Started, Talk About It, Keep Talking, Listening, Grammar, Reading and Writing, Extension, and Performance Check.

Unit Opener

Each Unit Opener includes photos and several related, work-focused questions. The photos and questions activate learners' prior knowledge by getting them to think and talk about the unit topic. The **Performance Preview**, which gives an overview of all the skills in the unit, helps teachers set goals and purposes for the unit. Optionally, teachers may want to examine the Performance Preview with learners before they begin the unit.

Getting Started

An initial **Team Work** activity presents key work skills, concepts, and language introduced in the unit. It consists of active critical thinking and peer teaching to activate the use of the new language and to preview the content of the unit. A **Partner Work** or **Practice the**

Dialog activity encourages learners to use the new language in communicative ways. A culminating class or group **Survey** encourages learners to relate the new language to themselves and their workplaces or career interests.

Talk About It

This page provides opportunities for spoken communication. **Practice the Dialog** provides a model for conversation. **Partner Work** presents an activity that allows learners to use Practice the Dialog as a model for their own conversations.

The **Useful Language** box contains related words, phrases, and expressions for learners to use as they complete activities.

The **ASAP Project** is a long-term project learners complete over the course of the unit. Learners create items such as a class telephone roster, a workplace safety booklet, and a file of tax and payroll forms they can use outside of the classroom.

Keep Talking

The Keep Talking page contains additional conversation models and speaking tasks. It also includes the **Personal Dictionary** feature. This feature allows learners to record the language relevant to the unit topic that they need to do their jobs. Because each learner's job is different, this personalized resource enables learners to focus on the language that is most useful to them. In addition, learners can use this feature in conjunction with Steck-Vaughn's *Workforce Writing Dictionary* to create a completely customized lexicon of key words and phrases they need to know.

Listening

The Listening page develops SCANS-based listening skills. Activities include listening to and understanding customer requests, employee performance reviews, safety instructions, and workplace meetings.

All the activities develop the skill of **focused listening.** Learners learn to recognize the information they need and to listen selectively for only that information. They do not have to understand every word; rather, they have to filter out everything except the relevant information. This essential skill is used by native speakers of all languages.

Many of the activities involve **multi-task listening.** In these activities, called **Listen Again** and **Listen Once More**, learners listen to the same selection several times and complete a different task each time. First they might listen for the main idea. They might listen again for specific information. They might listen a third time in order to draw conclusions or make inferences.

Culminating discussion questions allow learners to relate the information they have heard to their own needs and interests.

A complete Listening Transcript for all dialogs recorded on the Audiocassettes but not appearing on the Student Book pages is at the back of the Student Book and Teacher's Edition. All the Listening selections are recorded on the Audiocassettes.

Grammar

Grammar, a two-page spread, presents key grammatical structures that complement the unit competencies. Language boxes show the new language in a clear, simple format that allows learners to make generalizations about the new language. Oral and written exercises provide contextualized reinforcement relevant to the workplace.

Reading and Writing

Reading selections, such as help-wanted ads, meeting agendas, and company rules, focus on

To the Teacher

items learners encounter at work. Exercises and discussion questions develop reading skills and help learners relate the content of the selections to their workplaces or career interests.

The writing tasks, often related to the reading selection, help learners develop writing skills, such as completing job applications, filling out a Social Security form and completing a personal calendar/planner.

Extension

The Extension page enriches the previous instruction. As in other sections, realia is used extensively. Oral and written exercises help learners master the additional skills, language, and concepts, and relate them to their workplaces and career interests.

CultureNotes **Culture Notes**, a feature that appears on each Extension page, sparks lively, engaging discussion. Topics include holidays across cultures, the importance of customer service, and using active listening during meetings.

Performance Check

The two-page Performance Check allows teachers and learners to track learners' progress and to meet the learner verification needs of schools, companies, or programs. All work skills are tested in the same manner they are presented in the units, so formats are familiar and non-threatening, and success is built in. The **Performance Review** at the end of each test alerts teachers and learners to the work skills that are being evaluated. The check-off boxes allow learners to track their success and gain a sense of accomplishment and satisfaction. Finally, a culminating discussion allows learners to relate their new skills to their development as effective workers.

Teaching Techniques

Make Your Classroom Mirror the Workplace

Help learners develop workplace skills by setting up your classroom to mirror a workplace. Use any of these suggestions.

◆ Establish policies on lateness and absence similar to those a business might have.

◆ Provide learners with a daily agenda of the activities they will complete that day, including partner work and small group assignments. Go over the agenda with learners at the beginning and end of class.

◆ With learner input, establish a list of goals for the class. Goals can include speaking, reading, and writing English every day; using effective teamwork skills; or learning ten new vocabulary words each day. Go over the goals with learners at regular intervals.

◆ Assign learners regular jobs and responsibilities, such as arranging the chairs in a circle, setting up the overhead projector, or making copies for the class.

Presenting a Unit Opener

The unit opener sets the stage for the unit. Use the photos and questions to encourage learners to:

◆ Speculate about what the unit might cover.

◆ Activate prior knowledge.

◆ Relate what they see in the photos to their own work environments.

Peer Teaching

Because each adult learner brings rich life experience to the classroom, *English ASAP* is designed to help you use each learner's expertise as a resource for peer teaching.

Here are some practical strategies for peer teaching:

◆ Have learners work in pairs/small groups to clarify new language concepts for each other.

◆ If a learner possesses a particular work skill, appoint that learner as "class consultant" in that area and have learners direct queries to that individual.

To the Teacher

◆ Set up a reference area in a corner of your classroom. Include dictionaries, career books, and other books your learners will find useful.

Partner Work and Team Work

The abundance of Partner Work and Team Work activities in *English ASAP* serves the dual purposes of developing learners' communicative competence and providing learners with experience using key SCANS interpersonal skills, such as working in teams, teaching others, leading, negotiating, and working well with people from culturally diverse backgrounds. To take full advantage of these activities, follow these suggestions.

◆ Whenever learners work in groups, appoint, or have learners select, a leader.

◆ Use multiple groupings. Have learners work with different partners and teams, just as workers do in the workplace. For different activities, you might group learners according to language ability, skill, or learner interest.

◆ Make sure learners understand that everyone on the team is responsible for the team's work.

◆ At the end of each activity, have teams report the results to the class.

◆ Discuss with learners their teamwork skills and talk about ways teams can work together effectively. Learners can discuss how to clarify roles and responsibilities, resolve disagreements effectively, communicate openly, and make decisions together.

Purpose Statement

Each page after the unit opener begins with a brief purpose statement that summarizes the work skills presented on that page. When learners first begin working on a page, focus their attention on the purpose statement and help them read it. Ask them what the page will be about. Discuss with the class why the skill is important. Ask learners to talk about their prior knowledge of the skill. Finally, show learners how using the skill will help them become more effective on their jobs.

Survey

The **Survey** on each **Getting Started** page helps learners relate the new language and skills to their own lives. Before learners begin the activity, help them create questions they'll need to ask. Assist them in deciding how they'll record their answers. You may need to model taking notes, using tally marks, and other simple ways to record information. Assist learners in setting a time limit before they begin. Remember to allow learners to move about the room as they complete the activity.

Many Survey results can be summarized in a bar graph or pie chart.

◆ A bar graph uses bars to represent numbers. Bar graphs have two scales, a vertical scale and a horizontal scale. For example, to graph the number of learners who get paid by check versus those paid by direct deposit, the vertical scale can represent numbers of learners, such as 2, 4, 6, 8, etc. The horizontal scale can consist of two bars. One bar represents the number of learners paid by check. The other bar represents the number of learners paid by direct deposit. The two bars can be different colors to set them apart. Bars should be the same width.

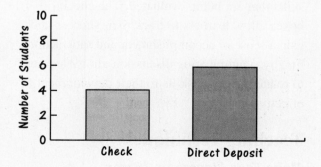

To the Teacher

◆ A pie chart shows the parts that make up a whole set of facts. Each part of the pie is a percentage of the whole. For example, a pie chart might show 40% of learners are paid by check and 60% are paid by direct deposit.

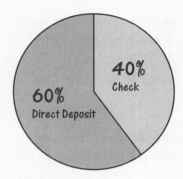

Presenting a Dialog

To present a dialog, follow these suggested steps:

◆ Play the tape or say the dialog aloud two or more times. Ask one or two simple questions to make sure learners understand.

◆ Say the dialog aloud line-by-line for learners to repeat chorally, by rows, and then individually.

◆ Have learners say or read the dialog together in pairs.

◆ Have several pairs say or read the dialog aloud for the class.

Presenting the Personal Dictionary

The Personal Dictionary enables learners to focus on the vocabulary in each unit that is relevant to their particular jobs. To use this feature, have learners work in teams to brainstorm vocabulary words they might put in their dictionaries. Have team reporters share their ideas with the class. Then allow learners a few minutes to add to their dictionaries. Remind learners to continue adding words throughout the unit.

For further vocabulary development, learners can enter the words from their Personal Dictionary into their *Workforce Writing Dictionary.*

Presenting a Listening Activity

Use any of these suggestions:

◆ To activate learners' prior knowledge, have them look at the illustrations, if any, and say as much as they can about them. Encourage learners to make inferences about the content of the listening selection.

◆ Have learners read the directions. To encourage them to focus their listening, have them read the questions before they listen so that they know exactly what to listen for.

◆ Play the tape or read the Listening Transcript aloud as learners complete the activity. Rewind the tape and play it again as necessary.

◆ Help learners check their work.

In multi-task listening, remind learners that they will listen to the same passage several times and answer different questions each time. After learners complete a section, have them check their own or each other's work before you rewind the tape and proceed to the next questions.

Presenting a Tip

Tip A variety of Tips throughout each unit present valuable advice on how to be a successful employee and/or language learner. To present a Tip, help learners read the Tip. Discuss it with them. Ask them how it will help them. For certain Tips, such as those in which learners make lists, you may want to allow learners time to start the activity.

Presenting a Discussion

English ASAP provides a variety of whole-class and team discussions. Always encourage learners to state their ideas and respond appropriately to other learners' comments. At the end of each discussion, have team reporters summarize their team's ideas and/or help the class come to a consensus about the topic.

Prereading

To help learners read the selections with ease and success, establish a purpose for reading and call on learners' prior knowledge to make inferences about the reading. Use any of these techniques:

◆ Have learners look over and describe any photographs, realia, and/or illustrations. Ask them to use the illustrations to say what they think the selection might be about.

◆ Have learners read the title and any heads or sub-heads. Ask them what kind of information they think is in the selection and how it might be organized. Ask them where they might encounter such information outside of class and why they would want to read it.

◆ To help learners focus their reading, have them review the comprehension activities before they read the selection. Ask them what kind of information they think they will find out when they read. Restate their ideas and/or write them on the board in acceptable English.

◆ Remind learners that they do not have to know all the words in order to understand the selection.

Evaluation

To use the Performance Check pages successfully, follow these suggested procedures:

Before and during each evaluation, create a relaxed, affirming atmosphere. Chat with the learners for a few minutes and review the material. When you and the learners are ready, have learners read the directions and look over each exercise before they complete it. If at any time you sense that learners are becoming frustrated, stop to provide additional review. Resume when learners are ready. The evaluation formats follow two basic patterns:

1. **Speaking** competencies are checked in the format used to present them in the unit. Have learners read the instructions. Make sure learners know what to do. Then have learners complete the evaluation in one of these ways:

   Self- and Peer Evaluation: Have learners complete the spoken activity in pairs. Learners in each pair evaluate themselves and/or each other and report the results to you.

   Teacher/Pair Evaluation: Have pairs complete the activity as you observe and evaluate their work. Begin with the most proficient learners. As other learners who are ready to be evaluated wait, have them practice in pairs. Learners who complete the evaluation successfully can peer-teach those who are waiting or those who need additional review.

   Teacher/Individual Evaluation: Have individuals complete the activity with you as their partner. Follow the procedures in Teacher/Pair Evaluation.

2. **Listening, reading,** and **writing** competencies are also all checked in the same format used to present them in the unit. When learners are ready to begin, have them read the instructions. Demonstrate the first item and have learners complete the activity. In Listening activities, play the tape or read the listening transcript aloud two or more times. Then have learners check their work. Provide any review needed, and have learners try the activity again.

When learners demonstrate mastery of a skill to your satisfaction, have them record their success by checking the appropriate box in the Performance Review. The Teacher's Edition also contains charts for you to reproduce to keep track of individual and class progress.

Steck-Vaughn

English ASAP™

Connecting English to the Workplace

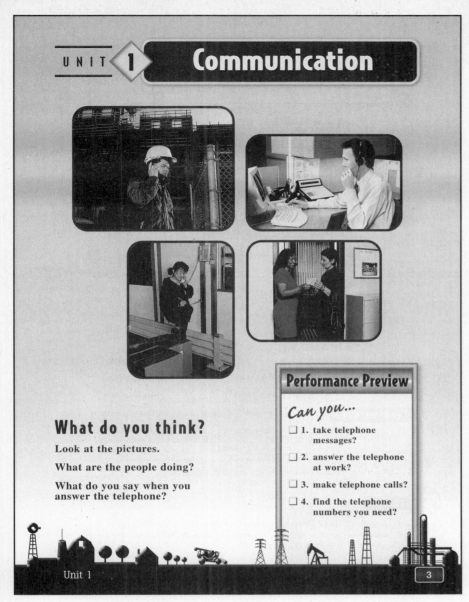

UNIT 1 Communication

What do you think?

Look at the pictures.

What are the people doing?

What do you say when you answer the telephone?

Performance Preview

Can you...

☐ 1. take telephone messages?

☐ 2. answer the telephone at work?

☐ 3. make telephone calls?

☐ 4. find the telephone numbers you need?

Unit 1 — 3

Unit 1 Overview
—SCANS Competencies—

★ Serve customers

★ Interpret and communicate information

★ Understand technological systems

Workforce Skills

● Take telephone messages

● Answer the telephone at work

● Make telephone calls

● Find telephone numbers

Materials

● Picture cards or realia for a Rolodex, answering machine, and telephone

● An oversized roster with commonly called phone numbers at your school or workplace, telephone message pads, and a variety of business cards

● Several blank Rolodex cards and an index card for each learner

Unit Warm-Up

To motivate learners to begin thinking about the unit topic, model a telephone call such as a customer asking about a shipment. Encourage learners to talk about when they have made or taken business-related telephone calls. What did they say?

★　　★　　★　　★　　★

WORKFORCE SKILLS (page 3)

Make telephone calls

★　　★　　★　　★　　★

PREPARATION

Display the picture cards or realia for the telephone-related objects. Help the learners identify the items. Encourage learners to use peer teaching to clarify any unfamiliar vocabulary.

PRESENTATION

1. Focus attention on the photographs. Ask learners to speculate on what the unit might be about. Write their ideas on the board and/or restate them in acceptable English.

2. Have learners talk about the pictures. Have them identify the objects they see and say what the people are doing.

3. Help learners read the questions. Discuss the questions with the class.

4. You may want to use the Performance Preview to provide learners with an overview of the skills in the unit. Have learners read the list of skills and discuss what they will learn in the unit.

FOLLOW-UP

Telephone Technology: Have teams list different types of telephone technology, such as pagers, cell phones, or pay phones. Have team reporters share their lists with the class.

♦ Discuss with learners how the different items are used.

WORKBOOK

Unit 1, Exercises 1A–1B

★   ★   ★   ★   ★

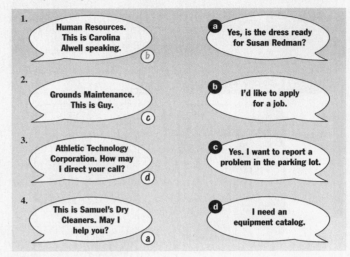

Getting Started — Making and answering telephone calls

TEAM WORK

Work with a team. Match the caller and the person answering the telephone. Then say the telephone conversations aloud.

1. Human Resources. This is Carolina Alwell speaking. (b)
2. Grounds Maintenance. This is Guy. (c)
3. Athletic Technology Corporation. How may I direct your call? (d)
4. This is Samuel's Dry Cleaners. May I help you? (a)

a. Yes, is the dress ready for Susan Redman?
b. I'd like to apply for a job.
c. Yes. I want to report a problem in the parking lot.
d. I need an equipment catalog.

PARTNER WORK

Practice the dialog. Then use the dialog to make calls for your job.

A Shipping department. This is Lou.

B This is Paul Smith. May I please speak to the manager?

 SURVEY

How do you answer the telephone at work? Write down what you say. Compare your answers with your classmates' answers. What is the most common way to answer the telephone?

4   Unit 1

Teaching Note

Use this page to introduce the new language in the unit. Whenever possible, encourage peer teaching. Supply any new language learners need.

PREPARATION

Ask teams to list as many ways to answer the telephone at work or school as they can. Have team reporters share their information with the class.

PRESENTATION

1. Have learners read and discuss the Purpose Statement. For more information, see "Purpose Statement" on page viii.

2. Focus attention on the speech balloons. Encourage learners to say as much as they can about them. Write their ideas on the board and/or restate them in acceptable English.

3. Have teams read the Team Work instructions. Make sure each team knows what to do. If necessary, model the first item. Remind the teams that

they are responsible for making sure that each member understands the new language. Then have teams complete the activity. If learners need help, encourage them to consult other teams. Have team reporters share their answers with the class.

4. Have partners read the Partner Work instructions. Make sure each pair knows what to do. If necessary, model the activity. Then have pairs complete the activity. Have learners switch partners and repeat the activity. Supply any language needed. Have several partners present their dialogs to the class.

 **5.** Read the Survey instructions. Make sure each person knows what to do. If necessary, model the activity. Then have learners complete

the activity. For more information, see "Survey" on page viii.

FOLLOW-UP

Table: Help the class use the information from the Survey to create a table that shows several of the most common ways that learners answer the telephone and the number of learners who answer that way. Have learners discuss the table.

◆ Have teams talk about what they say when they hang up the phone. Have team reporters share their ideas with the class.

WORKBOOK

Unit 1, Exercises 2A–2C

Talk About It

Getting telephone numbers

PRACTICE THE DIALOG

A This is Ana Smith. May I help you?

B Ana, it's Marta. Do you know Ruby Lee's number? It's not on my telephone roster or in my Rolodex.

A Ruby Lee's number? I have it. It's 555-7913.

B 555-7913. Thanks, Ana. Bye.

PARTNER WORK

Take turns asking for telephone numbers in Ana's Rolodex. Use the dialog and Useful Language above.

ASAP PROJECT

Make a class telephone roster. Team 1 puts names in alphabetical order. Team 2 gets the telephone numbers. Team 3 gets the best times for people to call. Complete this project as you work through this unit.

Useful Language

I'm looking for Ruby's telephone number.

I can look it up for you.

 Tip Carry important telephone numbers in your purse or wallet.

Unit 1

5

ASAP PROJECT

Have learners read the instructions. Discuss the project and its purpose with learners. Make sure that everyone understands. Help learners assign themselves to teams based upon their knowledge, skills, interests, or other personal strengths. Have each team select a leader, and have the team leaders or the whole class select an overall project leader. Throughout the rest of the unit, allow time for learners to work on the project. Have the teams agree on a deadline when the project will be finished. For more information, see "ASAP Project" on page vi.

PREPARATION

Preteach the new language in the lesson. Act out finding a telephone number using the large telephone roster. Then ask learners for telephone numbers. Say, *I'm looking for (person's) telephone number. Do you know/have it?* Then have learners ask you for telephone numbers from the roster. Respond with *I can look it up for you.* To preteach **Rolodex,** use a real Rolodex, a picture of one, or the illustration on the page. Explain that a Rolodex is a card file for organizing people's names, addresses, and telephone numbers.

PRESENTATION

1. Have learners read and discuss the Purpose Statement. For more information, see "Purpose Statement" on page viii.

 2. Focus attention on the Rolodex cards in the picture. Encourage learners to say as much as they can about them. Have them read the telephone numbers and the names. Then present the dialog. See "Presenting a Dialog" on page ix.

3. Have partners read the Partner Work instructions. Focus attention on the Useful Language box. Help learners read the expressions. If necessary, model pronunciation. Then have learners complete the activity. Have learners switch partners and repeat the activity. Have one or two pairs present their dialogs to the class.

Tip Have learners read the Tip independently. Have learners discuss how the advice will

help them. For more information, see "Presenting a Tip" on page ix.

FOLLOW-UP

Dialogs: Have pairs use the large roster to create dialogs in which they ask for and give telephone numbers. Have several pairs present their dialogs to the class.

♦ Have learners write their dialogs. Post the dialogs for everyone to examine.

WORKBOOK

Unit 1, Exercises 3A–3C

WORKFORCE SKILLS (page 6)

Answer the telephone at work

Make telephone calls

★　　★　　★　　★　　★

Culture Note

You might tell learners that in some workplaces, the telephone rings or lights up a certain way to let workers know if the call is coming from within the company or outside the company. This can help employees decide how to answer the telephone. Employees might, for example, answer outside calls more formally than inside calls.

Personal Dictionary

Have learners add the words in their Personal Dictionary to their *Workforce Writing Dictionary*. For more information, see "Workforce Writing Dictionary" on page v.

Keep Talking　Answering telephone calls

PRACTICE THE DIALOG

A Thanks for calling Pizza House. Can I take your order?

B Yes, I'd like a small pizza with mushrooms.

A What's your name and address?

B Carmen Diaz. D-I-A-Z. I'm at 16 Bank Street.

A A small pizza with mushrooms for Diaz at 16 Bank Street. We'll be there in thirty minutes.

B Great! Thanks.

PARTNER WORK

Take turns ordering a pizza. Write your partner's order on the form. Write the name and address. Use the dialog and Useful Language.

Useful Language

Thanks for calling . . .

Would you like . . . ?

How do you spell that?

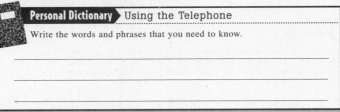

Personal Dictionary ▶ Using the Telephone

Write the words and phrases that you need to know.

_____

_____

_____

6　　　　　　　　　　　　　　　　　　　　　Unit 1

PREPARATION

Preteach the new language in the lesson. Use the speech balloons on page 4 to review ways to answer the telephone. Then model language from the Useful Language box by acting out taking an order over the telephone. Clarify using *Would you like . . . ?* to offer a suggestion and *How do you spell that?* to ask for the correct spelling.

PRESENTATION

1. Have learners read the Purpose Statement. For more information, see "Purpose Statement" on page viii.

 2. Focus attention on the pizza order form. Encourage learners to say as much as they can about it. Then present the dialog. See "Presenting a Dialog" on page ix.

3. Have partners read the Partner Work instructions. Make sure each pair knows what to do. If necessary, model the activity on the board. Then have pairs complete the activity. Ask pairs to share their completed order forms with the class.

4. Have learners read the Personal Dictionary instructions. Then use the Personal Dictionary procedures on page ix. Remind learners to continue to add words to their dictionaries throughout the unit.

FOLLOW-UP

Workplace Telephone Calls: Have pairs write simple dialogs for calls that they make to workplaces or calls that they receive at work. Have learners read their dialogs aloud to the class.

♦ Discuss learners' dialogs with the class. Ask the class questions such as *Who called? Who answered the telephone? What did the caller want?*

WORKBOOK

Unit 1, Exercise 4

　　　　　　　　　　　　　　　　　　　　　　　　English ASAP

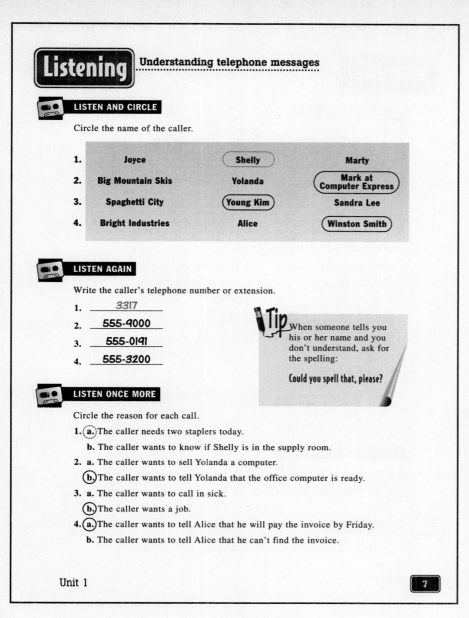

Listening ·········· Understanding telephone messages

LISTEN AND CIRCLE

Circle the name of the caller.

1.	Joyce	(Shelly)	Marty
2.	Big Mountain Skis	Yolanda	(Mark at Computer Express)
3.	Spaghetti City	(Young Kim)	Sandra Lee
4.	Bright Industries	Alice	(Winston Smith)

LISTEN AGAIN

Write the caller's telephone number or extension.

1. _____3317_____
2. __555-9000__
3. __555-0191__
4. __555-3200__

> **Tip** When someone tells you his or her name and you don't understand, ask for the spelling:
>
> **Could you spell that, please?**

LISTEN ONCE MORE

Circle the reason for each call.

1. (a.) The caller needs two staplers today.
   b. The caller wants to know if Shelly is in the supply room.
2. a. The caller wants to sell Yolanda a computer.
   (b.) The caller wants to tell Yolanda that the office computer is ready.
3. a. The caller wants to call in sick.
   (b.) The caller wants a job.
4. (a.) The caller wants to tell Alice that he will pay the invoice by Friday.
   b. The caller wants to tell Alice that he can't find the invoice.

Unit 1   7

SCANS Note

Point out to learners that communicating by telephone is an important part of working on a team, serving customers, and serving coworkers. For most businesses, the telephone is as important as in-person communication.

PREPARATION

Preteach the new language in the lesson. Model leaving a telephone message. Write the message on the board or overhead projector. Have learners identify the parts of a message (caller's name, person called, time and date, the message, the caller's telephone number). If necessary, contrast **telephone number** and **extension**.

PRESENTATION

1. Have learners read and discuss the Purpose Statement. For more information, see "Purpose Statement" on page viii.

 2. Have learners read the Listen and Circle instructions. Then have them read the names in the box. Use peer teaching to

clarify any unfamiliar vocabulary. Make sure that everyone understands the instructions. If necessary, model the first item. Then play the tape or read the Listening Transcript aloud two or more times as learners complete the activity. Have learners check their work. For more information, see "Presenting a Listening Activity" on page ix.

 3. Have learners read the Listen Again instructions. Then follow the procedures in 2.

 4. Have learners read the Listen Once More instructions. Then follow the procedures in 2.

 Have learners read the Tip independently. Have learners discuss how the advice will help them. Then have them practice

asking for spelling verification in pairs. For more information, see "Presenting a Tip" on page ix.

FOLLOW-UP

More Telephone Messages: Bring in or make a variety of typical telephone messages from a workplace. Have each pair examine one or two to figure out who called and why. Have several pairs share their messages with the class.

♦ Have teams write dialogs to match the telephone messages. Have volunteers present their dialogs to the class.

WORKBOOK

Unit 1, Exercises 5A–5B

WORKFORCE SKILLS (pages 8–9)

Answer the telephone at work

Find telephone numbers

★   ★   ★   ★   ★

 **Grammar**   Learning the language you need

A. Study the Examples

I'm He's She's It's	in the hall.

You're We're They're	in the hall.

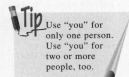 **Tip** Use "you" for only one person. Use "you" for two or more people, too.

COMPLETE THE SENTENCES

Use the language in A.

1. I am the supervisor. I **'m** in my office.

2. The workers are in the factory. They **'re** at a team meeting.

3. My boss is named Martina. She **'s** at her desk.

4. Carlos, Margo, and I work together. We **'re** a good team.

5. My extension is new. It **'s** 2287.

6. You and Jim work hard. You **'re** always busy.

7. Mark makes a lot of decisions. He **'s** very busy.

B. Study the Examples

I We You They	answer the telephone.

He She It	answers the telephone.

COMPLETE THE SENTENCES

1. I **take** (take) messages.

2. He **opens** (open) the mail.

3. We **ask** (ask) questions.

4. They **help** (help) customers.

 PARTNER WORK

Use the language in B. Talk about the work you do.

8   Unit 1

PREPARATION

Review the language in the grammar boxes with learners before they open their books, if necessary.

PRESENTATION

1. Have learners read and discuss the Purpose Statement. For more information, see "Purpose Statement" on page viii.

2. Have learners read the grammar boxes in A. Have learners use the language in the boxes to say as many sentences as possible. Tell learners that they can use the grammar boxes throughout the unit to review or check sentence structures.

3. Have learners read the instructions for Complete the Sentences. If necessary, model the first item. Allow learners to complete the activity. Have learners check each other's work in pairs. Ask several learners to read their sentences aloud while the rest of the class checks their work.

4. Focus attention on the grammar boxes in B. Follow the procedures in 2.

5. Focus attention on Complete the Sentences. If necessary, model the first item. Allow learners to complete the activity. Have learners check each other's work in pairs. Ask several learners to read their sentences aloud while the rest of the class checks their work.

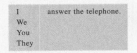 **6.** Have pairs read the Partner Work instructions. Make sure each pair knows what to do. If necessary, model the activity. Then have pairs complete the activity. Have

learners switch partners and repeat the activity. Ask several pairs to present their conversations to the class.

Tip Have learners read the Tip independently. Provide any clarification needed. For more information, see "Presenting a Tip" on page ix.

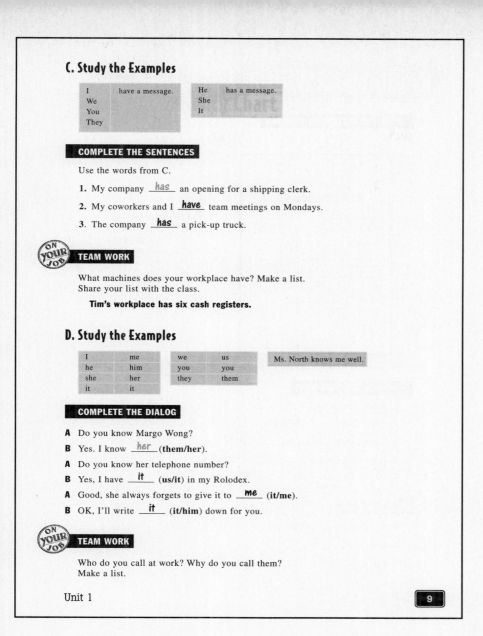

C. Study the Examples

I	have a message.	He	has a message.
We		She	
You		It	
They			

COMPLETE THE SENTENCES

Use the words from C.

1. My company __has__ an opening for a shipping clerk.

2. My coworkers and I __have__ team meetings on Mondays.

3. The company __has__ a pick-up truck.

 TEAM WORK

What machines does your workplace have? Make a list.
Share your list with the class.

Tim's workplace has six cash registers.

D. Study the Examples

I	me	we	us	Ms. North knows me well.
he	him	you	you	
she	her	they	them	
it	it			

COMPLETE THE DIALOG

A Do you know Margo Wong?

B Yes. I know __her__ (them/her).

A Do you know her telephone number?

B Yes, I have __it__ (us/it) in my Rolodex.

A Good, she always forgets to give it to __me__ (it/me).

B OK, I'll write __it__ (it/him) down for you.

 TEAM WORK

Who do you call at work? Why do you call them?
Make a list.

Unit 1

9

---

7. Focus attention on the grammar boxes in C. Follow the procedures in 2.

8. Have learners read the instructions for Complete the Sentences. If necessary, model the first item. Then have learners complete the activity independently. Have a different learner read each sentence aloud as the rest of the class checks their answers.

9. Have teams read the Team Work instructions. Make sure each team knows what to do. If necessary, model the activity. Then have teams complete the activity.

10. Focus attention on the grammar boxes in D. Follow the procedures in 2.

11. Focus attention on Complete the Dialog. If necessary, model the first item. Then have learners complete the activity independently. Have a pair of learners read the dialog aloud as the rest of the class checks their answers.

12. Have teams read the Team Work instructions. Make sure each team knows what to do. If necessary, model the activity. Then have teams complete the activity. Have team reporters share their lists with the class.

FOLLOW-UP

I Know You! Divide the class into teams. Have teams sit in circles so learners can see each other. Demonstrate the activity by thinking of a learner and giving two or three clues about that learner. For example, say *I have blue eyes. I'm always early. I repair cars. Do you know me?* A volunteer answers *I know you!*

You're (learner's name). Have teams play the game until each learner has a chance to give clues.

♦ Give each learner an index card. Have them write their names with 3 or 4 clues about themselves. Then redistribute the cards and let learners play *I Know You.* Have individuals read the clues on the cards aloud in order for the rest of the class to figure out the names on the cards.

WORKBOOK

Unit 1, Exercises 6A–6D

BLACKLINE MASTERS

Blackline Master: Unit 1

Unit 1

9

★　　★　　★　　★　　★

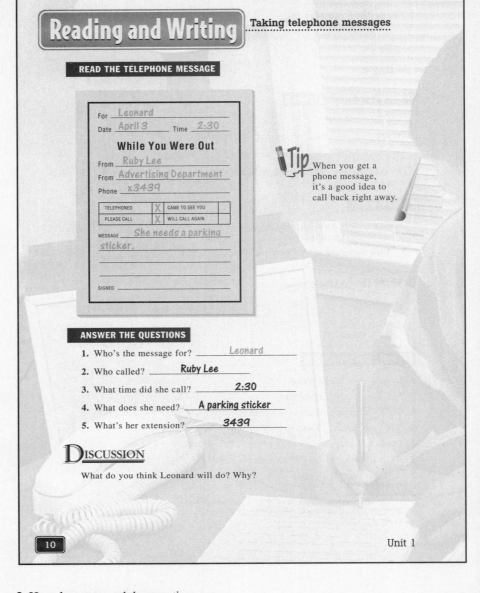

Teaching Note

You might have learners peer-edit each other's telephone messages. Monitor learners' peer editing. If a learner makes a questionable edit, focus both learners' attention on the edit and help them decide what to do.

PREPARATION

If necessary, review answering the telephone and taking a message. Model writing a message on the board. Display or give each learner a copy of a telephone message slip. Help learners identify the information in a telephone message.

PRESENTATION

1. Have learners read and discuss the Purpose Statement. For more information, see "Purpose Statement" on page viii.

2. Have learners preview the telephone message before they read. Encourage learners to say everything they can about the telephone message. Write their ideas on the board or restate them in acceptable English. Then have them read the message independently.

3. Have learners read the questions in Answer the Questions. Make sure everyone knows what to do. Then have learners complete the activity independently. Have learners review each other's work in pairs. Ask several learners to share their answers with the class while the rest of the class checks their work.

4. Have learners read the Discussion questions. Make sure everyone knows what to do. Then have learners work in teams to discuss what Leonard will do. Have team reporters share their ideas with the class. Have teams compare ideas.

Tip Have learners read the Tip independently. Have learners discuss how the advice will help them. For more information, see "Presenting a Tip" on page ix.

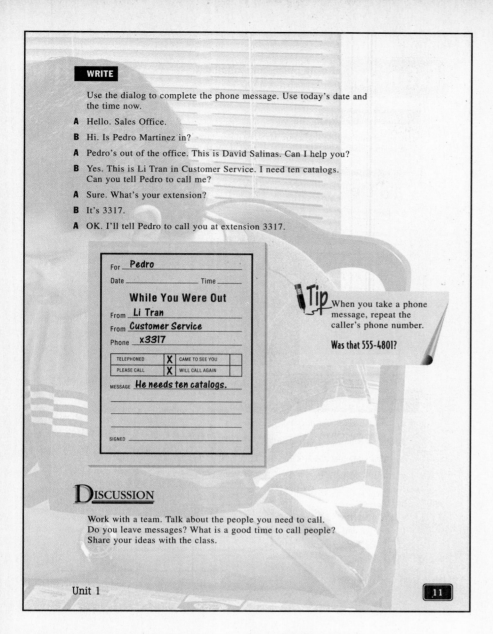

WRITE

Use the dialog to complete the phone message. Use today's date and the time now.

A Hello. Sales Office.

B Hi. Is Pedro Martinez in?

A Pedro's out of the office. This is David Salinas. Can I help you?

B Yes. This is Li Tran in Customer Service. I need ten catalogs. Can you tell Pedro to call me?

A Sure. What's your extension?

B It's 3317.

A OK. I'll tell Pedro to call you at extension 3317.

For _Pedro_

Date _____ Time _____

While You Were Out

From _Li Tran_

From _Customer Service_

Phone _x3317_

| TELEPHONED | X | CAME TO SEE YOU | |
| PLEASE CALL | X | WILL CALL AGAIN | |

MESSAGE _He needs ten catalogs._

_____

_____

_____

SIGNED _____

Tip When you take a phone message, repeat the caller's phone number.

Was that 555-4801?

DISCUSSION

Work with a team. Talk about the people you need to call. Do you leave messages? What is a good time to call people? Share your ideas with the class.

Unit 1

11

---

5. Have pairs of learners read the instructions for Write. Make sure everyone knows what to do. If necessary, model the activity. Then have pairs complete the activity. Have volunteers share their telephone messages with the class.

6. Have learners read the Discussion instructions. Model the activity if necessary by talking about your own telephone calling habits. Have teams discuss their ideas. Have team reporters share their ideas with the class.

Tip Have learners read the Tip independently. Have learners discuss how the advice will help them. For more information, see "Presenting a Tip" on page ix.

FOLLOW-UP

Telephone Messages: Have learners work in teams. Ask each team to imagine a telephone call that they would make to a workplace. Ask each team to write a telephone message for their call. Have them share their telephone messages with the class.

♦ Discuss voicemail and answering machines with learners. Ask learners to write the voicemail messages they would leave instead of the paper-and-pencil messages they just wrote. Have several pairs share their messages with the class.

WORKBOOK

Unit 1, Exercise 7

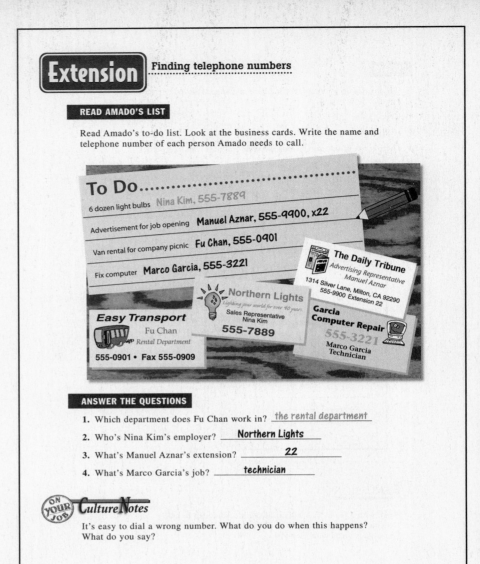

Extension — Finding telephone numbers

READ AMADO'S LIST

Read Amado's to-do list. Look at the business cards. Write the name and telephone number of each person Amado needs to call.

To Do...

6 dozen light bulbs — Nina Kim, 555-7889

Advertisement for job opening — Manuel Aznar, 555-9900, x22

Van rental for company picnic — Fu Chan, 555-0901

Fix computer — Marco Garcia, 555-3221

The Daily Tribune
Advertising Representative
Manuel Aznar
1314 Silver Lane, Milton, CA 92290
555-9900 Extension 22

Northern Lights
Lighting your world for over 40 years.
Sales Representative
Nina Kim
555-7889

Easy Transport
Fu Chan
Rental Department
555-0901 • Fax 555-0909

Garcia Computer Repair
555-3221
Marco Garcia
Technician

ANSWER THE QUESTIONS

1. Which department does Fu Chan work in? _the rental department_
2. Who's Nina Kim's employer? __Northern Lights__
3. What's Manuel Aznar's extension? __22__
4. What's Marco Garcia's job? __technician__

ON YOUR JOB — Culture Notes

It's easy to dial a wrong number. What do you do when this happens? What do you say?

12   Unit 1

PREPARATION

Show learners several business cards. Help them read the cards. Ask learners where they have seen business cards. Do they have any business cards in their purses or wallets? They may have business cards from doctors' offices, restaurants, or friends. Help learners generalize about the information on a business card. For example, the company name is usually the biggest name on the card.

PRESENTATION

1. Have learners read and discuss the Purpose Statement. For more information, see "Purpose Statement" on page viii.

2. Have learners preview the business cards and to-do list. Encourage them to say everything they can about them.

Write their ideas on the board or restate them in acceptable English.

3. Have learners read the instructions for Read Amado's List. If necessary, model the first item. Allow learners to complete the activity. Have learners review each other's work in pairs. Ask several learners to read their answers aloud while the rest of the class checks their work.

4. Have learners read the questions in Answer the Questions. If necessary, model the first item. Allow learners to complete the activity. Have learners review each other's work in pairs. Ask several learners to read their answers aloud while the rest of the class checks their work.

 5. Have learners read Culture Notes and talk over their responses in teams.

Have team reporters share their ideas with the class.

FOLLOW-UP

A Rolodex File: Have learners complete Rolodex cards for themselves, for 2 or 3 coworkers, and/or for businesses they call at home or work. If learners are not working, have them create a Rolodex card for a company they would like to work for. Be sure they include the name of the business, a work address, phone number, and extension. Have learners share their cards with the class.

♦ Have the class alphabetize all the Rolodex cards. If necessary, review alphabetical order and alphabetizing.

WORKBOOK

Unit 1, Exercise 8

 **How well can you use the skills in this unit?**

Complete the activities. Go over your work with a partner or your teacher. Then complete the Performance Review on page 14.

| SKILL 1 | TAKE TELEPHONE MESSAGES |

Listen to the telephone calls. Who's calling? Circle the letter.

1. a. Martin Valdez

    (b.) John Drummond

2. a. Ms. Mars

    (b.) Cindy Grey

Listen again. What's the message? Circle the letter.

1.(a.) Call back.

    b. Meet him at 4:00.

2. a. The meeting will be at 4:30.

    (b.) She needs to cancel the meeting.

| SKILL 2 | ANSWER TELEPHONE CALLS AT WORK |

You're answering the telephone at Lee's Chinese Restaurant. What do you say? Work with a partner or with your teacher.

| SKILL 3 | MAKE TELEPHONE CALLS |

You're ordering a sandwich from The Lunch Stop. What do you say? Work with a partner or with your teacher.

Unit 1   **13**

PRESENTATION

Use any of the procedures in "Evaluation," page x, with pages 13 and 14. Record individuals' results on the Unit 1 Individual Competency Chart. Record the class's results on the Class Cumulative Competency Chart.

Write the correct telephone extension next to the name.

Landry, Bill . . . . Ext. 7790
Maintenance Department . . . . Ext. 7789
Research and Development . . . Ext. 7870
Santiago, Ernesto . . . . Ext. 9547
Security Department . . . . Ext. 9077

Ernesto Santiago _____**9547**_____

Security Department _____**9077**_____

Research and Development _____**7870**_____

Bill Landry _____**7790**_____

Performance Review

I can...

☐ 1. take telephone messages.
☐ 2. answer the telephone at work.
☐ 3. make telephone calls.
☐ 4. find the telephone numbers I need.

DISCUSSION

Work with a team. How will your new skills help you?
Make a list. Share your list with the class.

14   Unit 1

PRESENTATION

Follow the instructions on page 13.

INFORMAL WORKPLACE-SPECIFIC ASSESSMENT

Ask learners to use the telephone roster with commonly called phone numbers to look up one or more numbers.

WORKBOOK

Unit 1, Exercise 9

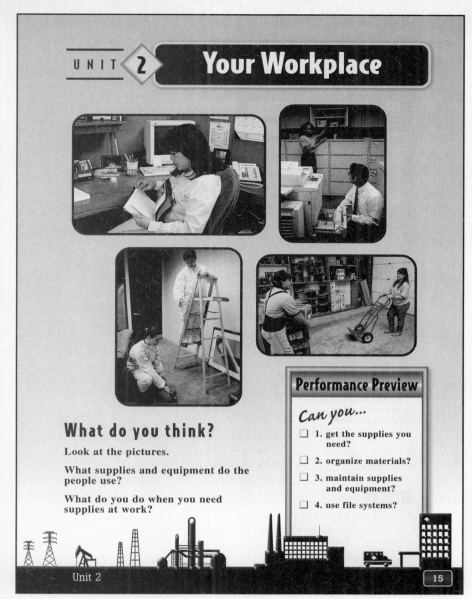

What do you think?

Look at the pictures.

What supplies and equipment do the people use?

What do you do when you need supplies at work?

Performance Preview

Can you...

☐ 1. get the supplies you need?

☐ 2. organize materials?

☐ 3. maintain supplies and equipment?

☐ 4. use file systems?

Unit 2   15

Unit 2 Overview
—SCANS Competencies—

★ Organize information

★ Understand organizational systems

★ Allocate materials

Workforce Skills

● Get supplies

● Organize materials

● Maintain supplies and equipment

● Use filing systems

Materials

● Buttons in various sizes and colors, and nails of various sizes

● Picture cards, photographs of, and/or real supplies and equipment in the unit and at learners' workplace(s); index cards; file folders

● Catalogs from various supply companies

● Shelves in your classroom or a poster of a supply shelf

Unit Warm-Up

To get learners thinking about the unit topic, model organizing buttons or nails by size. Ask learners to talk about supplies they use at work or school and how the supplies are organized.

★   ★   ★   ★   ★

WORKFORCE SKILLS (page 15)

Identify supplies

★   ★   ★   ★   ★

PREPARATION

Show the learners several picture cards of supplies and identify them as supplies. Have them talk about where they keep the supplies.

PRESENTATION

1. Focus attention on the photographs. Ask learners what the unit might be about. Write their ideas on the board and/or restate them in acceptable English.

2. Have learners talk about the pictures. Have them identify the supplies and equipment as well as the work situations, and say what the people are

doing. Help learners relate the supplies in the pictures to the supplies depicted on the picture cards.

3. Help learners read the questions. Discuss the questions with the class.

4. You may want to use the Performance Preview to provide learners with an overview of the skills in the unit. Have learners read the list of skills and discuss what they will learn in the unit.

FOLLOW-UP

Charades: Divide the class into two teams. Use picture cards of supplies or real supplies. One learner pantomimes using one of the supplies. Members of the other team identify the supply.

◆ Have teams write lists of the supplies that were acted out in the game.

WORKBOOK

Unit 2, Exercises 1A–1B

★　　★　　★　　★　　★

SCANS Note

You may want to point out that many workplaces have a system for workers to get supplies, such as completing a supply requisition. This helps the company to allocate materials, maintain inventories, and stay organized. Ask learners to talk about the methods for getting supplies at their workplaces.

Teaching Note

Use this page to introduce the new language in the unit. Whenever possible, encourage peer teaching. Supply any language learners need.

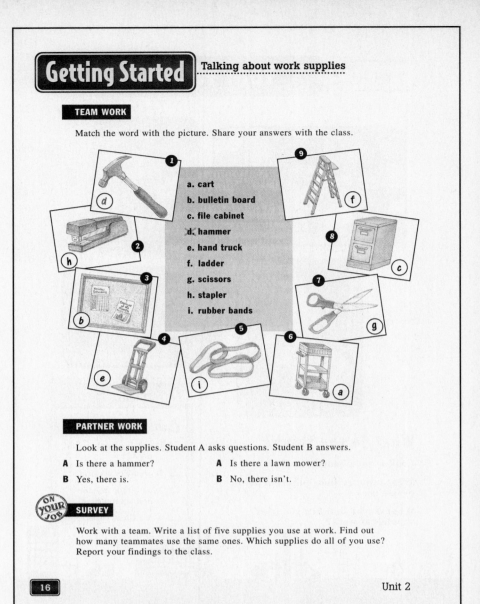

Getting Started — Talking about work supplies

TEAM WORK

Match the word with the picture. Share your answers with the class.

a. cart
b. bulletin board
c. file cabinet
d. hammer
e. hand truck
f. ladder
g. scissors
h. stapler
i. rubber bands

PARTNER WORK

Look at the supplies. Student A asks questions. Student B answers.

A Is there a hammer?
B Yes, there is.

A Is there a lawn mower?
B No, there isn't.

ON YOUR JOB — SURVEY

Work with a team. Write a list of five supplies you use at work. Find out how many teammates use the same ones. Which supplies do all of you use? Report your findings to the class.

16   Unit 2

PREPARATION

Ask teams to name several work supplies. Have teams share their information with the class.

PRESENTATION

1. Have learners read and discuss the Purpose Statement. For more information, see "Purpose Statement" on page viii.

2. Focus attention on the illustrations. Encourage learners to say as much as they can about them.

3. Have teams read the Team Work instructions. Make sure each team knows what to do. Remind teams that they are responsible for making sure that each member understands the new language. Then have teams complete

the activity. If learners need help, encourage them to consult other teams. Have team reporters share their answers with the class.

4. Have partners read the Partner Work instructions. Make sure each pair knows what to do. If necessary, model the activity. Then have pairs complete the activity. Have learners switch partners and repeat the activity. Supply any language needed. Have one or two partners present their dialogs to the class.

 5. Have partners read the Survey instructions. Make sure each person knows what to do. Then have pairs complete the activity. Have pairs share their answers with the class. For more information, see "Survey" on page viii.

FOLLOW-UP

Table: Help the class use the information from the Survey to create a class table showing the number of learners who use each kind of supply. Have learners discuss the table.

◆ Help learners use the table to create a bar graph. The horizontal axis should show the names of the supplies and the vertical axis the number of users. Have learners discuss the graph. For more information, see "Survey," page viii.

WORKBOOK

Unit 2, Exercises 2A–2B

 **Talk About It** .... Getting supplies

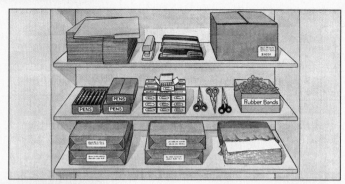

 **PRACTICE THE DIALOG**

A Excuse me. Where's the paper?

B It's on the bottom shelf.

A Where are the rubber bands?

B They're on the middle shelf.

A On the middle shelf?

B Yes, that's right.

A OK, thanks.

Useful Language

I need a . . .

I need some . . .

top	paper clips
middle	pen
bottom	file folder

a box of . . .

a roll of . . .

PARTNER WORK

You and your partner are getting supplies for your work areas. Talk about the supplies you need. Use the dialog and the Useful Language above.

ASAP
PROJECT

Choose a shelf in a supply room at your workplace or school and take inventory. Count all of the supplies. Make a list of the amount of each supply. Complete this project as you work through this unit.

Unit 2

Get supplies

Organize supplies

★   ★   ★   ★   ★

ASAP
PROJECT

Have learners read the instructions. Discuss the project and its purpose with learners. Make sure that everyone understands and that learners can inventory the area assigned to them in a reasonable amount of time. Choose a specific class time for learners to work on the project. For more information, see "ASAP Project" on page vi.

PREPARATION

Use the poster you made, shelves in your classroom, or the picture on the page to present or review **top, middle,** and **bottom.** Then model the Useful Language by asking for supplies in the picture. Use real supplies to model **paper clips, pens, file folders, a box of,** and **a roll of.**

PRESENTATION

1. Have learners read and discuss the Purpose Statement. For more information, see "Purpose Statement" on page viii.

 2. Focus attention on the illustration. Encourage learners to say as much as they can about it. Have them identify the supplies and their location. Then present the dialog. See "Presenting a Dialog" on page ix.

3. Have partners read the Partner Work instructions. Focus attention on the Useful Language box. Help learners read the expressions. If necessary, model pronunciation. Then have learners complete the activity. Have learners switch partners and repeat the activity. Have one or two pairs present their dialogs to the class.

FOLLOW-UP

Dialogs: Have pairs use the poster of a supply shelf, a real supply shelf, or shelves in your classroom that you've stocked with supplies to create dialogs in which learners ask for supplies and identify the supplies' locations. Have several pairs present their dialogs to the class.

♦ Have pairs write their dialogs and post them in the room.

WORKBOOK

Unit 2, Exercise 3

WORKFORCE SKILLS (page 18)

Get supplies

Maintain supplies

★　　★　　★　　★　　★

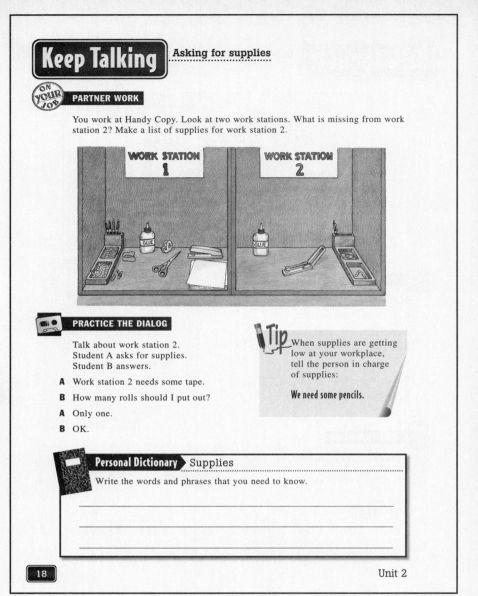

Keep Talking · Asking for supplies

ON YOUR JOB · PARTNER WORK

You work at Handy Copy. Look at two work stations. What is missing from work station 2? Make a list of supplies for work station 2.

WORK STATION 1 · WORK STATION 2

PRACTICE THE DIALOG

Talk about work station 2.
Student A asks for supplies.
Student B answers.

A Work station 2 needs some tape.

B How many rolls should I put out?

A Only one.

B OK.

Tip When supplies are getting low at your workplace, tell the person in charge of supplies:

We need some pencils.

Personal Dictionary ▸ Supplies

Write the words and phrases that you need to know.

18 · Unit 2

Personal Dictionary

Have learners add the words in their Personal Dictionary to their *Workforce Writing Dictionary.* For more information, see "Workforce Writing Dictionary" on page v.

PREPARATION

Use the picture cards or real supplies to review supplies on the page. Encourage learners to use peer teaching to clarify any unfamiliar vocabulary.

PRESENTATION

1. Have learners read the Purpose Statement. For more information, see "Purpose Statement" on page viii.

ON YOUR JOB 2. Have partners read the Partner Work instructions. Make sure each pair knows what to do. Then have pairs complete the activity. Ask several pairs to share their lists with the class.

 3. Have partners read the instructions for Practice the Dialog. Then present the

dialog. See "Presenting a Dialog" on page ix. Then have learners read the instructions again. Make sure everyone knows what to do. Allow learners time to complete the activity. Have learners change partners and repeat the activity. Have several pairs present their dialogs to the class.

4. Have learners read the Personal Dictionary instructions. Then use the Personal Dictionary procedures on page ix. Remind learners to continue to add words to their dictionaries throughout the unit.

Tip Have learners read the Tip independently. Have learners discuss how the advice will help them. For more information, see "Presenting a Tip" on page ix.

FOLLOW-UP

Catalog Scavenger Hunt: Provide teams with supply catalogs from different companies and a list of work-place supplies. Have teams find as many of the supplies as possible in their catalogs and list the page numbers and the headings (if any) under which the supplies were categorized. Have team reporters share their findings with the class.

♦ Have teams compare the prices for the supplies in the different catalogs. Are the prices similar? Which catalogs have the lowest prices?

WORKBOOK

Unit 2, Exercise 4

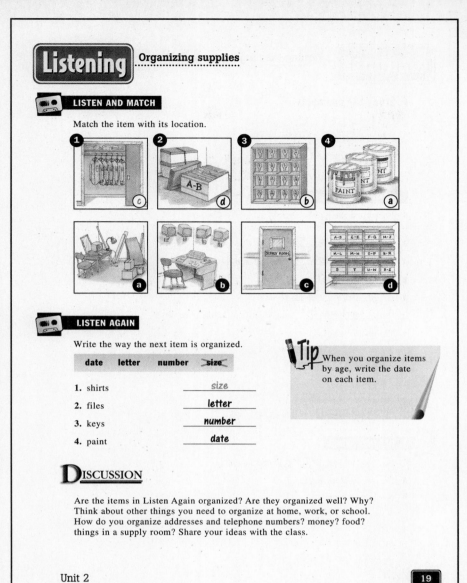

Listening — Organizing supplies

LISTEN AND MATCH

Match the item with its location.

LISTEN AGAIN

Write the way the next item is organized.

date	letter	number	size

1. shirts — *size*
2. files — *letter*
3. keys — *number*
4. paint — *date*

Tip When you organize items by age, write the date on each item.

DISCUSSION

Are the items in Listen Again organized? Are they organized well? Why? Think about other things you need to organize at home, work, or school. How do you organize addresses and telephone numbers? money? food? things in a supply room? Share your ideas with the class.

Unit 2   **19**

Language Note

Help learners brainstorm a list of kinds of storage facilities, such as supply rooms, closets, stock rooms, warehouses, and so on.

PREPARATION

Preteach **size, letter, number,** and **date** by describing things that are organized in each way such as clothes in a store or names in a telephone book. Clarify that a **storage room** is a place people keep unused objects.

PRESENTATION

1. Have learners read and discuss the Purpose Statement. For more information, see "Purpose Statement" on page viii.

 2. Have learners read the Listen and Match instructions. Then have them look at the pictures. Help the learners identify the objects and the rooms. Clarify that picture b is a security room and that picture 1 is a closet. Make sure that

everyone understands the instructions. Then play the tape or read the Listening Transcript aloud two or more times as learners complete the activity. Have learners check their work. For more information, see "Presenting a Listening Activity" on page ix.

 3. Have learners read the Listen Again instructions. Make sure that everyone understands the instructions. Then play the tape or read the Listening Transcript aloud one or more times as learners complete the activity. Have learners check their work. For more information, see "Presenting a Listening Activity" on page ix.

4. Have learners read the Discussion questions. Have teams discuss the questions. Have team reporters share their ideas with the class.

Tip Have learners read the Tip. Have learners discuss how the advice will help them. For more information, see "Presenting a Tip" on page ix.

FOLLOW-UP

More Workplace Organization: Have pairs choose a supply relevant to their workplace and discuss how they would organize the supply. Have pairs share their ideas with the class.

♦ Have pairs switch supplies. Have each pair think of a different way to organize the supply. Let the pairs share their ideas with the class.

WORKBOOK

Unit 2, Exercise 5

Get supplies

Maintain supplies and equipment

★   ★   ★   ★   ★

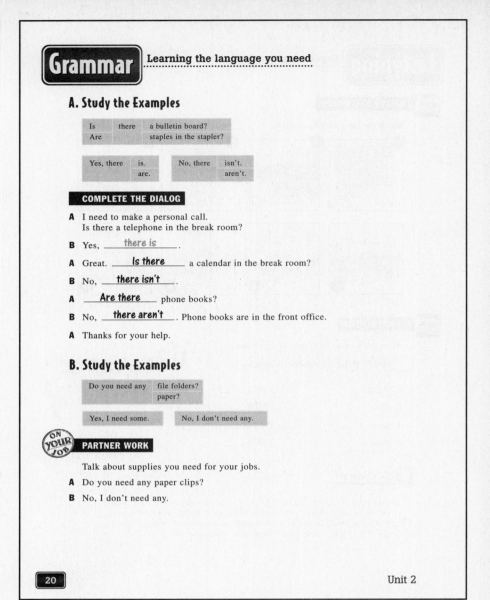

Grammar .... Learning the language you need

A. Study the Examples

| Is | there | a bulletin board? |
| Are | | staples in the stapler? |

| Yes, there | is. | | No, there | isn't. |
| | are. | | | aren't. |

COMPLETE THE DIALOG

A I need to make a personal call.
Is there a telephone in the break room?

B Yes, ____there is____ .

A Great. ____Is there____ a calendar in the break room?

B No, ____there isn't____ .

A ____Are there____ phone books?

B No, ____there aren't____ . Phone books are in the front office.

A Thanks for your help.

B. Study the Examples

| Do you need any | file folders? |
| | paper? |

| Yes, I need some. | No, I don't need any. |

PARTNER WORK

Talk about supplies you need for your jobs.

A Do you need any paper clips?

B No, I don't need any.

20   Unit 2

PREPARATION

Review the language in the grammar boxes with learners before they open their books, if necessary.

PRESENTATION

1. Have learners read and discuss the Purpose Statement. For more information, see "Purpose Statement" on page viii.

2. Have learners read the grammar boxes in A. Have learners use the language in the boxes to say as many sentences as possible. Tell learners that they can use the grammar boxes throughout the unit to review or check sentence structures.

3. Have learners read Complete the Dialog. If necessary, model the first item. Allow learners to complete the activity. Have learners check each other's work in pairs. Have them practice the dialog in pairs. Ask several pairs to read the dialog aloud while the rest of the class checks their work.

4. Focus attention on the grammar boxes in B. Follow the procedures in 2.

5. Have pairs read the Partner Work instructions. Make sure each learner knows what to do. If necessary, model the activity with a learner. Allow learners to complete the activity. Have learners switch partners and repeat the activity. Ask several pairs to present their conversations to the class.

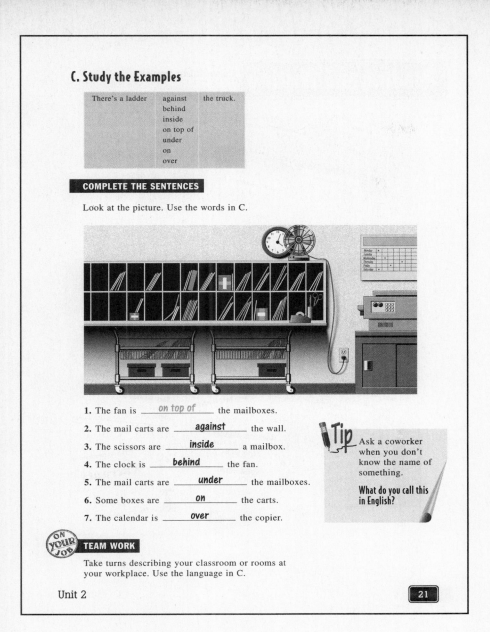

C. Study the Examples

There's a ladder	against	the truck.
	behind	
	inside	
	on top of	
	under	
	on	
	over	

COMPLETE THE SENTENCES

Look at the picture. Use the words in C.

1. The fan is ___on top of___ the mailboxes.

2. The mail carts are ___against___ the wall.

3. The scissors are ___inside___ a mailbox.

4. The clock is ___behind___ the fan.

5. The mail carts are ___under___ the mailboxes.

6. Some boxes are ___on___ the carts.

7. The calendar is ___over___ the copier.

Tip Ask a coworker when you don't know the name of something.

What do you call this in English?

TEAM WORK

Take turns describing your classroom or rooms at your workplace. Use the language in C.

---

6. Focus attention on the grammar box in C. Follow the procedure in 2.

7. Have learners read the instructions for Complete the Sentences. Then focus attention on the illustration. Have learners say as much as they can about it. Make sure everyone understands what to do. If necessary, model the first item. Then have learners complete the activity independently. Have a different learner read each sentence aloud as the rest of the class checks their answers.

 8. Have teams read the Team Work instructions. Make sure each team knows what to do. If necessary, model the activity. Then have teams complete the activity. Have team reporters share their answers with the class.

Tip Have learners read the Tip independently. Provide any clarification needed. Ask learners to give a few examples. For more information, see "Presenting a Tip" on page ix.

FOLLOW-UP

What Is It? Use items in your classroom to play this game. Demonstrate by thinking of an object in your classroom and giving two or three clues. For example, say, *It's against the wall. It's behind me. What is it?* Learners will answer, *It's your desk.* Divide the class into small teams and have them play the game until each learner has a chance to give clues.

♦ Have learners give clues about objects in other rooms at their workplaces or school.

WORKBOOK

Unit 2, Exercises 6A–6C

BLACKLINE MASTERS

Blackline Master: Unit 2

Use filing systems

Organize materials

★   ★   ★   ★   ★

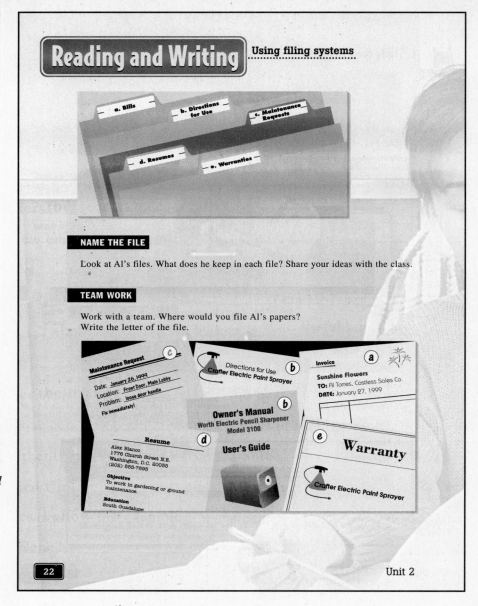

Reading and Writing — Using filing systems

NAME THE FILE

Look at Al's files. What does he keep in each file? Share your ideas with the class.

TEAM WORK

Work with a team. Where would you file Al's papers?
Write the letter of the file.

22   Unit 2

Teaching Note

Point out to learners that they should think carefully before naming a file. If a name is specific, for example, "Electric Bills," they may end up with lots of files that aren't very full. If the name is too broad, such as "All Bills," they may end up with a few files that are too full.

PREPARATION

Preteach or review the vocabulary on the page. Clarify that a **filing system** is a way to organize documents in files. Explain that a **maintenance request** is a form to complete at work when you want something fixed. A **warranty** is a form stating that if something you buy breaks or doesn't work, the company that made it will fix or replace it. A **resume** is a list of a person's work history and education. An **owner's manual** or **user's guide** explains how to use and/or take care of something you buy. If possible, bring in examples of each item.

PRESENTATION

1. Have learners read and discuss the Purpose Statement. For more information, see "Purpose Statement" on page viii.

2. Have learners preview the names of Al's files and the papers he needs to file before they begin the activities on the page. Encourage learners to say everything they can. Write their ideas on the board or restate them in acceptable English.

3. Have learners read the instructions for Name the File. Make sure everyone knows what to do. Then have learners complete the activity in teams. Have a team secretary keep a list of the team's ideas. Ask each team to share its ideas with the class.

4. Have learners read the Team Work instructions. Make sure each team knows what to do. If necessary, model the activity. Then have teams complete the activity. Have teams share their

ideas with the class. Ask teams to compare ideas.

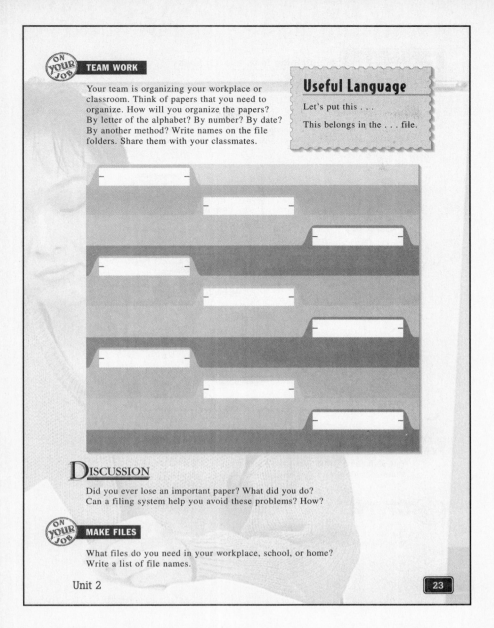

TEAM WORK

Your team is organizing your workplace or classroom. Think of papers that you need to organize. How will you organize the papers? By letter of the alphabet? By number? By date? By another method? Write names on the file folders. Share them with your classmates.

Useful Language

Let's put this . . .

This belongs in the . . . file.

DISCUSSION

Did you ever lose an important paper? What did you do? Can a filing system help you avoid these problems? How?

ON YOUR JOB **MAKE FILES**

What files do you need in your workplace, school, or home? Write a list of file names.

Unit 2

23

---

5. Have teams read the Team Work instructions. Make sure each team knows what to do. If necessary, model the activity. Then have teams complete the activity. Have team reporters share their file names with the class. (If learners' occupations do not involve organizing papers, have learners discuss how to organize objects they work with.)

6. Have learners read the Discussion questions. Model the activity if necessary by talking about your own filing system and how you keep track of papers. Then have learners complete the activity independently. Have them discuss their ideas. Have team reporters share their ideas with the class.

ON YOUR JOB **7.** Have learners read the instructions for Make Files. Model the activity if necessary by naming files that you need. Then have learners complete the activity independently. Have several learners share their lists with the class.

FOLLOW-UP

Filing: Have learners work in teams. Ask each team to imagine a project, such as buying equipment, moving to a different office, starting a new job, filing invoices, or paying monthly bills. Ask them to come up with a list of papers that their project is likely to produce. Ask each team to create two or three file names for their papers and to share their file names with the class.

♦ Have teams label actual folders with their file names. Then, have each team read its file names and show their file folders.

WORKBOOK

Unit 2, Exercises 7A–7B

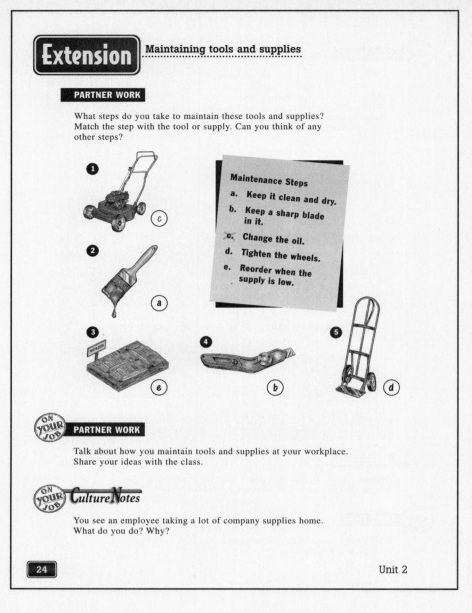

Extension — Maintaining tools and supplies

PARTNER WORK

What steps do you take to maintain these tools and supplies? Match the step with the tool or supply. Can you think of any other steps?

Maintenance Steps

a. Keep it clean and dry.

b. Keep a sharp blade in it.

c. Change the oil.

d. Tighten the wheels.

e. Reorder when the supply is low.

PARTNER WORK

Talk about how you maintain tools and supplies at your workplace. Share your ideas with the class.

Culture Notes

You see an employee taking a lot of company supplies home. What do you do? Why?

24   Unit 2

PREPARATION

1. Display picture cards with the tools and supplies from this page. Have learners identify the supplies and equipment. Encourage learners to use peer teaching to clarify any unfamiliar vocabulary.

2. Ask learners to talk about how they take care of the tools and supplies. Supply any new language learners need. Ask learners to talk about why it's important to take care of tools and supplies. Elicit or present the steps in the list of maintenance steps on the page. Supply any language needed.

PRESENTATION

1. Have learners read and discuss the Purpose Statement. For more information, see "Purpose Statement" on page viii.

2. Have learners read the instructions for Partner Work. If necessary, model the first item. Allow learners to complete the activity. Have learners review each other's work in pairs. Ask several learners to read their answers aloud while the rest of the class checks their work.

3. Have learners read the instructions for the second Partner Work activity. If necessary, model the activity with a volunteer. Then have pairs complete the activity. Ask several pairs to share their conversations with the class.

4. Have learners read Culture Notes and talk over their responses in teams. Have team reporters share their ideas with the class. Ask the teams to compare each other's ideas.

FOLLOW-UP

My Tools: Have learners think of one tool or supply that they use often. Have them write a list of steps to maintain that tool or supply. Encourage them to include even simple maintenance steps, such as *Keep it clean*. Have learners share their lists with the class.

♦ Encourage the class to come up with an additional maintenance step for each tool or supply that is presented. Let each learner decide if he or she will add it to his or her list. Post the lists in the class.

WORKBOOK

Unit 2, Exercise 8

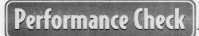 **How well can you use the skills in this unit?** ....

Complete the activities. Go over your work with a partner or your teacher. Then complete the Performance Review on page 26.

SKILL 1 GET THE SUPPLIES I NEED

You are stocking your workplace with supplies. Tell your partner or teacher what supplies you need.

SKILL 2 ORGANIZE MATERIALS

How are the things organized? Circle the answer.

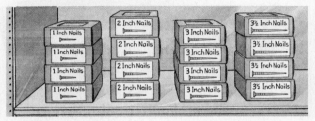

1. (size)   letter of the alphabet

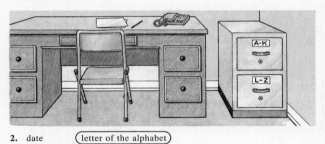

2. date   (letter of the alphabet)

SKILL 3 MAINTAIN SUPPLIES AND EQUIPMENT

What supplies and equipment do you use at your workplace or school? How do you maintain them? Tell your partner or teacher.

Unit 2   25

PRESENTATION

Use any of the procedures in "Evaluation," page x, with pages 25 and 26. Record individuals' results on the Unit 2 Individual Competency Chart. Record the class's results on the Class Cumulative Competency Chart.

SKILL 4   USE FILE SYSTEMS

Read the file names. Read the papers. Where would you file the papers?
Write the letter of the file.

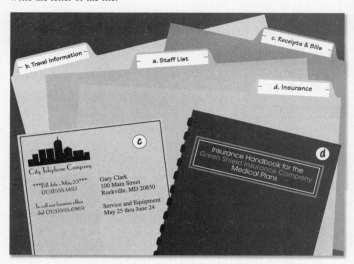

b. Travel Information

a. Staff List

c. Receipts & Bills

d. Insurance

City Telephone Company

Bill date - May 23
(703)555-1452

To call our business office
dial (703)555-6869

Gary Clark
100 Main Street
Rockville, MD 20850

Service and Equipment
May 25 thru June 24

c

Insurance Handbook for the
Green Shield Insurance Company
Medical Plans

d

Performance Review

I can...

☐ **1.** get the supplies I need.

☐ **2.** organize materials.

☐ **3.** maintain supplies and equipment.

☐ **4.** use file systems.

Discussion

Work with a team. How will your new skills help you? Make a list.
Share your list with the class.

26   Unit 2

PRESENTATION

Follow the instructions on page 25.

INFORMAL WORKPLACE-SPECIFIC ASSESSMENT

Ask learners to name supplies they use
at work, say how they get the supplies,
and say how the supplies are organized.

WORKBOOK

Unit 2, Exercise 9

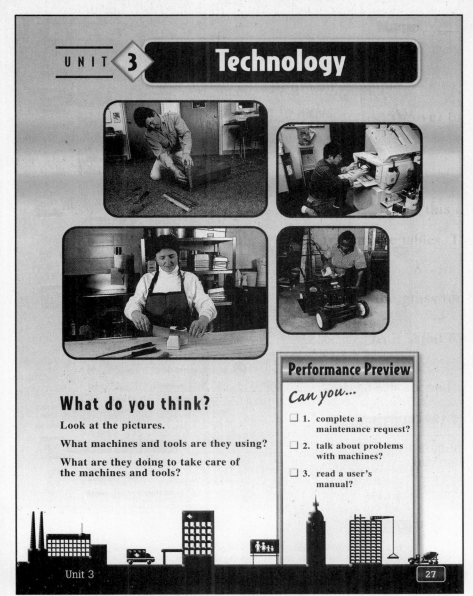

UNIT 3

Technology

What do you think?

Look at the pictures.

What machines and tools are they using?

What are they doing to take care of the machines and tools?

Performance Preview
Can you...

☐ 1. complete a maintenance request?

☐ 2. talk about problems with machines?

☐ 3. read a user's manual?

Unit 3

27

Unit 3 Overview
—SCANS Competencies—

★ Monitor and correct performance

★ Maintain and troubleshoot technology

★ Select equipment and tools

★ Apply technology to specific tasks

Workforce Skills

● Complete a maintenance report

● Talk about problems with machines

● Read a user's manual

Materials

● Picture cards of machines and supplies in the unit, other machines relevant to learners, and people maintaining machines (including a plumber and an electrician)

● Sample user manuals for machines

● Blank service request forms similar to those on page 34, and blank maintenance report forms

● A pack of index cards

Unit Warm-Up

To get learners thinking about the unit topic, show one or two picture cards of machines. Have learners name the machines they use. Ask if the machines ever break. What do they do then?

★   ★   ★   ★   ★

WORKFORCE SKILLS (page 27)

Talk about problems with machines

★   ★   ★   ★   ★

PREPARATION

Display the picture cards of machines. Help learners identify the machines. Encourage learners to use peer teaching to clarify any unfamiliar vocabulary.

PRESENTATION

1. Focus attention on the photographs. Ask learners to speculate about what the unit might be about. Write their ideas on the board and/or restate them in acceptable English.

2. Have learners talk about the pictures. Have them identify the machines and tools, and speculate about what the people are doing in each picture.

3. Help the learners read the questions. Discuss the questions with the class.

4. You may want to use the Performance Preview to provide learners with an overview of the skills in the unit. Have learners read the list of skills and discuss what they will learn in the unit.

FOLLOW-UP

Machine Maintenance: Divide the class into teams. Have team members make a list of supplies needed to repair a machine they use at work.

♦ Have the teams write the maintenance steps for the machines. Have them post their ideas on a bulletin board.

WORKBOOK

Unit 3, Exercises 1A–1B

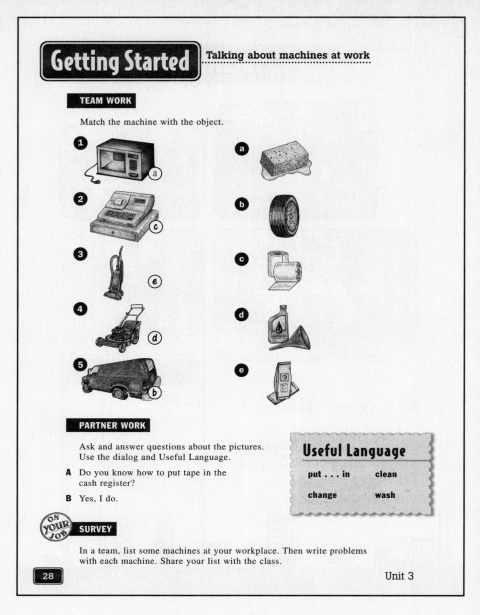

Getting Started — Talking about machines at work

TEAM WORK

Match the machine with the object.

1   a
2   b
3   c
4   d
5   e

PARTNER WORK

Ask and answer questions about the pictures. Use the dialog and Useful Language.

A   Do you know how to put tape in the cash register?

B   Yes, I do.

Useful Language

put . . . in	clean
change	wash

SURVEY

In a team, list some machines at your workplace. Then write problems with each machine. Share your list with the class.

28   Unit 3

Teaching Note

Use this page to introduce the new language in the unit. Whenever possible, encourage peer teaching. Supply any language learners need.

PREPARATION

Display the picture cards showing people maintaining machines. Ask learners what the people are doing and what supplies they are using.

PRESENTATION

1. Have learners read and discuss the Purpose Statement. For more information, see "Purpose Statement" on page viii.

2. Focus attention on the illustrations. Encourage learners to say as much as they can about them.

3. Have teams read the Team Work instructions. Make sure each team knows what to do. If necessary, model the first item. Remind the teams that they are responsible for making sure that each member understands the new language. Then have teams complete the activity. If learners need help, encourage them to consult other teams. Have team reporters share their answers with the class.

4. Have partners read the Partner Work instructions. Then focus attention on the Useful Language box. Help learners read the expressions. Make sure each pair knows what to do. If necessary, model the activity. Then have pairs complete it. Have learners switch partners and repeat the activity several times. Supply any language needed. Have one or two partners present their dialogs to the class.

 5. Have teams read the Survey instructions. Make sure each person knows what to do. If necessary, model the activity.

Then have teams complete the activity. Have teams share their answers with the class. For more information, see "Survey" on page viii.

FOLLOW-UP

Machines and Supplies: Distribute pictures of machines and of supplies used to maintain them. Each learner should get a different picture. Have learners find the classmate whose machine matches their supply, or vice versa.

♦ Ask teams to talk about how they get supplies. Do learners get them from the supply room, special-order them, or obtain them from another person, such as their boss?

WORKBOOK

Unit 3, Exercises 2A–2C

Talking about problems with machines

PRACTICE THE DIALOG

A The vacuum cleaner is broken.

B Did you ask Diane for help?
She can usually fix it.

A Yes, I did. She told me to take it to the maintenance department.

B Good. Tell the maintenance department we need the vacuum cleaner repaired today.

PARTNER WORK

Talk about the problems with the machines in the picture. Figure out solutions. Use the dialog and Useful Language above.

ASAP PROJECT

As a team, make a user's manual for a machine. Choose a machine you all use. Write instructions for the machine. Include a drawing. List common problems with the machine. Tell what to do to fix the problem. Complete this project as you work through this unit.

Useful Language

Can you help me with . . .

The coffee maker isn't working/is leaking/ is out of order.

You need to fill out a maintenance request.

You should call a plumber/ electrician.

Unit 3

`29`

ASAP PROJECT

Have learners read the instructions. Discuss the project and its purpose with learners. Make sure that everyone understands. If possible, bring in real manuals for the machines that learners choose. Have learners use these as models for their own manuals. Help learners assign themselves to teams based upon their knowledge, skills, interests, or other individual strengths. Have each team select a leader, and have the team leaders or the whole class select an overall project leader. Throughout the rest of the unit, allow time for learners to work on the project. Have the teams agree on a deadline when the project will be finished. For more information, see "ASAP Project" on page vi.

PREPARATION

1. Use picture cards to preteach or review the names of the objects on the page.

2. Model reporting a problem with a machine. Introduce the Useful Language by modeling different ways to report a problem. Report various problems to different learners. Then let learners report machine problems to you. Use pictures to clarify **plumber, electrician,** and **maintenance request form.**

PRESENTATION

1. Have learners read and discuss the Purpose Statement. For more information, see "Purpose Statement" on page viii.

 2. Focus attention on the picture. Encourage learners to say as much as they can

about it. Have them identify the machines and say the problem with each one. Then present the dialog. See "Presenting a Dialog" on page ix.

3. Have partners read the Partner Work instructions. Focus attention on the Useful Language box. Help learners read the expressions. If necessary, model pronunciation. Then have learners complete the activity. Have learners switch partners and repeat the activity. Have one or two pairs present their dialogs to the class.

FOLLOW-UP

Dialogs: Have pairs use the picture cards of machines to create dialogs in which they report a problem with a machine and suggest how to handle it.

Have several pairs present their dialogs to the class.

◆ Have pairs write their dialogs.

WORKBOOK

Unit 3, Exercises 3A–3B

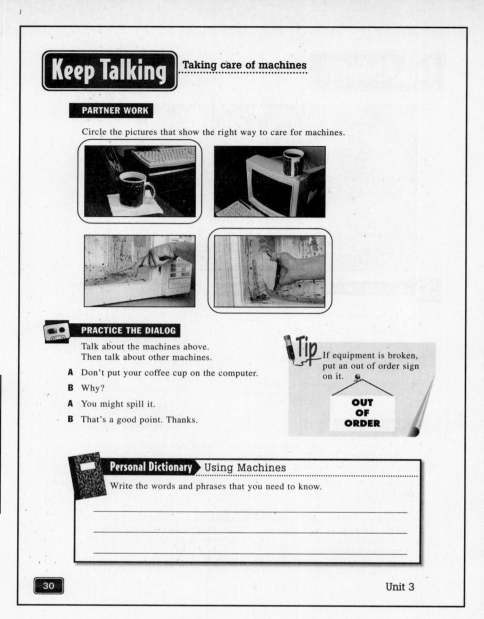

Keep Talking   Taking care of machines

PARTNER WORK

Circle the pictures that show the right way to care for machines.

PRACTICE THE DIALOG

Talk about the machines above.
Then talk about other machines.

A   Don't put your coffee cup on the computer.

B   Why?

A   You might spill it.

B   That's a good point. Thanks.

Tip   If equipment is broken, put an out of order sign on it.

OUT OF ORDER

Personal Dictionary ▷ Using Machines

Write the words and phrases that you need to know.

_____

_____

_____

30   Unit 3

Personal Dictionary ▷

Have learners add the words in their Personal Dictionary to their *Workforce Writing Dictionary*. For more information, see "Workforce Writing Dictionary" on page v.

PREPARATION

Use the picture cards to review names of machines. Act out an incorrect way to care for a machine. Help learners describe what you're doing.

PRESENTATION

1. Have learners read the Purpose Statement. For more information, see "Purpose Statement" on page viii.

2. Focus attention on the pictures. Encourage learners to say as much as they can about them. Write their ideas on the board or restate them in acceptable English.

3. Have partners read the Partner Work instructions. Make sure each pair knows what to do. If necessary, model the

activity on the board. Then have pairs complete the activity.

4. Present the dialog. See "Presenting a Dialog" on page ix. Then have partners read the instructions for Practice the Dialog. Model, if necessary. Allow the learners time to complete the activity. Have learners change partners and repeat. Have several pairs present their dialogs to the class.

5. Have learners read the Personal Dictionary instructions. Then use the Personal Dictionary procedures on page ix. Remind learners to continue to add words to their dictionaries throughout the unit.

 Tip   Have learners read the Tip independently. Have learners discuss how the advice will

help them and why it's important. For more information, see "Presenting a Tip" on page ix.

FOLLOW-UP

Machine Care: Have learners work in pairs. Use the picture cards of people maintaining machines to prompt learners. Have learners write a sentence describing the activity shown on the card. Then, under each sentence, have pairs list as many machines as they can think of that need such care.

♦ Have learners compare their lists. As a class, compile a master list and post it.

WORKBOOK

Unit 3, Exercise 4

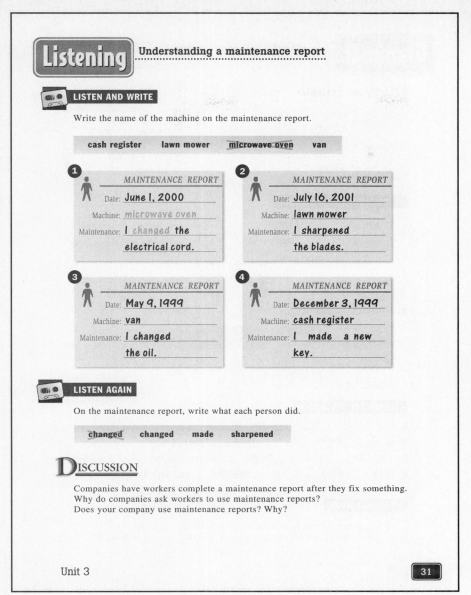

Listening **Understanding a maintenance report**

LISTEN AND WRITE

Write the name of the machine on the maintenance report.

cash register   lawn mower   microwave oven   van

1
MAINTENANCE REPORT
Date: June 1, 2000
Machine: *microwave oven*
Maintenance: I changed the
electrical cord.

2
MAINTENANCE REPORT
Date: July 16, 2001
Machine: lawn mower
Maintenance: I sharpened
the blades.

3
MAINTENANCE REPORT
Date: May 9, 1999
Machine: van
Maintenance: I changed
the oil.

4
MAINTENANCE REPORT
Date: December 3, 1999
Machine: cash register
Maintenance: I made a new
key.

LISTEN AGAIN

On the maintenance report, write what each person did.

changed   changed   made   sharpened

DISCUSSION

Companies have workers complete a maintenance report after they fix something.
Why do companies ask workers to use maintenance reports?
Does your company use maintenance reports? Why?

Unit 3

31

PREPARATION

Use the picture cards to present or review the names of the machines and the maintenance procedures on the page. Use picture cards and pantomime to clarify **cord, blades, oil, key, change, make,** and **sharpen.**

PRESENTATION

1. Have learners read and discuss the Purpose Statement. For more information, see "Purpose Statement" on page viii.

2. Focus attention on the maintenance reports. Have learners discuss the parts of the maintenance report and their purpose.

 3. Have learners read the Listen and Write instructions. Then have them read the words in the box. Make sure that

everyone understands the instructions. If necessary, model the first item. Then play the tape or read the Listening Transcript aloud two or more times as learners complete the activity. Have learners check their work. For more information, see "Presenting a Listening Activity" on page ix.

 4. Have learners read the Listen Again instructions. Then follow the procedures in 3.

5. Have learners read the Discussion instructions. Make sure everyone knows what to do. Then have learners work in teams to discuss their ideas. Have team reporters share their ideas with the class. Ask the teams to compare their ideas.

FOLLOW-UP

Think About Maintenance: Have learners work in teams of four. Provide each team with a blank maintenance report form. Have each team complete the form. Have teams share their forms with the class.

♦ Have teams list the people to whom they might report malfunctioning machines. The list may include their supervisor or coworkers. Have them explain why each person is on the list.

WORKBOOK

Unit 3, Exercise 5

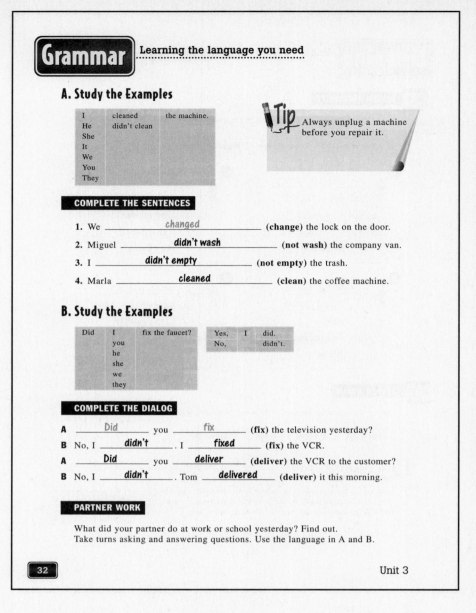

| **Grammar** | Learning the language you need |

A. Study the Examples

I	cleaned	the machine.
He	didn't clean	
She		
It		
We		
You		
They		

Tip Always unplug a machine before you repair it.

COMPLETE THE SENTENCES

1. We _____changed_____ (change) the lock on the door.
2. Miguel _____didn't wash_____ (not wash) the company van.
3. I _____didn't empty_____ (not empty) the trash.
4. Marla _____cleaned_____ (clean) the coffee machine.

B. Study the Examples

Did	I	fix the faucet?		Yes,	I	did.
	you			No,		didn't.
	he					
	she					
	we					
	they					

COMPLETE THE DIALOG

A _____Did_____ you _____fix_____ (fix) the television yesterday?

B No, I _____didn't_____ . I _____fixed_____ (fix) the VCR.

A _____Did_____ you _____deliver_____ (deliver) the VCR to the customer?

B No, I _____didn't_____ . Tom _____delivered_____ (deliver) it this morning.

PARTNER WORK

What did your partner do at work or school yesterday? Find out.
Take turns asking and answering questions. Use the language in A and B.

32   Unit 3

PREPARATION

Review the language in the grammar boxes with learners before they open their books, if necessary.

PRESENTATION

1. Have learners read and discuss the Purpose Statement. For more information, see "Purpose Statement" on page viii.

2. Have learners read the grammar box in A. Have learners use the language in the box to say as many sentences as possible. Tell learners that they can use the grammar boxes throughout the unit to review or check sentence structures.

3. Focus attention on Complete the Sentences. Make sure learners know what to do. If necessary, model the first item. Allow learners to complete the activity. Have learners check each other's work in pairs. Ask several learners to read their sentences aloud while the rest of the class checks their work.

4. Focus attention on the grammar boxes in B. Follow the procedures in 2.

5. Focus attention on Complete the Dialog. Make sure learners know what to do. If necessary, model the first item. Allow learners to complete the activity. Have learners check each other's work in pairs. Ask several pairs to read their dialogs aloud while the rest of the class checks their work.

6. Have partners read the Partner Work instructions. Make sure each pair knows what to do. If necessary, model the activity. Then have pairs complete the activity. Ask volunteers to present their conversations to the class.

Tip Have learners read the Tip independently. Provide any clarification needed. Ask learners to say why the advice is important. For more information, see "Presenting a Tip" on page ix.

C. Study the Examples

| I | went | to the meeting. |
| | didn't go | |

Irregular Verbs

bring	brought
buy	bought
go	went
have	had
make	made
send	sent
take	took

COMPLETE THE DIALOG

1. I _____went_____ (**go**) to the post office.

2. I _____bought_____ (**buy**) twenty stamps for Mrs. Li.

3. She _____had_____ (**have**) several letters to send.

4. She _____sent_____ (**send**) them to Korea.

5. I _____didn't send_____ (**not send**) a package.

6. After the post office, I _____had_____ (**have**) to go to the bank.

7. I _____made_____ (**make**) a deposit for Mrs. Li

WRITE A REPORT

Finish the report about Ernesto's work.

━━━ WORK REPORT ━━━

Worker: Ernesto Peta

Date: February 12, 1999

Mr. Johnson _____brought_____ (**bring**) a lawn mower to the shop this morning. It _____had_____ (**have**) a broken blade. I _____replaced_____ (**replace**) the blade and _____took_____ (**take**) the mower back to Mr. Johnson.

PARTNER WORK

Think about a bad experience you had with a machine. What happened? How did you fix it? Tell your partner. Share your experiences with the class.

Unit 3   33

---

7. Focus attention on the grammar boxes in C. Follow the procedure in 2.

8. Focus attention on Complete the Sentences. If necessary, model the first item. Allow learners to complete the activity. Have learners check each other's work in pairs. Ask several learners to read their sentences aloud while the rest of the class checks their work.

9. Have learners read the instructions for Write a Report. If necessary, model the first item. Then have learners complete the activity independently. Have a different learner read each sentence aloud as the rest of the class checks their answers.

10. Have partners read the Partner Work instructions. Make sure each pair knows what to do. If necessary, model the activity. Then have pairs complete the activity. Supply any language needed. Have several learners share their experiences with the class.

FOLLOW-UP

I Did It! Have learners act out something that they did at their workplace yesterday for the rest of the class to figure out. Demonstrate by acting out something in your workday. For example, you went to school/class. You took some books. As you act, have learners ask you yes/no questions about what you did. *Did you go to school/class? Yes, I did. Did you take something? Yes, I did. Did you take scissors? No, I didn't.* Divide the class into small teams and have them play the game until each learner has a chance to act out something from their workday.

♦ Have learners write two or three things that they did at work on separate index cards. Collect them in a pile. Have learners play I Did It! by picking a card from the pile and acting out the activity for the rest of the class to figure out.

WORKBOOK

Unit 3, Exercises 6A–6D

BLACKLINE MASTERS

Blackline Master: Unit 3

★   ★   ★   ★   ★

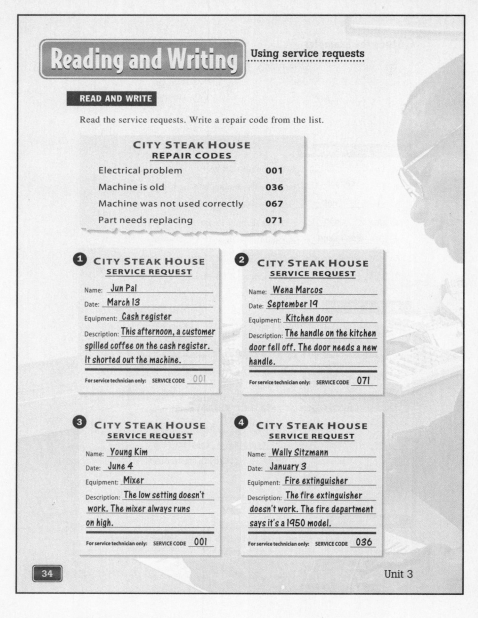

PREPARATION

Use one of the blank service request forms to introduce new vocabulary. Explain that employees use a service request form to ask for needed repairs. Help learners name the information that goes in each part of the form.

PRESENTATION

1. Have learners read and discuss the Purpose Statement. For more information, see "Purpose Statement" on page viii.

2. Have learners preview the service requests and the repair code list before they complete the activity. Encourage learners to say everything they can about the service requests. Write their ideas on the board or restate them in acceptable English.

3. Have learners read the instructions for Read and Write. Make sure everyone knows what to do. Then have learners complete the activity independently. Have learners review each other's work in pairs. Ask several pairs to share their answers with the class while the rest of the class checks their work.

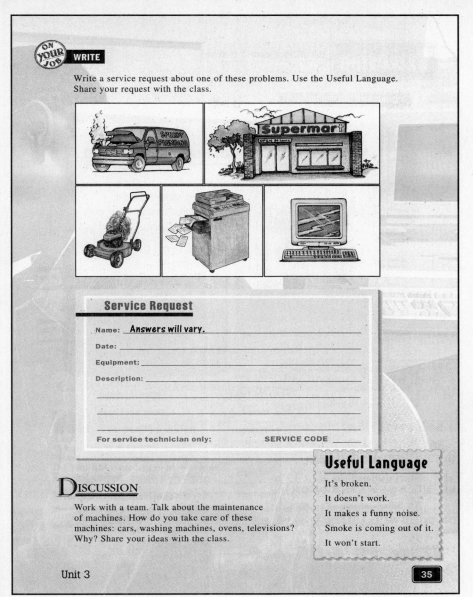

WRITE

Write a service request about one of these problems. Use the Useful Language. Share your request with the class.

Service Request

Name: _Answers will vary._

Date: _____

Equipment: _____

Description: _____

_____

_____

_____

For service technician only: SERVICE CODE _____

DISCUSSION

Work with a team. Talk about the maintenance of machines. How do you take care of these machines: cars, washing machines, ovens, televisions? Why? Share your ideas with the class.

Useful Language

It's broken.

It doesn't work.

It makes a funny noise.

Smoke is coming out of it.

It won't start.

Unit 3

35

Language Note

In addition to the sentences in the Useful Language box, you may want to introduce other language describing machine malfunctions, such as **It burned out, A warning light is flashing,** *and* **It's jammed.**

4. Have teams read the instructions for Write. Then focus attention on the illustrations. Discuss with learners what's wrong in each picture. Refer learners to the Useful Language box. Help learners read the expressions. Make sure each team knows what to do. If necessary, model the activity. Then have teams complete the activity. Have team reporters share their service requests with the class.

5. Have learners read the Discussion instructions. Model the activity, if necessary, by describing the maintenance of a machine in your daily life. Have learners discuss their ideas. Have team reporters share their ideas with the class.

FOLLOW-UP

Service Requests: Help the class brainstorm categories of problems with machines. Then have learners assign a repair code to each category. List the categories and repair codes on the board.

♦ Have learners work in pairs. Give each pair a blank service request form. Ask them to write a service request for a machine they know. Have them include the repair code on their service request.

WORKBOOK

Unit 3, Exercises 7A–7B

★   ★   ★   ★   ★

SCANS Note

You might talk about the value of regular maintenance in preventing problems with tools and machines. Point out to learners that it is usually easier and less expensive to prevent a problem than to fix a problem.

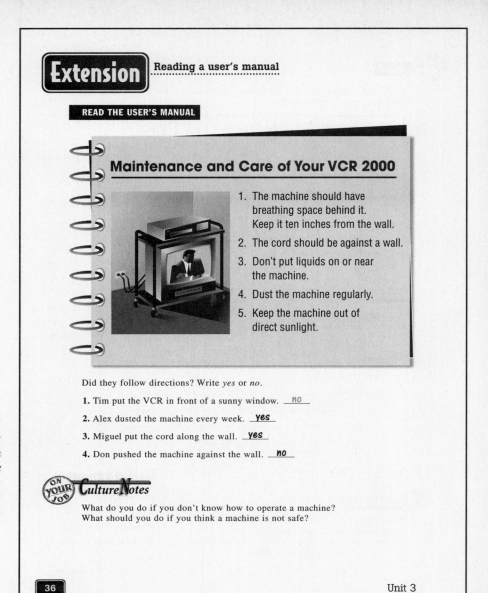

Extension — Reading a user's manual

READ THE USER'S MANUAL

Maintenance and Care of Your VCR 2000

1. The machine should have breathing space behind it. Keep it ten inches from the wall.
2. The cord should be against a wall.
3. Don't put liquids on or near the machine.
4. Dust the machine regularly.
5. Keep the machine out of direct sunlight.

Did they follow directions? Write *yes* or *no*.

1. Tim put the VCR in front of a sunny window. __no__
2. Alex dusted the machine every week. __yes__
3. Miguel put the cord along the wall. __yes__
4. Don pushed the machine against the wall. __no__

ON YOUR JOB — *Culture Notes*

What do you do if you don't know how to operate a machine? What should you do if you think a machine is not safe?

36   Unit 3

PREPARATION

Preteach the new language in the user's manual. Display a real user's manual and identify it. Use a real cord to clarify **cord.** Ask learners to name examples of machines with cords or point out any machines in the classroom with cords attached. Give examples of **liquids** and identify them as liquids. Pantomime **dusting** furniture and identify the action. Draw a picture of the sun and its rays, or point out real sunlight in the classroom, to identify **sunlight.**

PRESENTATION

1. Have learners read and discuss the Purpose Statement. For more information, see "Purpose Statement" on page viii.

2. Have learners preview the user's manual before they complete the activity. Encourage them to say everything they can about it. Write their ideas on the board or restate them in acceptable English. Then have learners read the user's manual independently.

3. Have learners read the instructions for Read the User's Manual. If necessary, model the first item. Allow learners to complete the activity independently. Have learners review each other's work in pairs. Ask several learners to read their answers aloud while the rest of the class checks their work.

 4. Have learners read Culture Notes and talk over their responses in teams. Have team reporters share their ideas with the class. Ask the teams to discuss each other's ideas.

FOLLOW-UP

User's Manual: Have teams look at a real user's manual and find information about taking care of a machine. Then have them share the maintenance steps with the class.

♦ Have learners discuss the maintenance steps. Which steps can they do themselves? Which steps do they need help with? Who would they ask? Have them discuss their reasons.

WORKBOOK

Unit 3, Exercise 8

Performance Check
How well can you use the skills in this unit?

Complete the activities. Go over your work with a partner or your teacher.
Then complete the Performance Review on page 38.

SKILL 1	COMPLETE A MAINTENANCE REQUEST

Your vacuum cleaner, cash register, or another machine is not working.
Complete the service request. Use today's date.

Service Request

Name: **Answers will vary.** _____

Date: _____

Equipment: _____

Description: _____

_____

_____

_____

_____

_____

For service technician only: SERVICE CODE _____

SKILL 2	TALK ABOUT PROBLEMS WITH MACHINES

Think of a problem with a machine at your workplace or school.
Who can you ask for help? What do you say? Tell your partner
or your teacher.

Unit 3   37

PRESENTATION

Use any of the procedures in
"Evaluation," page x, with pages 37
and 38. Record individuals' results
on the Unit 3 Individual Competency
Chart. Record the class's results on the
Class Cumulative Competency Chart.

Are they following the user's manual? Write *yes* or *no*.

Care of Your Microwave Oven

Tips

- Keep the microwave oven about 15 inches or more from the wall.
- Keep the oven away from water.

1. Lin put the microwave oven 15 inches from the wall. __yes__
2. Al put a glass of water on top of the microwave. __no__

Performance Review

I can...

- ☐ 1. complete a maintenance request.
- ☐ 2. talk about problems with machines.
- ☐ 3. read a user's manual.

DISCUSSION

Work with a team. How will your new skills help you? Make a list. Share your list with the class.

38   Unit 3

PRESENTATION

Follow the instructions on page 37.

INFORMAL WORKPLACE-SPECIFIC ASSESSMENT

Ask learners to name a machine at their workplace and say how they maintain it.

WORKBOOK

Unit 3, Exercise 9

What do you think?

Look at the schedules.

Do you use schedules at work?

How do you manage your time?

Performance Preview

Can you...

☐ 1. understand schedules?

☐ 2. interpret a holiday schedule?

☐ 3. use calendars and planners?

Unit 4

39

Unit 4 Overview
—SCANS Competencies—

★ Allocate time

★ Interpret information

★ Understand organizational systems

Workforce Skills

• Understand schedules

• Interpret a holiday schedule

• Use calendars and planners

Materials

• A large calendar showing one month

• Self-stick notes

• Large paper

• An assortment of calendars, planners, and schedules (such as holiday, work, class, and bus schedules)

• A teaching clock with movable hands

• A calendar for the current year, including major holidays

Unit Warm-Up

To get the learners thinking about the unit topic, display a large calendar. Ask volunteers about their responsibilities for an average week. Ask learners to each write one responsibility on a self-stick note. Have them put the notes on the calendar. Then have learners discuss their schedules and responsibilities.

★   ★   ★   ★   ★

WORKFORCE SKILLS (page 39)

Understand schedules

★   ★   ★   ★   ★

PREPARATION

Display the various calendars and schedules and help learners examine them. Have learners talk about the kind of information usually found on schedules. Encourage learners to use peer teaching to clarify any unfamiliar vocabulary.

PRESENTATION

1. Focus attention on the photographs. Ask learners to speculate about what the unit might be about. Write their ideas on the board and/or restate them in acceptable English.

2. Have learners talk about the photographs. Have them identify the schedules they see in the photographs. Help learners relate the photographs to the calendars and schedules that you showed.

3. Help learners read the questions. Discuss the questions with the class.

4. You may want to use the Performance Preview to provide learners with an overview of the skills in the unit. Have learners read the list of skills and discuss what they will learn in the unit.

FOLLOW-UP

My Schedules: Have teams discuss ways that their school or workplace uses schedules and calendars. Ask, *Where does your workplace post work*

schedules? How do workers find out about schedule changes?

♦ Help learners write on the board a one-month schedule of when your class meets. Ask volunteers to copy the schedule onto a large piece of paper and post it in your classroom.

WORKBOOK

Unit 4, Exercises 1A–1B

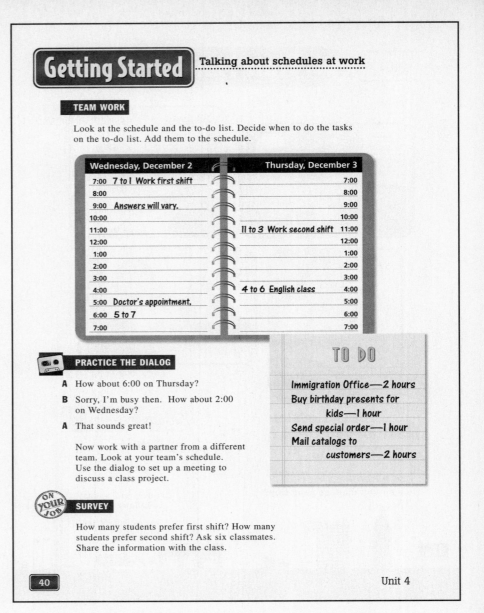

Getting Started — Talking about schedules at work

TEAM WORK

Look at the schedule and the to-do list. Decide when to do the tasks on the to-do list. Add them to the schedule.

Wednesday, December 2		Thursday, December 3	
7:00	7 to 1 Work first shift		7:00
8:00			8:00
9:00	Answers will vary.		9:00
10:00			10:00
11:00		11 to 3 Work second shift	11:00
12:00			12:00
1:00			1:00
2:00			2:00
3:00			3:00
4:00		4 to 6 English class	4:00
5:00	Doctor's appointment,		5:00
6:00	5 to 7		6:00
7:00			7:00

PRACTICE THE DIALOG

A How about 6:00 on Thursday?

B Sorry, I'm busy then. How about 2:00 on Wednesday?

A That sounds great!

Now work with a partner from a different team. Look at your team's schedule. Use the dialog to set up a meeting to discuss a class project.

TO DO

Immigration Office—2 hours
Buy birthday presents for
 kids—1 hour
Send special order—1 hour
Mail catalogs to
 customers—2 hours

SURVEY

How many students prefer first shift? How many students prefer second shift? Ask six classmates. Share the information with the class.

40   Unit 4

Teaching Note

Use this page to introduce the new language in the unit. Whenever possible, encourage peer teaching. Supply any language learners need.

SCANS Note

Explain to learners that there are many different types of calendars and planners to help people manage time and organize activities. If possible, display some examples. Point out that learners can make their own calendars and planners easily. A simple piece of paper with the date and a list of tasks can help learners organize their time.

PREPARATION

Preteach the new language in the lesson. Use the datebook on the page to preteach **schedule**. Point to the times and the items listed and say, *This is the schedule for December 2 and 3*. Explain to learners that people use schedules to manage time and organize activities. If necessary, clarify other words in the datebook and to-do list.

PRESENTATION

1. Have learners read and discuss the Purpose Statement. For more information, see "Purpose Statement" on page viii.

2. Encourage learners to say as much as they can about the datebook. Write their ideas on the board and/or restate them in acceptable English.

3. Have teams read the Team Work instructions. Make sure each team knows what to do. Remind the teams to make sure each member understands the new language. Then have teams complete the activity. If learners need help, encourage them to consult other teams. Have team reporters share their answers with the class.

4. Focus attention on Practice the Dialog and present the dialog. See "Presenting a Dialog" on page ix. Then have partners read the instructions. Make sure each pair knows what to do. Then have pairs complete the activity. Have one or two partners present their dialogs to the class.

5. Have learners read the Survey instructions. Make sure each person knows what to do.

If necessary, model the activity. Then have learners complete it and share their answers with the class. See "Survey" on page viii.

FOLLOW-UP

Table: Help the class use the information from the Survey to create a table showing the work shifts that learners prefer. Have learners discuss the table.

♦ Help teams create a bar graph. The horizontal axis should show the work shifts. The vertical axis should show how many learners prefer each shift.

WORKBOOK

Unit 4, Exercises 2A–2C

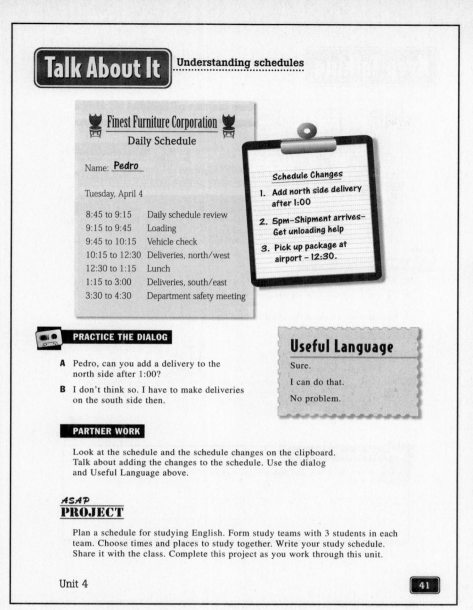

Talk About It · Understanding schedules

Finest Furniture Corporation
Daily Schedule

Name: Pedro

Tuesday, April 4

8:45 to 9:15	Daily schedule review
9:15 to 9:45	Loading
9:45 to 10:15	Vehicle check
10:15 to 12:30	Deliveries, north/west
12:30 to 1:15	Lunch
1:15 to 3:00	Deliveries, south/east
3:30 to 4:30	Department safety meeting

Schedule Changes

1. Add north side delivery after 1:00
2. 5pm–Shipment arrives– Get unloading help
3. Pick up package at airport – 12:30.

 PRACTICE THE DIALOG

A Pedro, can you add a delivery to the north side after 1:00?

B I don't think so. I have to make deliveries on the south side then.

Useful Language

Sure.

I can do that.

No problem.

PARTNER WORK

Look at the schedule and the schedule changes on the clipboard. Talk about adding the changes to the schedule. Use the dialog and Useful Language above.

ASAP PROJECT

Plan a schedule for studying English. Form study teams with 3 students in each team. Choose times and places to study together. Write your study schedule. Share it with the class. Complete this project as you work through this unit.

Unit 4

41

ASAP PROJECT

Have learners read the instructions. Discuss the project and its purpose with learners. Make sure that everyone understands. Help learners assign themselves to teams based upon their knowledge, skills, interests, or other personal strengths. Have each team select a leader, and have the team leaders or the whole class select an overall project leader. Throughout the rest of the unit, allow time for learners to work on the project. Have the teams agree on a deadline when the project will be finished. For more information, see "ASAP Project" on page vi.

PREPARATION

1. Preteach the new language. For **loading**, pantomime loading a cart with books. Say, *I'm loading the cart.* Explain that cars and trucks are **vehicles.** Use pantomime, real items, and/or drawings to preteach **delivery, shipment, package,** and **airport.**

2. Present the language in the Useful Language box by having learners make small requests of you. Respond with the target phrases. Then carry out the requests.

PRESENTATION

1. Have learners read and discuss the Purpose Statement. For more information, see "Purpose Statement" on page viii.

2. Focus attention on the Daily Schedule and Schedule Changes on the page. Encourage learners to say as much as they can about each one. Have them identify the tasks and the times. Then present the dialog. See "Presenting a Dialog" on page ix.

3. Have partners read the Partner Work instructions. Make sure everyone understands what to do. Focus attention on the Useful Language box. Help learners read the expressions. If necessary, model pronunciation. Then have learners complete the activity. Have learners switch partners and repeat the activity. Have one or two pairs present their dialogs to the class.

FOLLOW-UP

Dialogs: Have learners work in pairs. Ask learners to write their schedules for tomorrow on sheets of paper. Have learners share their schedules with the class.

♦ In the next class, have learners talk about the schedules they made. Did they follow them? Were they useful?

WORKBOOK

Unit 4, Exercise 3

★   ★   ★   ★   ★

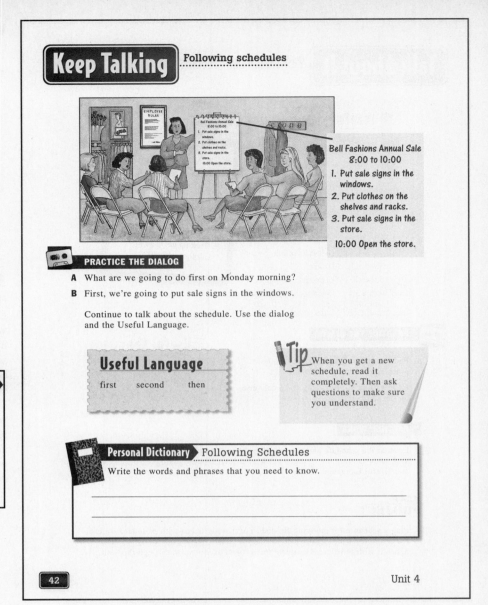

Keep Talking — Following schedules

Bell Fashions Annual Sale
8:00 to 10:00
1. Put sale signs in the windows.
2. Put clothes on the shelves and racks.
3. Put sale signs in the store.

10:00 Open the store.

PRACTICE THE DIALOG

A   What are we going to do first on Monday morning?

B   First, we're going to put sale signs in the windows.

Continue to talk about the schedule. Use the dialog and the Useful Language.

Useful Language
first   second   then

Tip When you get a new schedule, read it completely. Then ask questions to make sure you understand.

Personal Dictionary ▷ Following Schedules
Write the words and phrases that you need to know.

_____

_____

42   Unit 4

Personal Dictionary

Have learners add the words in their Personal Dictionary to their *Workforce Writing Dictionary*. For more information, see "Workforce Writing Dictionary" on page v.

PREPARATION

Present or review the words in the Useful Language box by talking about your daily work routine. Encourage learners to make sentences about the sequence of events in their daily schedules. *First, I get to work. Then, I open the store for customers.*

PRESENTATION

1. Have learners read the Purpose Statement. For more information, see "Purpose Statement" on page viii.

2. Focus attention on the schedule. Present the language in the schedule by acting out each activity in the schedule. Have learners figure out which activity you are acting out.

3. Focus attention on Practice the Dialog and present the dialog. See "Presenting a Dialog" on page ix. Then have partners read the instructions. Model if necessary. Allow learners time to complete the activity. Have learners change partners and repeat. Have several pairs present their dialogs to the class.

4. Have learners read the Personal Dictionary instructions. Then use the Personal Dictionary procedures on page ix. Remind learners to continue to add words to their dictionaries throughout the unit.

Tip Have learners read the Tip independently. Have learners discuss how the advice will help them. For more information, see "Presenting a Tip" on page ix.

FOLLOW-UP

My Plans For Tomorrow: Have learners work in pairs. Have them use the Useful Language to ask each other about their plans for tomorrow. For example, *What are you going to do first tomorrow?* If they are employed, encourage them to talk about their work schedules.

♦ Discuss these questions: *Why does it help you to write a schedule? Why does it help to review the schedule occasionally? Where is a good place to keep your schedule? How can you make your schedule easier?*

WORKBOOK

Unit 4, Exercise 4

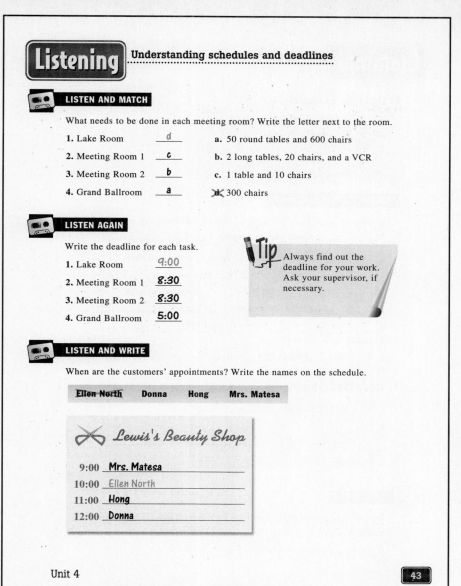

Listening ·········· Understanding schedules and deadlines

 LISTEN AND MATCH

What needs to be done in each meeting room? Write the letter next to the room.

1. Lake Room _____d_____   **a.** 50 round tables and 600 chairs

2. Meeting Room 1 _____c_____   **b.** 2 long tables, 20 chairs, and a VCR

3. Meeting Room 2 _____b_____   **c.** 1 table and 10 chairs

4. Grand Ballroom _____a_____   ~~d.~~ 300 chairs

 LISTEN AGAIN

Write the deadline for each task.

1. Lake Room ___9:00___

2. Meeting Room 1 ___8:30___

3. Meeting Room 2 ___8:30___

4. Grand Ballroom ___5:00___

> **Tip** Always find out the deadline for your work. Ask your supervisor, if necessary.

 LISTEN AND WRITE

When are the customers' appointments? Write the names on the schedule.

~~Ellen North~~   Donna   Hong   Mrs. Matesa

✂ Lewis's Beauty Shop

9:00 __Mrs. Matesa__

10:00 __Ellen North__

11:00 __Hong__

12:00 __Donna__

Unit 4

Language Note

*Discuss with learners different ways to write the time of day in English: **9:00, nine o'clock, 9 a.m., 9 p.m.; 12:00, noon, midnight**, etc.*

PREPARATION

Use the teaching clock to review saying the time in English. Display times and have learners say and write them. Then display times and have learners say what they have to do today or tomorrow at those times.

PRESENTATION

1. Have learners read and discuss the Purpose Statement. For more information, see "Purpose Statement" on page viii.

 2. Have learners read the Listen and Match instructions. Make sure that everyone understands the instructions. If necessary, model the first item. Then play the tape or read the Listening Transcript aloud two or more times as learners complete the activity. Check learners' work. For more information, see "Presenting a Listening Activity" on page ix.

3. Have learners read the Listen Again instructions. Then follow the procedures in 2.

4. Have learners read the Listen and Write instructions. Then follow the procedures in 2.

Have learners read the Tip independently. Have learners discuss how the advice will help them. For more information, see "Presenting a Tip" on page ix.

FOLLOW-UP

Deadlines: Have learners make a list of deadlines for upcoming tasks they have to do. Have volunteers share their lists with the class.

♦ Have learners work in pairs. Ask partners to help each other prioritize their tasks to meet their deadlines.

WORKBOOK

Unit 4, Exercises 5A–5B

Unit 4

Understand schedules

Use calendars and planners

★   ★   ★   ★   ★

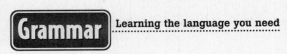

Grammar · Learning the language you need

A. Study the Examples

I We You They	have to don't have to	deliver these packages.
He She	has to doesn't have to	deliver these packages.

COMPLETE THE SENTENCES

1. Workers ____have to open____ (**open**) mail every day.

2. The manager ____doesn't have to explain____ (**not explain**) special tasks.

3. Workers ____have to put____ (**put**) postage on all mail.

4. Regular mail ____doesn't have to be____ (**not be**) ready until 3:30.

5. Overnight mail ____has to be____ (**be**) ready by 1:30.

6. Customers ____don't have to send____ (**not send**) packages first class.

7. ____Do____ we ____have to go____ (**go**) to the post office every day?

8. Yes, you ____have to take____ (**take**) the packages there every day at 3:30.

B. Study the Examples

Do	I we you they	have to sign the attendance sheet?
Does	he she	

 TEAM WORK

What do you have to do? Ask and answer questions about your workplaces.

1. punch in on a time clock   2. work on weekends

3. go to department meetings   4. get to work early

Unit 4

PREPARATION

Review the language in the grammar boxes with learners before they open their books, if necessary.

PRESENTATION

1. Have learners read and discuss the Purpose Statement. For more information, see "Purpose Statement" on page viii.

2. Have learners read the grammar boxes in A. Have learners use the language in the boxes to say as many sentences as possible. Tell learners that they can use the grammar boxes throughout the unit to review or check sentence structures.

3. Focus attention on Complete the Sentences. Make sure learners know what to do. If necessary, model the first item. Allow learners to complete the

activity. Have learners check each other's work in pairs. Ask several learners to read their sentences aloud while the rest of the class checks their work.

4. Focus attention on the grammar box in B. Follow the procedures in 2.

 5. Have teams read the Team Work instructions. Make sure each team knows what to do. If necessary, model the activity with a learner. Allow learners to complete the activity. Have learners switch teams and repeat the activity. Ask several teams to present their answers to the class.

English ASAP

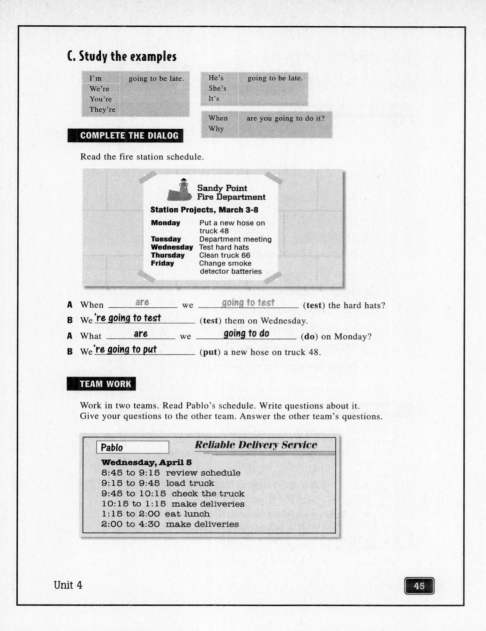

C. Study the examples

I'm We're You're They're	going to be late.

He's She's It's	going to be late.

When Why	are you going to do it?

COMPLETE THE DIALOG

Read the fire station schedule.

Sandy Point Fire Department

Station Projects, March 3-8

Monday	Put a new hose on truck 48
Tuesday	Department meeting
Wednesday	Test hard hats
Thursday	Clean truck 66
Friday	Change smoke detector batteries

A When ___are___ we ___going to test___ (**test**) the hard hats?

B We___'re going to test___ (**test**) them on Wednesday.

A What ___are___ we ___going to do___ (**do**) on Monday?

B We___'re going to put___ (**put**) a new hose on truck 48.

TEAM WORK

Work in two teams. Read Pablo's schedule. Write questions about it.
Give your questions to the other team. Answer the other team's questions.

Pablo	*Reliable Delivery Service*

Wednesday, April 5
8:45 to 9:15 review schedule
9:15 to 9:45 load truck
9:45 to 10:15 check the truck
10:15 to 1:15 make deliveries
1:15 to 2:00 eat lunch
2:00 to 4:30 make deliveries

Unit 4

45

---

6. Focus attention on the grammar boxes in C. Follow the procedures in 2.

7. Have learners read the instructions for Complete the Dialog. Read the schedule with learners. Clarify language as needed. If necessary, model the first item. Allow learners to complete the activity. Have learners check each other's work in pairs. Ask several pairs to read the dialog aloud while the rest of the class checks their work.

8. Focus attention on Pablo's schedule. Encourage learners to say as much as they can about it. Then have teams read the Team Work instructions. Make sure each team knows what to do. If necessary, model the activity. Then have teams complete the activity. Supply any language needed. Have each team share

one or two of its questions and answers with the class.

FOLLOW-UP

I'm Going To . . . Play "I'm Going To . . ." One learner starts by saying what he/she will do at work the next day: *I'm going to (make deliveries)*. The next learner repeats the first learner's statement and adds his/her own work plans: *Mohamed is going to make deliveries and I'm going to fix the copier.* Continue. If a learner cannot remember the whole list, he or she has to drop out of the game. Continue until only one person can say the list.

◆ Have learners write three sentences about what they're going to do at work the next day. Ask volunteers to share their sentences with the class.

WORKBOOK
Unit 4, Exercises 6A–6D

BLACKLINE MASTERS
Blackline Master: Unit 4

★   ★   ★   ★   ★

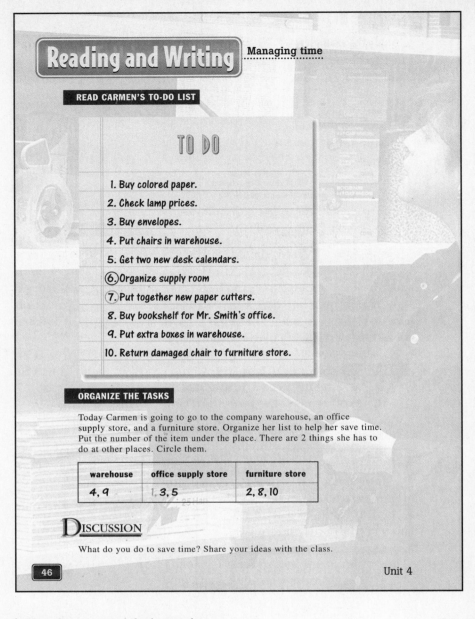

Reading and Writing — Managing time

READ CARMEN'S TO-DO LIST

TO DO

1. Buy colored paper.
2. Check lamp prices.
3. Buy envelopes.
4. Put chairs in warehouse.
5. Get two new desk calendars.
6. Organize supply room
7. Put together new paper cutters.
8. Buy bookshelf for Mr. Smith's office.
9. Put extra boxes in warehouse.
10. Return damaged chair to furniture store.

ORGANIZE THE TASKS

Today Carmen is going to go to the company warehouse, an office supply store, and a furniture store. Organize her list to help her save time. Put the number of the item under the place. There are 2 things she has to do at other places. Circle them.

warehouse	office supply store	furniture store
4, 9	1, 3, 5	2, 8, 10

DISCUSSION

What do you do to save time? Share your ideas with the class.

46   Unit 4

PREPARATION

Use pictures, realia, and/or pantomime to present or review key vocabulary on this page: **lamp, warehouse, paper cutter, bookshelf, damaged,** and **furniture.** Use each word in a sentence. Ask learners questions to encourage them to use the words in sentences, too.

PRESENTATION

1. Have learners read and discuss the Purpose Statement. For more information, see "Purpose Statement" on page viii.

2. Have learners preview Carmen's to-do list. Encourage learners to say everything they can about the tasks. Write their ideas on the board or restate them in acceptable English. Then have learners read the to-do list independently.

3. Have learners read the instructions for Organize the Tasks. Make sure everyone knows what to do. Then have learners complete the activity individually. Have learners review each other's work in pairs. Ask several learners to share their answers with the class while the rest of the class checks their work.

4. Have learners read the Discussion instructions. Then have learners work in teams to discuss ways that they save time. Have team reporters share their ideas with the class.

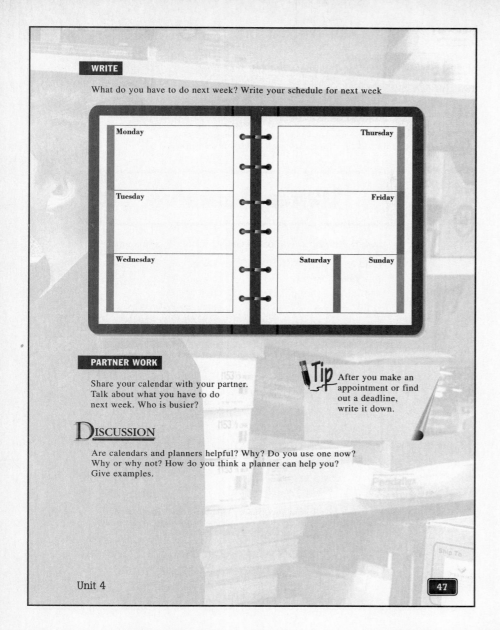

WRITE

What do you have to do next week? Write your schedule for next week

Monday		Thursday
Tuesday		Friday
Wednesday	Saturday	Sunday

PARTNER WORK

Share your calendar with your partner. Talk about what you have to do next week. Who is busier?

Tip After you make an appointment or find out a deadline, write it down.

DISCUSSION

Are calendars and planners helpful? Why? Do you use one now? Why or why not? How do you think a planner can help you? Give examples.

---

5. Have teams read the instructions for Write. Make sure each learner knows what to do. If necessary, model the activity. Then have learners complete the activity. Have several learners share their schedules with the class.

6. Have partners read the Partner Work instructions. Then have learners complete the activity. Do they have activities in common? When do they do them? Have learners switch partners and repeat the activity. Have one or two pairs present their ideas to the class. Who is busier?

7. Have learners read the Discussion instructions. Model the activity by displaying calendars and planners and talking about how you use calendars and planners in your own daily life. Then have teams complete the activity.

Have them discuss their ideas. Have team reporters share their ideas with the class. Ask the teams to compare each other's ideas.

Tip Have learners read the Tip independently. Have learners discuss how the advice will help them. For more information, see "Presenting a Tip" on page ix.

FOLLOW-UP

Our Responsibilities: Have learners write a to-do list of things that they have to do at their workplace or school. Then have learners share their lists with the class.

♦ Have learners organize their lists to help them save time. Ask volunteers to share their ideas.

WORKBOOK
Unit 4, Exercises 7A--7B

WORKFORCE SKILLS (page 48)

Interpret a holiday schedule

★　　★　　★　　★　　★

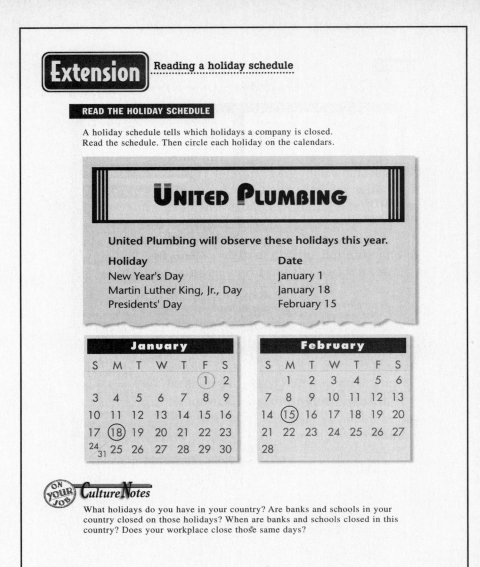

Extension ⋯⋯⋯ Reading a holiday schedule

READ THE HOLIDAY SCHEDULE

A holiday schedule tells which holidays a company is closed. Read the schedule. Then circle each holiday on the calendars.

UNITED PLUMBING

United Plumbing will observe these holidays this year.

Holiday	Date
New Year's Day	January 1
Martin Luther King, Jr., Day	January 18
Presidents' Day	February 15

January

S	M	T	W	T	F	S
					①	2
3	4	5	6	7	8	9
10	11	12	13	14	15	16
17	⑱	19	20	21	22	23
24 31	25	26	27	28	29	30

February

S	M	T	W	T	F	S
	1	2	3	4	5	6
7	8	9	10	11	12	13
14	⑮	16	17	18	19	20
21	22	23	24	25	26	27
28						

ON YOUR JOB *Culture Notes*

What holidays do you have in your country? Are banks and schools in your country closed on those holidays? When are banks and schools closed in this country? Does your workplace close those same days?

48   Unit 4

PREPARATION

1. Display a calendar. Show learners how holidays are noted on calendars. Help learners name the holidays on the calendar.

2. Ask teams to think of all the holidays they know in the U.S. Ask them to make a list. Which holidays do they have off from work? Have team reporters share their ideas with the class.

PRESENTATION

1. Have learners read and discuss the Purpose Statement. For more information, see "Purpose Statement" on page viii.

2. Have learners preview the holiday schedule and calendars on the page before they complete the activity. Encourage learners to say everything

they can about them. Which holidays do United Plumbing employees have off from work? Write their ideas on the board or restate them in acceptable English.

3. Have learners read the instructions for Read the Holiday Schedule. If necessary, model the first item. Allow learners to complete the activity. Have learners review each other's work in pairs. Ask several learners to read their answers aloud while the rest of the class checks their work.

 4. Have learners read Culture Notes and talk over their responses in teams. Have team reporters share their ideas with the class. Ask the teams to compare each other's ideas.

FOLLOW-UP

How Many Holidays? Have learners work in two teams. Give each team a calendar for the year. Ask one team to find all of the holidays in the first six months of the year. Ask the other team to find the holidays in the last six months of the year. Have team reporters list the holidays their teams found on the board. How many holidays did the teams find in total?

◆ Have learners keep personal calendars. Ask them to write the holiday schedule from their workplace or school on their calendars.

WORKBOOK

Unit 4, Exercise 8

 **Performance Check** | How well can you use the skills in this unit? ....

Complete the activities. Go over your work with a partner or your teacher. Then complete the Performance Review on page 50.

SKILL 1   **UNDERSTAND SCHEDULES**

Answer the questions about Ruben's schedule.

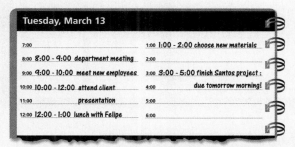

Tuesday, March 13

7:00	1:00 1:00 - 2:00 choose new materials
8:00 8:00 - 9:00 department meeting	2:00
9:00 9:00 - 10:00 meet new employees	3:00 3:00 - 5:00 finish Santos project :
10:00 10:00 - 12:00 attend client	4:00 due tomorrow morning!
11:00 presentation	5:00
12:00 12:00 - 1:00 lunch with Felipe	6:00

1. What time is Ruben going to meet new employees?   _9:00_

2. Does Ruben have time for another meeting in the morning?   _no_

3. What time is Ruben free in the afternoon?   _2:00_

SKILL 2   **INTERPRET A HOLIDAY SCHEDULE**

> November 28–29 . . . . . Thanksgiving
> December 25 . . . . Christmas

1. It's November 27. Is the company open? _yes_

2. It's December 24. Is the company open? _yes_

3. It's December 25. Is the company open? _no_

Unit 4   **49**

PRESENTATION

Use any of the procedures in "Evaluation," page x, with pages 49 and 50. Record individuals' results on the Unit 4 Individual Competency Chart. Record the class's results on the Class Cumulative Competency Chart.

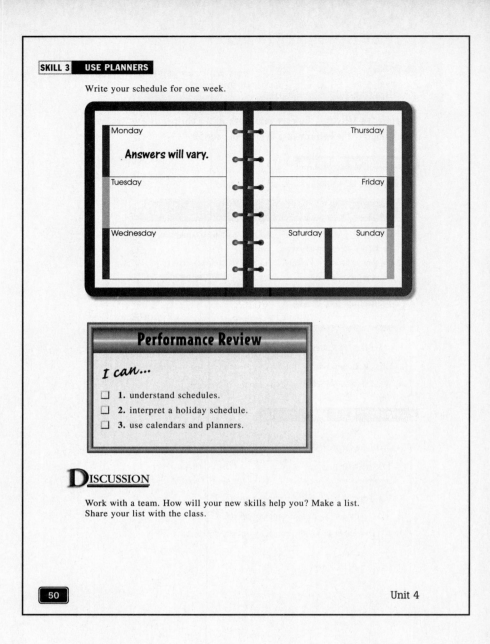

Write your schedule for one week.

Monday	Thursday
Answers will vary.	
Tuesday	Friday
Wednesday	Saturday / Sunday

Performance Review

I can...

☐ **1.** understand schedules.

☐ **2.** interpret a holiday schedule.

☐ **3.** use calendars and planners.

DISCUSSION

Work with a team. How will your new skills help you? Make a list. Share your list with the class.

50   Unit 4

PRESENTATION

Follow the instructions on page 49.

INFORMAL WORKPLACE-SPECIFIC ASSESSMENT

Have learners discuss a schedule from their workplace with you. Make sure learners clarify the main parts of the schedule.

WORKBOOK

Unit 4, Exercise 9

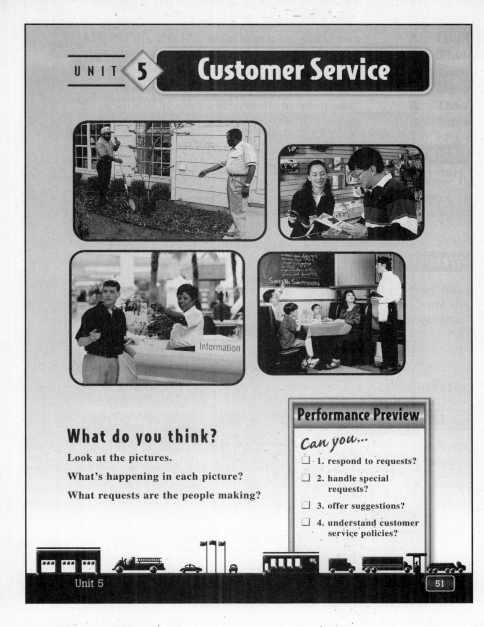

Customer Service

What do you think?

Look at the pictures.

What's happening in each picture?

What requests are the people making?

Performance Preview

Can you...

☐ 1. respond to requests?

☐ 2. handle special requests?

☐ 3. offer suggestions?

☐ 4. understand customer service policies?

Unit 5 Overview

—SCANS Competencies—

★ Serve customers

★ Interpret and communicate information

★ Work on teams

★ Work with cultural diversity

Workforce Skills

● Respond to requests

● Handle special requests

● Offer suggestions

● Understand customer service policies

Materials

● Picture cards of customers and workers in customer service situations

● A large menu with several meal specials, such as **Hamburger with French fries** and **Chicken with salad and baked potato,** or copies of real menus from local restaurants

● Receipts and blank return forms

Unit Warm-Up

To get learners thinking about the unit topic, act out courteous and rude customer service. Ask learners to say why the service was good or bad. Ask learners to share their own experiences as customers.

★ ★ ★ ★ ★

WORKFORCE SKILLS (page 51)

Respond to requests

Handle special requests

★ ★ ★ ★ ★

PREPARATION

Ask learners what they think customer service means. Do their workplaces have customer service policies? What are they?

PRESENTATION

1. Focus attention on the photographs. Ask learners what the unit might be about. Write their ideas on the board and/or restate them in acceptable English.

2. Have learners talk about the pictures. Have them identify the situations, the likely requests being made in each

situation, and likely responses to the requests.

3. Help learners read the questions. Discuss the questions with the class.

4. You may want to use the Performance Preview to provide learners with an overview of the skills in the unit. Have learners read the list of skills and discuss what they will learn in the unit.

FOLLOW-UP

What Do Customers Want? In teams, have learners answer the question *What do your customers want?* Have teams list their answers. Have team reporters share their lists with the class.

♦ Ask teams to discuss why customers want the things learners listed. Have teams share their ideas.

WORKBOOK

Unit 5, Exercises 1A–1B

WORKFORCE SKILLS (page 52)

Respond to requests

Handle special requests

★　　★　　★　　★　　★

Teaching Note

Use this page to introduce the new language in the unit. Whenever possible, encourage peer teaching. Supply any new language learners need.

Language Note

*Explain to learners that many requests begin with **Can I/you . . . ?** Point out other ways to begin a request, such as **Could I/you . . . ? May I . . . ?***

Getting Started · Responding to requests

TEAM WORK

Choose an answer for each picture. Discuss your choices with the class.

> a. Yes, I'd be happy to.
>
> b. I'm not sure. I need to check my schedule.
>
> c. I'm sorry. We give store credit only.

Can you deliver the boxes today?　　Can you give me some towels?　　Can I get a cash refund?

PARTNER WORK

Student A is a hotel guest. Student B is an employee. Student A makes requests. Student B responds.

A Can you get me two more pillows?

B Of course. I'll be right back.

 SURVEY

What are some common requests you get at work? Talk to your classmates about them. List three of the most common requests.

Unit 5

PREPARATION

Introduce the new language *Yes, I'd be happy to*; *I'm not sure. I need to check my schedule;* and *I'm sorry. We give store credit only.* Model a situation where an employee would give one of these responses to a customer request. Then have learners name situations where they would use the other responses.

PRESENTATION

1. Have learners read and discuss the Purpose Statement. For more information see "Purpose Statement" on page viii.

2. Focus attention on the photographs. Encourage learners to say as much as they can about them. Write their ideas on the board and/or restate them in acceptable English.

3. Have teams read the Team Work instructions. Make sure each team knows what to do. If necessary, model the first item. Remind the teams that they are responsible for making sure that each member understands the new language. Then have teams complete the activity. If learners need help, encourage them to consult other teams. Have team reporters share their answers with the class.

4. Have partners read the Partner Work instructions. Make sure each pair knows what to do. If necessary, model the activity. Then have pairs complete the activity. Have learners switch partners and repeat the activity. Supply any language needed. Have one or two partners present their dialogs to the class.

 5. Have partners read the Survey instructions. Make sure each pair knows what to

do. If necessary, model the activity. Then have pairs complete the activity. Have pairs share their answers with the class. For more information, see "Survey" on page viii.

FOLLOW-UP

So Many Requests: Write the categories *home, work,* and *school* on the board. Have learners write one or two requests they get under each category. Discuss the results with the class. How are the requests in each category different? How are they the same?

♦ Have learners brainstorm appropriate ways to respond to each request. Encourage them to think of both affirmative and negative responses.

WORKBOOK

Unit 5, Exercises 2A–2B

Making suggestions

PRACTICE THE DIALOG

A I finished putting down the carpet.

B When did you finish?

A Just before lunch. I need to clean up now.

B What can we do with this extra carpet?

A We can put it in the closet in the reception area.

B That's a good idea.

Useful Language

Why don't I...?

What about...?

Why not...?

Let's....

PARTNER WORK

You're the carpet layer. Your partner is the office manager. Talk about what else to do with the extra carpet. Use the dialog and Useful Language above.

ASAP
PROJECT

As a class, think of requests at your workplace or school. Divide into teams. One team thinks of requests. The other team makes suggestions for responding to the requests. Make a chart of the requests and responses. Complete this project as you work through this unit.

Unit 5

53

ASAP
PROJECT

Have learners read the instructions. Discuss the project and its purpose with learners. Make sure that everyone understands. Help learners assign themselves to teams based upon their knowledge, skills, interests, or other individual strengths. Have each team select a leader, and have the team leaders or the whole class select an overall project leader. Throughout the rest of the unit, allow time for learners to work on the project. Have the teams agree on a deadline when the project will be finished. For more information see "ASAP Project" on page vi.

PREPARATION

Select or set up a problem situation in your classroom, such as chairs blocking an aisle or a large item blocking learners' view of the board. Model the language in the Useful Language box by suggesting ways of solving the problem. Encourage learners to offer other suggestions. Supply any language learners need.

PRESENTATION

1. Have learners read and discuss the Purpose Statement. For more information, see "Purpose Statement" on page viii.

 2. Focus attention on the picture. Encourage learners to say as much as they can about it. Ask them what the speakers might be saying. Then present the dialog. See "Presenting a Dialog" on page ix.

3. Have partners read the Partner Work instructions. Then focus attention on the Useful Language box. Help learners read the expressions. If necessary, model pronunciation. Then have learners complete the activity. Have learners switch partners and repeat the activity. Have one or two pairs present their dialogs to the class.

FOLLOW-UP

Dialogs: Have pairs use the picture cards as prompts to create a customer service dialog. Have one learner act as the employee and make a suggestion. Have the other learner act as the customer and respond to the suggestion. Ask several pairs to present their dialogs to the class.

♦ Have pairs write their dialogs. Ask them to read their dialogs to the class.

WORKBOOK

Unit 5, Exercises 3A–3B

WORKFORCE SKILLS (page 54)

Respond to requests

Understand customer service policies

★　　★　　★　　★　　★

SCANS Note

Discuss with learners why workers can't always comply with a customer request. For example, the request may conflict with company rules. Explain to learners that there are many different, polite ways to turn down a customer's special request. Offer polite ways to say no, such as Substitutions aren't allowed, but you could order fries on the side.

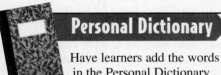

Personal Dictionary

Have learners add the words in the Personal Dictionary to their *Workforce Writing Dictionary*. For more information, see "Workforce Writing Dictionary" on page v.

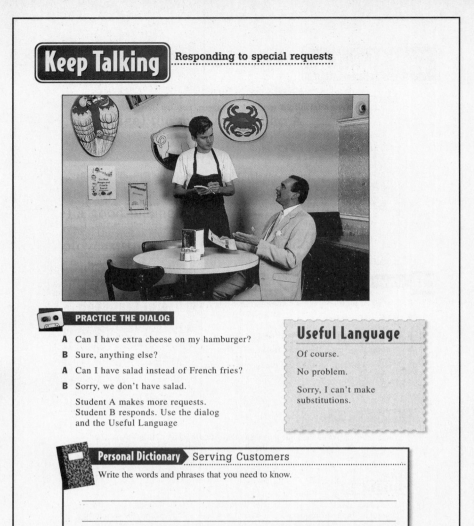

Keep Talking ············ Responding to special requests

PRACTICE THE DIALOG

A Can I have extra cheese on my hamburger?

B Sure, anything else?

A Can I have salad instead of French fries?

B Sorry, we don't have salad.

　Student A makes more requests.
　Student B responds. Use the dialog
　and the Useful Language

Useful Language

Of course.

No problem.

Sorry, I can't make substitutions.

Personal Dictionary ▶ Serving Customers

Write the words and phrases that you need to know.

_____

_____

_____

54　　　　　　　　　　　　　　　　　Unit 5

PREPARATION

1. Use the picture cards to review customer requests such as those on page 52. Model the responses in the Useful Language box: *Sorry, Of course,* and *No problem.*

2. Focus attention on the realia menu(s) to introduce or review food vocabulary. Have learners read the menu. Clarify **substitution** by saying that you want, for example, soup instead of salad with your meal. Have learners talk about which items on the menu could possibly be substituted. Supply any language learners need.

PRESENTATION

1. Have learners read the Purpose Statement. For more information, see "Purpose Statement" on page viii.

2. Focus attention on the picture. Encourage learners to say as much as they can about it. Ask them what the speakers might be saying. Then present the dialog. See "Presenting a Dialog" on page ix.

 3. Have partners read the instructions under the dialog. Model if necessary. Allow learners time to complete the activity using the large menu or menus. Have learners switch partners and repeat. Have several pairs present their dialogs to the class.

4. Have learners read the Personal Dictionary instructions. Then use the Personal Dictionary procedures on page ix. Remind learners to continue to add words to their dictionaries throughout the unit.

FOLLOW-UP

Can I . . . ? Can you . . . ? Have learners work in pairs. One learner is a department store clerk. The other is a customer. The customer makes requests of the clerk, such as *Can you deliver this computer today?* The clerk uses language from the unit to respond: *Sure. No problem.* Learners may wish to refer to page 52 to review requests and responses. Have pairs present their conversations to the class.

◆ Have learners write their dialogs.

WORKBOOK

Unit 5, Exercise 4

Handle special requests

★　　★　　★　　★　　★

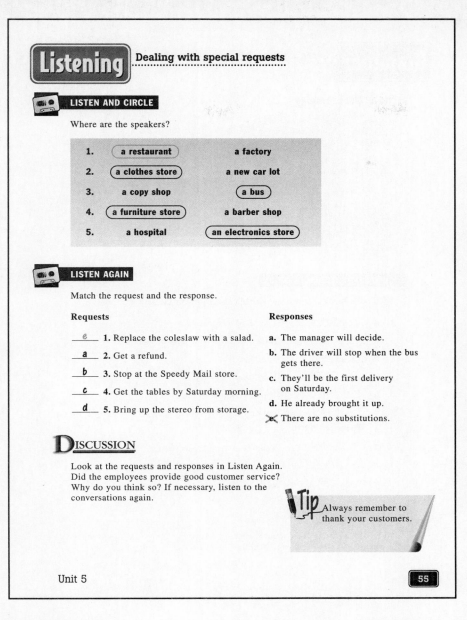

Listening Dealing with special requests

LISTEN AND CIRCLE

Where are the speakers?

1.	**a restaurant**	a factory
2.	**a clothes store**	a new car lot
3.	a copy shop	**a bus**
4.	**a furniture store**	a barber shop
5.	a hospital	**an electronics store**

LISTEN AGAIN

Match the request and the response.

Requests

_e_ 1. Replace the coleslaw with a salad.

_a_ 2. Get a refund.

_b_ 3. Stop at the Speedy Mail store.

_c_ 4. Get the tables by Saturday morning.

_d_ 5. Bring up the stereo from storage.

Responses

a. The manager will decide.

b. The driver will stop when the bus gets there.

c. They'll be the first delivery on Saturday.

d. He already brought it up.

e. There are no substitutions.

DISCUSSION

Look at the requests and responses in Listen Again. Did the employees provide good customer service? Why do you think so? If necessary, listen to the conversations again.

Tip Always remember to thank your customers.

Unit 5

55

Teaching Note

As learners become familiar with various kinds of classroom activities, give them more responsibility in organizing the activities. For example, learners can help lead discussions or decide the order in which groups will present their role plays to the class. This will help you create a more learner-centered classroom.

SCANS Note

*Explain to learners that workplaces may have both **internal** and **external** customers. Internal customers are coworkers who make requests of each other. External customers are people from outside the workplace who request services or goods.*

PREPARATION

Have learners think of a list of workplaces. Write the workplaces on the board. Ask learners to talk about requests that customers might make in these locations. How might employees respond to these requests? Clarify new vocabulary on this page: **barber shop, electronics store, storage,** etc., as needed.

PRESENTATION

1. Have learners read and discuss the Purpose Statement. For more information, see "Purpose Statement" on page viii.

2. Have learners read the Listen and Circle instructions. Make sure that everyone understands the instructions. If necessary, model the first item. Then play the tape or read the

Listening Transcript aloud two or more times as learners complete the activity. Have learners check their work. For more information, see "Presenting a Listening Activity" on page ix.

3. Have learners read the Listen Again instructions. Then follow the procedures in 2.

4. Have learners read the Discussion instructions. Make sure everyone knows what to do. Then have learners work in teams to discuss their ideas. If necessary, have learners listen again. Have team reporters share their ideas with the class. If learners think the service was poor, how would they improve it?

Tip Have learners read the Tip independently. Have learners discuss how the advice will

help them. For more information, see "Presenting a Tip" on page ix.

FOLLOW-UP

Customers at Work: Have learners work in teams. Have each team think of a workplace. In that workplace, who are the internal customers? Have each team discuss how internal customers' requests differ from external customers' requests. Have teams share their ideas with the class.

♦ Have teams write a dialog between two internal customers. Ask volunteers to present their dialogs to the class. Then have teams repeat the activity using external customers.

WORKBOOK

Unit 5, Exercise 5

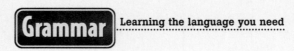

A. Study the Examples

Where	did you	buy this machine?
When		call the service center?
How		fix it?

I	bought it at the downtown store.
	called last week.
	fixed it with a new part.

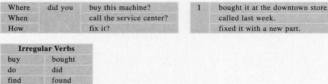

Irregular Verbs

buy	bought
do	did
find	found
get	got
make	made
pay	paid
see	saw
wear	wore
tell	told

COMPLETE THE CONVERSATION

Write *where*, *when*, or *how*. Write the correct form of the verb.

1. **A** ___Where___ did you find that jacket?

   B I ___found___ (**find**) it at a discount store downtown.

2. **A** ___When___ did you buy it?

   B I ___bought___ (**buy**) it on Thursday.

3. **A** ___How___ did you pay for it?

   B I ___paid___ (**pay**) for it with a check.

4. **A** ___Where (or When)___ did you wear it?

   B I ___wore___ (**wear**) it to the job interview.

5. **A** ___When___ did you get the job?

   B I ___got___ (**get**) the job on Friday.

 **PARTNER WORK**

Work with a partner. Talk about something that you bought for work or school. When did you buy it? Where? How did you buy it?

[56]   Unit 5

PREPARATION

Review the language in the grammar boxes with learners before they open their books, if necessary.

PRESENTATION

1. Have learners read and discuss the Purpose Statement. For more information, see "Purpose Statement" on page viii.

2. Have learners read the grammar boxes in A. Have learners use the language in the boxes to say as many sentences as possible. Tell learners that they can use the grammar boxes throughout the unit to review or check sentence structures.

3. Have learners read the instructions for Complete the Conversation. If necessary, model the first item. Allow learners to complete the activity. Have learners check each other's work in pairs. Ask a different pair of learners to read each question and answer aloud while the rest of the class checks their work.

 4. Have pairs read the Partner Work instructions. Make sure each pair knows what to do. If necessary, model the activity with a learner. Then have pairs complete the activity. Have learners switch partners and repeat the activity. Ask several pairs to present their conversations to the class.

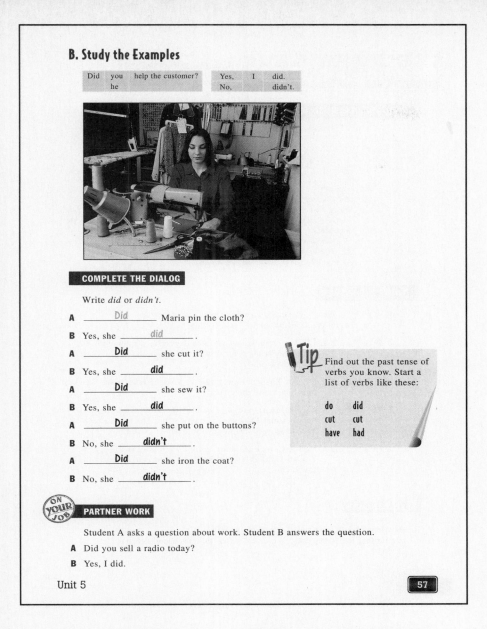

B. Study the Examples

| Did | you | help the customer? | Yes, | I | did. |
| | he | | No, | | didn't. |

COMPLETE THE DIALOG

Write *did* or *didn't*.

A _____Did_____ Maria pin the cloth?

B Yes, she _____did_____ .

A _____Did_____ she cut it?

B Yes, she _____did_____ .

A _____Did_____ she sew it?

B Yes, she _____did_____ .

A _____Did_____ she put on the buttons?

B No, she _____didn't_____ .

A _____Did_____ she iron the coat?

B No, she _____didn't_____ .

> **Tip** Find out the past tense of verbs you know. Start a list of verbs like these:
>
> do   did
> cut   cut
> have had

PARTNER WORK

Student A asks a question about work. Student B answers the question.

A Did you sell a radio today?

B Yes, I did.

---

5. Focus attention on the grammar boxes in B. Follow the procedures in 2.

6. Have learners read the instructions for Complete the Dialog. If necessary, model the first item. Allow learners to complete the activity. Have learners check each other's work in pairs. Ask several pairs to read the dialog aloud while the rest of the class checks their work.

 7. Have pairs read the Partner Work instructions. Tell learners to use verbs in the grammar boxes on page 56. Make sure each pair knows what to do. If necessary, model the activity with a learner. Then have pairs complete the activity. Have learners switch partners and repeat the activity. Ask several pairs to present their conversations to the class.

Tip Have learners read the Tip independently. Provide any clarification needed. Ask learners to give a few examples of verbs to include in their lists. Have learners add their lists to their Personal Dictionary. For more information, see "Presenting a Tip" on page ix.

FOLLOW-UP

All Done: Have learners work in pairs. Have them tell each other about a task that they recently finished at work or at school. Have them ask each other questions about the tasks and answer the questions. Have a few learners share with the class what their partners did.

♦ Have learners write two or three sentences about their recent task. Ask volunteers to share their sentences with the class.

WORKBOOK

Unit 5, Exercises 6A–6C

BLACKLINE MASTERS

Blackline Master: Unit 5

Handle special requests

Understand customer service policies

★   ★   ★   ★   ★

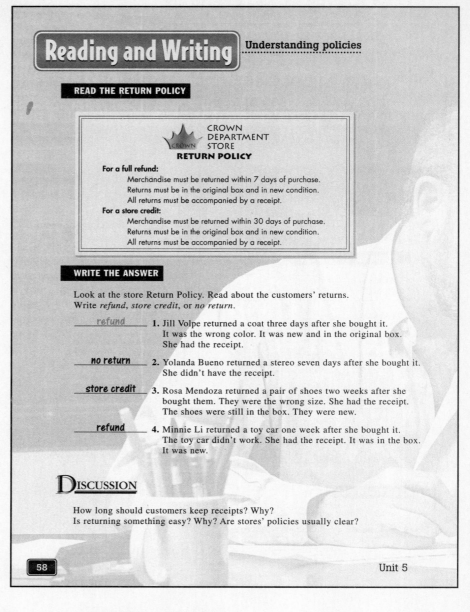

Reading and Writing — Understanding policies

READ THE RETURN POLICY

CROWN DEPARTMENT STORE
RETURN POLICY

For a full refund:
> Merchandise must be returned within 7 days of purchase.
> Returns must be in the original box and in new condition.
> All returns must be accompanied by a receipt.

For a store credit:
> Merchandise must be returned within 30 days of purchase.
> Returns must be in the original box and in new condition.
> All returns must be accompanied by a receipt.

WRITE THE ANSWER

Look at the store Return Policy. Read about the customers' returns.
Write *refund, store credit,* or *no return.*

refund 1. Jill Volpe returned a coat three days after she bought it. It was the wrong color. It was new and in the original box. She had the receipt.

no return 2. Yolanda Bueno returned a stereo seven days after she bought it. She didn't have the receipt.

store credit 3. Rosa Mendoza returned a pair of shoes two weeks after she bought them. They were the wrong size. She had the receipt. The shoes were still in the box. They were new.

refund 4. Minnie Li returned a toy car one week after she bought it. The toy car didn't work. She had the receipt. It was in the box. It was new.

Discussion

How long should customers keep receipts? Why?
Is returning something easy? Why? Are stores' policies usually clear?

58

Unit 5

PREPARATION

Preteach the new vocabulary on the page. Tell learners that the items a store sells are called **merchandise.** To **return** means to take an item back to the store from which it was purchased in order to get a new item or one's money back. Explain that a **return policy** is a list of rules for returning merchandise. Display a real receipt to teach **receipt.**

PRESENTATION

1. Have learners read and discuss the Purpose Statement. For more information, see "Purpose Statement" on page viii.

2. Have learners preview the return policy before they read. Encourage learners to say everything they can about the return policy. Write their ideas on the board and/or restate them in acceptable English. Then have them read the return policy independently.

3. Have learners read the instructions for Write the Answer. Make sure everyone knows what to do. Then have learners complete the activity independently. Have learners review each other's work in pairs. Ask volunteers to say their answers aloud while the class checks their work.

4. Have learners read the Discussion questions. Then have learners work in teams to discuss their ideas. Have team reporters share their ideas with the class. Ask teams to compare each other's ideas.

Use the receipts and the information on page 58 to complete the refund forms for
Rosa Mendoza and Minnie Li. Follow the example. The date is June 15.

CROWN DEPARTMENT STORE

RETURN FORM

Date of sale _June 12_   Date of Return _June 15_

Merchandise _Coat_

Reason _The coat was the wrong color._

Total Amount Due _$79.99_

Customer Signature _Jill Volpe_

Refund _✓_   Store Credit _____

Crown Department Store
Woodbridge Mall

June 12

Coat $79.99

Total $79.99

CROWN DEPARTMENT STORE

RETURN FORM

Date of sale _June 1_   Date of Return _June 15_

Merchandise _Shoes_

Reason _The shoes were the wrong size._

Total Amount Due _$75.75_

Customer Signature _Rosa Mendoza_

Refund _____   Store Credit _✓_

Crown Department Store
Woodbridge Mall

June 1

Shoes $75.75

Total $75.75

CROWN DEPARTMENT STORE

RETURN FORM

Date of sale _June 8_   Date of Return _June 15_

Merchandise _Toy car_

Reason _It didn't work._

Total Amount Due _$19.95_

Customer Signature _Minnie Li_

Refund _✓_   Store Credit _____

Crown Department Store
Woodbridge Mall

June 8

Toy car $19.95

Total $19.95

Unit 5   59

---

5. Have learners look over the return forms and receipts. Encourage learners to say everything they can about the forms. Write their ideas on the board and/or restate them in acceptable English.

6. Have teams read the instructions for Complete the Forms. Have learners work in pairs. Make sure each pair knows what to do. If necessary, model the activity. Then have pairs complete the activity. Ask several pairs to say their answers aloud as the rest of the class checks their work.

FOLLOW-UP

Returns: Have learners work in pairs to create dialogs between a clerk and a customer who wants to return something. Have pairs present their dialogs to the class.

♦ Distribute copies of the blank return forms to each pair. Have learners complete the form using information from the dialog they created.

WORKBOOK

Unit 5, Exercises 7A–7B

Respond to requests

Handle special requests

★   ★   ★   ★   ★

Extension   Answering customers' questions

READ AND CIRCLE

Read each customer's request. Choose the better response.
Talk about it with your classmates.

1. Can I get a box of paper clips?

   (a.) They come in boxes of 1,000 and 5,000. Which size box do you want?

   b. Which size box?

2. Can I leave my car in the no-parking zone for just a minute?

   (a.) It's really not a good idea. This is an emergency exit.

   b. No. Move your car now.

3. Would you please make twenty copies of this report? I need them right away.

   a. Can't you see I'm busy?

   (b.) Dana says she doesn't need her copies right away. I'll make yours now.

4. This toaster broke the first time I used it. May I talk to the manager?

   a. Why do you think it's our responsibility?

   (b.) I'm sure the manager can help you. Do you have your receipt?

5. John, please take this food to table ten.

   (a.) Sure. Just let me put this coffee pot down.

   b. I'm a cook, not a waiter.

TEAM WORK

Think of more good ways to answer these requests.
Share them with the class.

 *Culture Notes*

Why is good customer service important? What happens to companies
that offer poor service?

60   Unit 5

PREPARATION

1. Introduce the new vocabulary. Explain that a **zone** is an area. Say sentences using **responsibility,** such as *One of my responsibilities is to (come to class).* Ask learners to name a few of their responsibilities.

2. Review how to respond to requests. Make requests of learners: *May I sit here? Can I borrow your pen?* Let learners respond. Write their responses on the board in acceptable English. Talk about which responses are the politest, and why.

PRESENTATION

1. Have learners read and discuss the Purpose Statement. For more information, see "Purpose Statement" on page viii.

2. Have learners read the instructions for Read and Circle. If necessary, model the first item. Allow learners to complete the activity. Have learners review each other's work in pairs. Ask several learners to read their answers aloud while the rest of the class checks their work.

3. Have learners read the Team Work instructions. Make sure each team knows what to do. Then have teams complete the activity. Have team reporters share their answers with the class.

 4. Have learners read Culture Notes and discuss their responses in teams. Have team reporters share their ideas with the class. Ask the teams to compare each other's ideas.

FOLLOW-UP

Good Service: Have teams make a list of five requests that they have heard at a workplace. Have them write two polite responses to each request. One response should be affirmative (granting the request), and the other should deny the request. Ask team reporters to share their ideas with the class.

♦ Have teams make a list of adjectives to describe good customer service, such as **friendly, kind, pleasant,** and **nice.** Have teams share their lists with the class.

WORKBOOK

Unit 5, Exercise 8

 **How well can you use the skills in this unit?**

Complete the activities. Go over your work with a partner or your teacher. Then complete the Performance Review on page 62.

SKILL 1 RESPOND TO REQUESTS

Your partner or teacher wants you to help move the furniture in your classroom. How do you respond?

SKILL 2 HANDLE SPECIAL REQUESTS

Read The Copy Shop's store policies and the customer's special requests. What do you say? Talk about it with your teacher or partner.

1. A customer wants ten copies right away.

2. A customer wants 1,000 copies. He doesn't have money to pay in advance.

STORE POLICIES

1. Allow at least one hour for all copy orders.

2. Orders of 500 copies or more must be paid for in advance.

SKILL 3 OFFER SUGGESTIONS

You work at Quality Supermarket. A customer does not know what to fix for dinner. Make one or two suggestions. Follow the example:

How about hamburgers?

Unit 5

PRESENTATION

Use any of the procedures in "Evaluation," page x, with pages 61 and 62. Record individuals' results on the Unit 5 Individual Competency Chart. Record the class's results on the Class Cumulative Competency Chart.

Crystal Dining Elegance
Return Policy

- A full refund is available on returns within 30 days of purchase.

- All returns must be accompanied by a receipt.

- In-store credits are available on returns within 45 days of purchase.

- After 45 days, no credits and no returns are available.

Read the policy. Write *refund*, *store credit*, or *no return*.

refund   **1.** Kathy wants to return some water glasses she bought last week. She did not use them. She has the receipt.

no return   **2.** Ralph wants to return some plates he bought six months ago. He has the receipt.

Performance Review

I can...

☐ **1.** respond to requests.
☐ **2.** handle special requests.
☐ **3.** offer suggestions.
☐ **4.** understand customer service policies.

DISCUSSION

Work with a team. How will your new skills help you? Make a list. Share your list with the class.

62   Unit 5

PRESENTATION

Follow the instructions on page 61.

INFORMAL WORKPLACE-SPECIFIC ASSESSMENT

Ask learners to name one or two ways they can provide good customer service at their workplaces.

WORKBOOK

Unit 5, Exercise 9

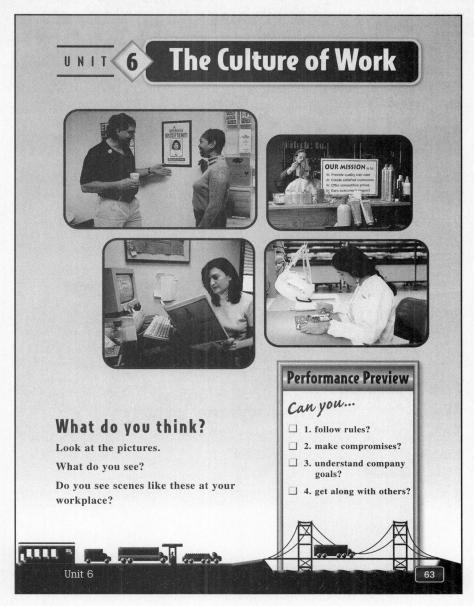

UNIT 6 ⬧ The Culture of Work

What do you think?

Look at the pictures.

What do you see?

Do you see scenes like these at your workplace?

Performance Preview

Can you...

☐ 1. follow rules?

☐ 2. make compromises?

☐ 3. understand company goals?

☐ 4. get along with others?

Unit 6

63

Unit 6 Overview
—SCANS Competencies—

★ Understand social systems

★ Interpret and communicate information

★ Work on teams

Workforce Skills

● Follow rules

● Make compromises

● Understand company goals

● Get along with others

Materials

● Copies of two different advertisements for similar products, such as cars or food items

● Copies of a company handbook from learners' workplaces or a workplace they know

Unit Warm-Up

To get the learners thinking about the unit topic, discuss rules in your classroom. Then ask learners to discuss rules they or their families follow at work, school, or home. List their ideas on the board. Discuss with learners why rules are important.

★　　★　　★　　★　　★

WORKFORCE SKILLS (page 63)

Understand company goals

★　　★　　★　　★　　★

PREPARATION

1. Write on the board your school's or company's mission statement or motto and identify it. Have learners discuss the statement. Encourage learners to talk about the purpose of the statement. Encourage learners to use peer teaching to clarify any unfamiliar vocabulary.

2. Ask learners to talk about the traits of a good employee. What happens to bad employees? How do companies encourage good employees?

PRESENTATION

1. Focus attention on the photographs. Ask learners what the unit might be about. Write their ideas on the board and/or restate them in acceptable English.

2. Have learners talk about the pictures. Have them identify the situations. How are the workers following workplace standards? Have learners think of positive work behaviors that are visible in the scenes.

3. Help learners read the questions. Discuss the questions with the class.

4. You may want to use the Performance Preview to provide learners with an overview of the skills in the unit. Have learners read the list of skills and discuss what they will learn in the unit.

FOLLOW-UP

Coworkers: Ask learners if they have ever worked with a bad coworker, such as someone who was constantly late or who couldn't get along with others. Have learners discuss how it made them feel to work with that person.

◆ Ask learners how that coworker could have improved his or her work habits.

WORKBOOK

Unit 6, Exercises 1A–1B

Follow rules

Understand company goals

★　　★　　★　　★　　★

Teaching Note

Use this page to introduce the new language in the unit. Whenever possible, encourage peer teaching. Supply any new language learners need.

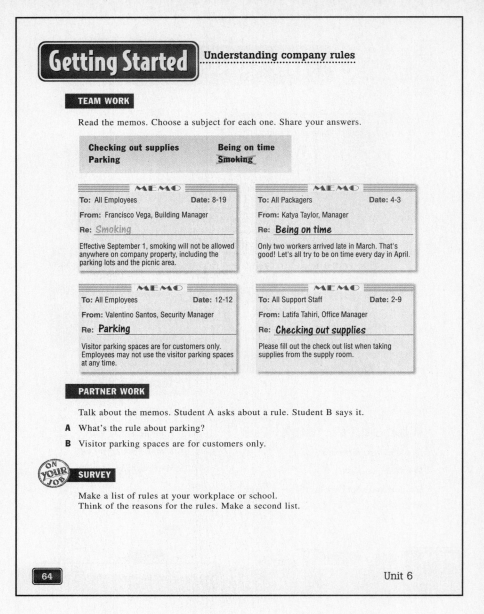

Getting Started — Understanding company rules

TEAM WORK

Read the memos. Choose a subject for each one. Share your answers.

Checking out supplies	**Being on time**
Parking	**Smoking**

MEMO

To: All Employees　　　　**Date:** 8-19

From: Francisco Vega, Building Manager

Re: *Smoking*

Effective September 1, smoking will not be allowed anywhere on company property, including the parking lots and the picnic area.

MEMO

To: All Packagers　　　　**Date:** 4-3

From: Katya Taylor, Manager

Re: *Being on time*

Only two workers arrived late in March. That's good! Let's all try to be on time every day in April.

MEMO

To: All Employees　　　　**Date:** 12-12

From: Valentino Santos, Security Manager

Re: *Parking*

Visitor parking spaces are for customers only. Employees may not use the visitor parking spaces at any time.

MEMO

To: All Support Staff　　　　**Date:** 2-9

From: Latifa Tahiri, Office Manager

Re: *Checking out supplies*

Please fill out the check out list when taking supplies from the supply room.

PARTNER WORK

Talk about the memos. Student A asks about a rule. Student B says it.

A What's the rule about parking?

B Visitor parking spaces are for customers only.

SURVEY

Make a list of rules at your workplace or school.
Think of the reasons for the rules. Make a second list.

64　　　　　　　　　　　　　　　　　　　　Unit 6

PREPARATION

1. Explain that a **check out list** is a list on which workers write what supplies they are taking from the supply room.

2. Ask learners what their workplaces' rules are for the topics on the page: checking out supplies, being on time, parking, and smoking.

PRESENTATION

1. Have learners read and discuss the Purpose Statement. For more information, see "Purpose Statement" on page viii.

2. Focus attention on the memos. Encourage learners to say as much as they can about them. Clarify any vocabulary as needed. Write learners' ideas on the board and/or restate them in acceptable English.

3. Have teams read the Team Work instructions. Make sure each team knows what to do. If necessary, model the first item. Remind the teams that they are responsible for making sure that each member understands the new language. Then have teams complete the activity. If learners need help, encourage them to consult other teams. Have team reporters share their answers with the class.

4. Have partners read the Partner Work instructions. Make sure each pair knows what to do. If necessary, model the activity. Then have pairs complete the activity. Have learners switch partners and repeat the activity. Supply any language needed. Have one or two partners present their dialogs to the class.

 5. Have partners read the Survey instructions. Make sure each person knows what

to do. If necessary, model the activity. Then have pairs complete the activity. Have pairs share their answers with the class. For more information, see "Survey" on page viii.

FOLLOW-UP

Table: Help the class use the information from the Survey to create a summary table showing typical work rules and policies and the reasons for them. Have learners discuss the table.

♦ Have volunteers take turns pantomiming breaking one of the work rules. The rest of the class should try to figure out what rule is being broken.

WORKBOOK

Unit 6, Exercises 2A–2B

Compromising

PRACTICE THE DIALOG

A Lee, we're going to be busier than usual tomorrow. Can you work from 7:00 to 12:00?

B I'm sorry, Virginia, I can't. My daughter has a doctor's appointment at 11:00.

A That's too bad. We have a lot of big holiday orders.

B I could come in from 6:00 to 9:00.

A That would help a lot. Thanks, Lee.

B No problem, Virginia.

> **Useful Language**
>
> I can't do it this time.
>
> I can come in for a couple of hours.
>
> How about. . . ?
>
> Sure.
>
> That sounds good.

PARTNER WORK

Ask your partner to work on Wednesday. Use the dialog and Useful Language above.

ASAP PROJECT

As a class, write rules and goals for your class. Make rules, such as "Be on time." Make goals, such as "Learn ten new words a week." Everybody should agree on all items. Post the list on your classroom wall. Complete this project as you work through this unit.

Unit 6   65

ASAP PROJECT

Have learners read the instructions. Discuss the project and its purpose with learners. Make sure that everyone understands. Choose a specific class time for learners to work on the project throughout the unit. Have learners agree on a deadline when the project will be finished. For more information, see "ASAP Project" on page vi.

PREPARATION

Present a dialog in which a volunteer is the boss and you are the employee. Have the volunteer ask *Can you work late tonight?* Use the language in the Useful Language box to answer. Have the volunteer repeat the question several times, and offer different answers each time. Clarify the language for learners as necessary.

PRESENTATION

1. Have learners read and discuss the Purpose Statement. For more information, see "Purpose Statement" on page viii.

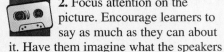 **2.** Focus attention on the picture. Encourage learners to say as much as they can about it. Have them imagine what the speakers

are saying. Then present the dialog. See "Presenting a Dialog" on page ix.

3. Have partners read the Partner Work instructions. Focus attention on the Useful Language box. Help learners read the expressions. If necessary, model pronunciation. Then have learners complete the activity. Have learners switch partners and repeat the activity. Have one or two pairs present their dialogs to the class.

FOLLOW-UP

Here's a Suggestion: Provide learners with several scenarios between a supervisor and an employee about schedule problems (someone left early; there are extra deliveries to be made, etc.). Have

pairs create dialogs that offer compromises and solutions. Ask several pairs to present their dialogs to the class.

♦ Have pairs write their dialogs.

WORKBOOK

Unit 6, Exercises 3A–3B

WORKFORCE SKILLS (page 66)

Get along with others

Make compromises

★　　★　　★　　★　　★

Personal Dictionary

Have learners add the words in their Personal Dictionary to their *Workforce Writing Dictionary*. For more information, see "Workforce Writing Dictionary" on page v.

Keep Talking · Getting along with others

PARTNER WORK

Look at the pictures. What's the matter?

PRACTICE THE DIALOG

A Excuse me, your smoke is coming in the window. Could you please smoke somewhere else?

B Sorry, I'll go over there.

Now talk about the other pictures above. Student A makes requests. Student B responds. Use the dialog and the Useful Language.

Useful Language

Is there a problem?

I'm sorry.

It's against company policy to. . .

Personal Dictionary ▷ Fitting in at Work

Write the words and phrases that you need to know.

_____

_____

_____

66   Unit 6

PREPARATION

Model making requests such as *It's against company policy to smoke inside. Could you please smoke outside?* Encourage learners to make requests of you.

PRESENTATION

1. Have learners read the Purpose Statement. For more information, see "Purpose Statement" on page viii.

2. Focus attention on the illustrations. Have learners say everything they can about them. Write their ideas on the board and/or restate them in acceptable English.

3. Have partners read the Partner Work instructions. Make sure each pair knows what to do. Have pairs share their answers with the class.

4. Focus attention on Practice the Dialog and present the dialog. See "Presenting a Dialog" on page ix. Then have learners read the instructions under the dialog. Model if necessary, using the language in the Useful Language box. Allow learners time to complete the activity. Have learners change partners and repeat. Have several pairs present their dialogs to the class.

5. Have learners read the Personal Dictionary instructions. Then use the Personal Dictionary procedures on page ix. Remind learners to continue to add words to their dictionaries throughout the unit.

FOLLOW-UP

Would You Mind . . . ? Have pairs role-play situations about getting along with others that would happen at their workplace or school. One learner makes a request. The other responds. Encourage learners to make realistic requests, to respond reasonably, and to offer compromises. Have learners present their role plays to the class.

◆ Discuss the role plays with the class. Were the requests fair? Were the responses fair? Did the people make compromises?

WORKBOOK

Unit 6, Exercises 4A–4B

Follow rules

Understand company goals

★   ★   ★   ★   ★♱

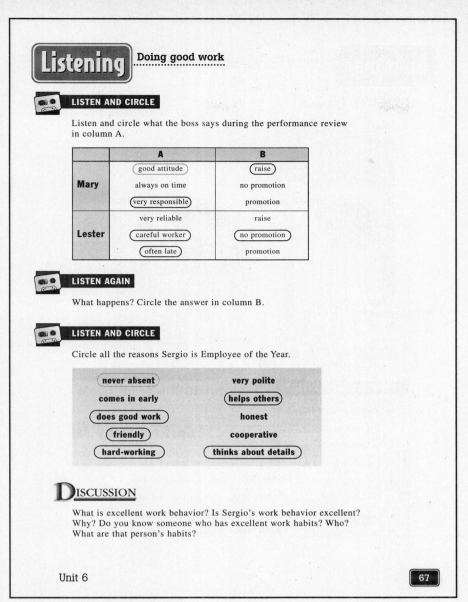

Listening ········· Doing good work

LISTEN AND CIRCLE

Listen and circle what the boss says during the performance review in column A.

	A	B
Mary	(good attitude)	(raise)
	always on time	no promotion
	(very responsible)	promotion
Lester	very reliable	raise
	(careful worker)	(no promotion)
	(often late)	promotion

LISTEN AGAIN

What happens? Circle the answer in column B.

LISTEN AND CIRCLE

Circle all the reasons Sergio is Employee of the Year.

(never absent)	(very polite)
comes in early	(helps others)
(does good work)	honest
(friendly)	cooperative
(hard-working)	(thinks about details)

DISCUSSION

What is excellent work behavior? Is Sergio's work behavior excellent? Why? Do you know someone who has excellent work habits? Who? What are that person's habits?

Unit 6

67

PREPARATION

Preteach or review **attitude, responsible, raise, promotion, reliable, careful, absent, honest, cooperative,** and **details.** Use each word in several sample sentences. Have learners figure out the meaning of each word based on the sample sentences. Encourage learners to create sentences of their own using the new words.

PRESENTATION

1. Have learners read and discuss the Purpose Statement. For more information, see "Purpose Statement" on page viii.

 2. Have learners read the Listen and Circle instructions. Then have them read the words in columns A and B. Use peer-teaching to clarify any unfamiliar vocabulary.

Make sure that everyone understands the instructions. If necessary, model the first item. Then play the tape or read the Listening Transcript aloud two or more times as learners complete the activity. Have learners check their work. For more information, see "Presenting a Listening Activity" on page ix.

 3. Have learners read the Listen Again instructions. Then follow the procedures in 2.

 4. Have learners read the Listen and Circle instructions. Have them read the boldface words. Then follow the procedures in 2.

5. Have learners read the Discussion questions. Then have learners work in teams to discuss their ideas. Have team reporters share their ideas with the class.

FOLLOW-UP

Bad Work Behaviors: Divide the class into teams. Each team brainstorms a list of all the bad work habits they know, such as sleeping on the job, returning late from lunch every day, and being unwilling to help coworkers. Have team reporters share their teams' lists with the class.

♦ Have teams discuss what to do when a coworker exhibits a behavior on their list. Do they tell their supervisor? Have teams share their ideas.

WORKBOOK

Unit 6, Exercises 5A–5B

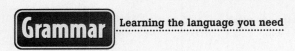

A. Study the Examples

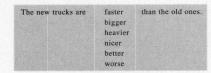

| The new trucks are | faster bigger heavier nicer better worse | than the old ones. |

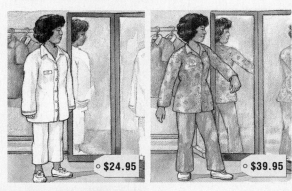

○ $24.95   ○ $39.95

COMPLETE THE SENTENCES

Ana needs a new uniform for work. Complete the sentences.

1. The pink pants are ___longer than___ (**long**) the white pants.

2. The white pants are ___shorter than___ (**short**) the pink pants.

3. The white blouse is ___larger than___ (**large**) the pink blouse.

4. The pink blouse is ___smaller than___ (**small**) the white blouse.

5. The white uniform is ___cheaper than___ (**cheap**) the pink uniform.

6. The pink uniform is ___prettier than___ (**pretty**) the white uniform.

7. The pink uniform is ___better than___ (**better**) the white uniform.

68   Unit 6

PREPARATION

Review the language in the grammar boxes with learners before they open their books, if necessary.

PRESENTATION

1. Have learners read and discuss the Purpose Statement. For more information, see "Purpose Statement" on page viii.

2. Have learners read the grammar box in A. Have learners use the language in the box to say as many sentences as possible. Tell learners that they can use the grammar boxes throughout the unit to review or check sentence structures.

3. Have learners read the instructions for Complete the Sentences. If necessary, model the first item. Allow learners to complete the activity. Have learners check each other's work in pairs. Ask several learners to read their sentences aloud while the rest of the class checks their work.

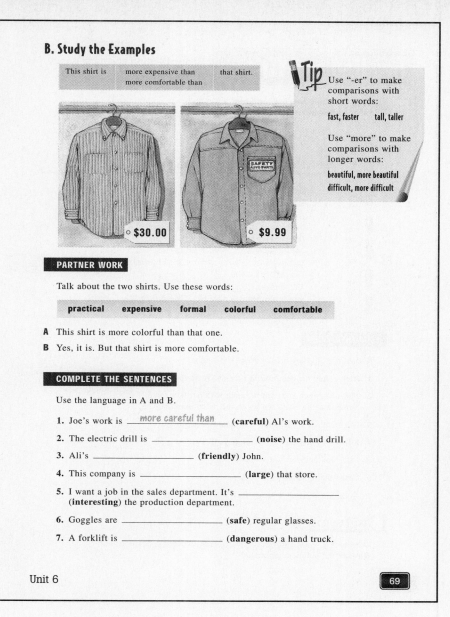

B. Study the Examples

| This shirt is | more expensive than | that shirt. |
| | more comfortable than | |

Tip

Use "-er" to make comparisons with short words:

fast, faster   tall, taller

Use "more" to make comparisons with longer words:

beautiful, more beautiful

difficult, more difficult

$30.00

$9.99

PARTNER WORK

Talk about the two shirts. Use these words:

| practical | expensive | formal | colorful | comfortable |

A This shirt is more colorful than that one.

B Yes, it is. But that shirt is more comfortable.

COMPLETE THE SENTENCES

Use the language in A and B.

1. Joe's work is _____more careful than_____ (**careful**) Al's work.

2. The electric drill is _____ (**noise**) the hand drill.

3. Ali's _____ (**friendly**) John.

4. This company is _____ (**large**) that store.

5. I want a job in the sales department. It's _____ (**interesting**) the production department.

6. Goggles are _____ (**safe**) regular glasses.

7. A forklift is _____ (**dangerous**) a hand truck.

Unit 6

69

Teaching Note

After learners read the Tip, help learners brainstorm a list of adjectives that they know. Write their words on the board. Divide them by single-syllable adjectives and multisyllable adjectives. Have learners copy the list for use throughout the unit. Encourage them to continue adding words to the list.

4. Focus attention on the grammar box in B. Follow the procedures in 2.

5. Have pairs read the Partner Work instructions. Make sure each pair knows what to do. If necessary, model the activity with a learner. Allow learners to complete the activity. Have learners switch partners and repeat the activity. Ask several pairs to present their conversations to the class.

6. Have learners read the instructions for Complete the Sentences. If necessary, model the first item. Then have learners complete the activity independently. Have a different learner read each sentence aloud while the rest of the class checks their answers.

 Tip Have learners read the Tip independently. Provide any clarification needed. Ask

learners to give additional examples. For more information, see "Presenting a Tip" on page ix.

FOLLOW-UP

Which Is Better? Have learners work in pairs. Display the two advertisements for similar products. Have learners look at the advertisements and compare the products. Tell learners to write their comparisons in list form.

♦ Have two pairs join together and compare lists. Then have each group of four decide which of the items they would choose to buy. Take a class poll.

WORKBOOK

Unit 6, Exercises 6A–6B

BLACKLINE MASTERS

Blackline Master: Unit 6

Follow rules

Understand company goals

★　　★　　★　　★　　★

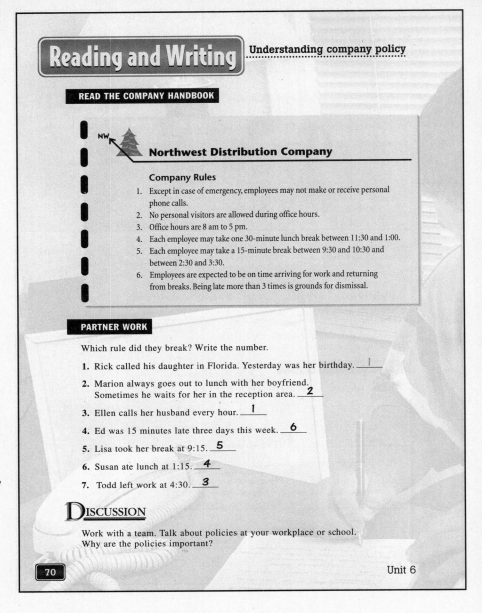

Reading and Writing   Understanding company policy

READ THE COMPANY HANDBOOK

NW 🌲 **Northwest Distribution Company**

Company Rules

1. Except in case of emergency, employees may not make or receive personal phone calls.
2. No personal visitors are allowed during office hours.
3. Office hours are 8 am to 5 pm.
4. Each employee may take one 30-minute lunch break between 11:30 and 1:00.
5. Each employee may take a 15-minute break between 9:30 and 10:30 and between 2:30 and 3:30.
6. Employees are expected to be on time arriving for work and returning from breaks. Being late more than 3 times is grounds for dismissal.

PARTNER WORK

Which rule did they break? Write the number.

1. Rick called his daughter in Florida. Yesterday was her birthday. __1__

2. Marion always goes out to lunch with her boyfriend. Sometimes he waits for her in the reception area. __2__

3. Ellen calls her husband every hour. __1__

4. Ed was 15 minutes late three days this week. __6__

5. Lisa took her break at 9:15. __5__

6. Susan ate lunch at 1:15. __4__

7. Todd left work at 4:30. __3__

DISCUSSION

Work with a team. Talk about policies at your workplace or school. Why are the policies important?

70   Unit 6

SCANS Note

Explain that different workplaces have different policies and rules. For example, restaurant employees follow health policies by washing their hands often. Construction site employees follow safety rules by wearing special clothing.

PREPARATION

1. Present a company handbook from a learner's workplace (if possible) or from a workplace the learners know. Ask learners why companies have rules and why it is important to follow them.

2. Preteach or review the vocabulary **emergency, personal,** and **dismissal.** Introduce **emergency** by providing examples, such as a fire. Explain that a **personal** phone call is a phone call that is not about work, while **dismissal** means losing your job.

PRESENTATION

1. Have learners read and discuss the Purpose Statement. For more information, see "Purpose Statement" on page viii.

2. Have learners preview the company handbook. Encourage learners to say

everything they can about the handbook. Clarify any vocabulary as needed. Write their ideas on the board or restate them in acceptable English. Then have them read the handbook in pairs.

3. Have learners read the Partner Work instructions. Make sure everyone knows what to do. Then have learners complete the activity in pairs. Ask several pairs to share their answers with the class while the rest of the class checks their work.

4. Have learners read the Discussion instructions. Make sure everyone knows what to do. Then have learners work in teams to discuss their ideas. Have team reporters share their ideas with the class.

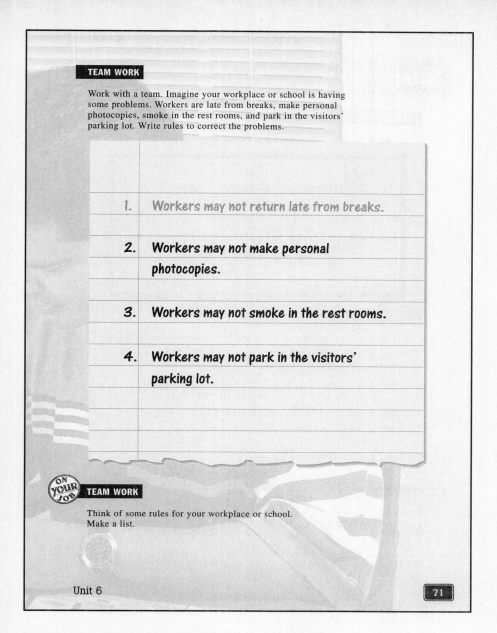

Work with a team. Imagine your workplace or school is having some problems. Workers are late from breaks, make personal photocopies, smoke in the rest rooms, and park in the visitors' parking lot. Write rules to correct the problems.

1. Workers may not return late from breaks.

2. Workers may not make personal photocopies.

3. Workers may not smoke in the rest rooms.

4. Workers may not park in the visitors' parking lot.

 TEAM WORK

Think of some rules for your workplace or school. Make a list.

Unit 6   71

5. Have teams read the Team Work instructions. Make sure each team knows what to do. If necessary, model the activity. Then have teams complete the activity. Have team reporters share their answers with the class. Ask teams to compare ideas.

6. Have teams read the Team Work instructions. Then have teams complete the activity. Have team reporters share their lists with the class.

FOLLOW-UP

Company Rules: Bring copies of company handbooks and have learners discuss them in teams. What are some of the rules in the books? Ask team reporters to report the rules they find to the class.

♦ Have learners list actions that are grounds for dismissal. Ask learners to give reasons companies do not want employees who do these things.

WORKBOOK

Unit 6, Exercises 7A–7B

★   ★   ★   ★   ★

Extension — Understanding company goals

READ THE MISSION STATEMENT

A company's mission statement tells employees the company's goals.

Express Delivery Company

Our Mission Is To
- Deliver each and every package on time
- Keep packages safe and clean
- Offer competitive rates
- Greet customers with a smile
- Answer customers' questions politely
- Handle customers' special requests

WRITE YES OR NO

Are the employees following Express Delivery Company's mission?

__no__ **1.** It's five o'clock. A driver doesn't deliver the last three packages on the schedule.

__yes__ **2.** A customer asks for a weekend delivery. A clerk says he will find a driver to make the delivery.

__yes__ **3.** A clerk smiles and says, "May I help you?"

__yes__ **4.** A driver delivers a package on a specific day by customer request.

__no__ **5.** A driver leaves packages in the rain.

 Culture Notes

When you see a worker who isn't following company rules, what do you do? Why?

72   Unit 6

PREPARATION

1. Write on the board your school's or workplace's mission statement or motto to review the purpose of mission statements. Discuss how the mission statement or motto explains your school's or company's goals. Ask volunteers to describe how they follow the mission or motto of their workplace or school.

2. Clarify that **competitive rates** means prices that are low or similar to other companies' prices.

PRESENTATION

1. Have learners read and discuss the Purpose Statement. For more information, see "Purpose Statement" on page viii.

2. Have learners preview the mission statement before they read. Encourage them to say everything they can about it.

Clarify any vocabulary needed. Write their ideas on the board or restate them in acceptable English. Have learners read the mission statement independently.

3. Have learners read the instructions for Write *Yes* or *No*. If necessary, model the first item. Allow learners to complete the activity. Have learners review each other's work in pairs. Ask several learners to read their answers aloud while the rest of the class checks their work.

4. Have learners read Culture Notes and talk over their responses in teams. Have team reporters share their ideas with the class. Ask the teams to compare each other's ideas. What would happen in the learners' home countries? How is that the same or different from in the U.S.?

FOLLOW-UP

Our Class Mission Statement: Divide the class into teams. Have each team write a mission statement for your classroom. Have teams share their mission statements.

♦ Have learners agree on the main points of their mission statements. Have them compile their thoughts into one mission statement. Have them write the statement and post it in your classroom.

WORKBOOK

Unit 6, Exercise 8

---

72   English ASAP

Performance Check

How well can you use the skills in this unit?
....

Complete the activities. Go over your work with a partner or your teacher. Then complete the Performance Review on page 74.

SKILL 1   FOLLOW RULES

Work starts at 9:00, and employees must fill out the check-out list when they get supplies. Tell your teacher which employees are following the rules.

SKILL 2   MAKE COMPROMISES

Your partner or teacher asks you to work an extra day next week. You have plans for that afternoon. What do you say?

Unit 6   73

PRESENTATION

Use any of the procedures in "Evaluation," page x, with pages 73 and 74. Record individuals' results on the Unit 6 Individual Competency Chart. Record the class's results on the Class Cumulative Competency Chart.

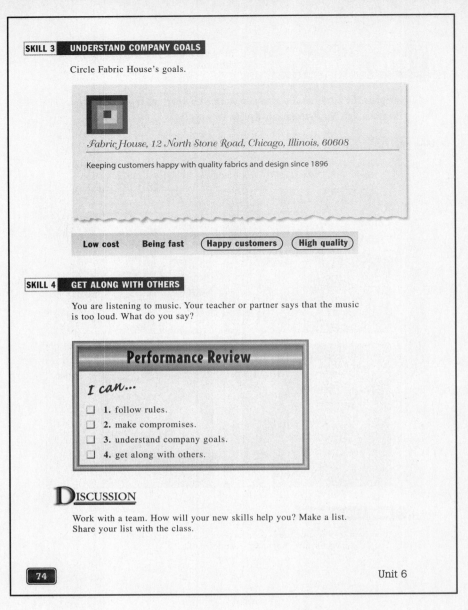

SKILL 3 UNDERSTAND COMPANY GOALS

Circle Fabric House's goals.

Fabric House, 12 North Stone Road, Chicago, Illinois, 60608

Keeping customers happy with quality fabrics and design since 1896

| Low cost | Being fast | (Happy customers) | (High quality) |

SKILL 4 GET ALONG WITH OTHERS

You are listening to music. Your teacher or partner says that the music is too loud. What do you say?

Performance Review

I can...

☐ **1.** follow rules.
☐ **2.** make compromises.
☐ **3.** understand company goals.
☐ **4.** get along with others.

DISCUSSION

Work with a team. How will your new skills help you? Make a list. Share your list with the class.

74   Unit 6

PRESENTATION

Follow the instructions on page 73.

INFORMAL WORKPLACE-SPECIFIC ASSESSMENT

Ask learners to state one or two of their company's or department's goals. Have learners say what they do to meet those goals.

WORKBOOK

Unit 6, Exercise 9

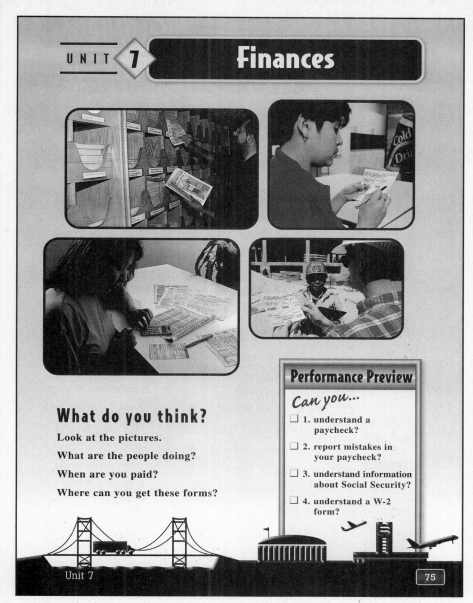

UNIT 7 — Finances

What do you think?

Look at the pictures.

What are the people doing?

When are you paid?

Where can you get these forms?

Performance Preview

Can you...

- ☐ 1. understand a paycheck?
- ☐ 2. report mistakes in your paycheck?
- ☐ 3. understand information about Social Security?
- ☐ 4. understand a W-2 form?

Unit 7

75

Unit 7 Overview
—SCANS Competencies—

★ Acquire and evaluate data
★ Interpret and communicate information
★ Allocate money
★ Understand organizational systems

Workforce Skills

- Understand a paycheck
- Report mistakes in your paycheck
- Understand Social Security
- Understand a W-2 form

Materials

- Large samples of a paycheck with pay stub attached, a W-2 form, and a Social Security card
- Copies of simple, blank tax forms such as 1040EZ or 1040A
- A large sample of a timecard

Unit Warm-Up

To get learners thinking about the unit topic, ask them what they do when they get a paycheck. Do they verify that the amount is correct? Do they look at what deductions were made? Do they save their paycheck stubs? Discuss with learners why checking this information and keeping financial records can be useful.

★   ★   ★   ★   ★

WORKFORCE SKILLS (page 75)

Understand a paycheck

Understand a W-2 form

★   ★   ★   ★   ★

PREPARATION

Display the large paycheck and W-2 form. Have learners identify them and say what they're for. Ask if their paychecks look like the sample check. Do they get paid every week, every other week, once a month, or on some other schedule? Ask them to name places to deposit or cash checks.

PRESENTATION

1. Focus attention on the photographs. Ask learners what the unit might be about. Write their ideas on the board and/or restate them in acceptable English.

2. Have learners talk about the pictures. Have them identify the paychecks and forms. Help learners relate the pictures to the samples of the paycheck and the W-2 form.

3. Help learners read the questions. Discuss the questions with the class.

4. You may want to use the Performance Preview to provide learners with an overview of the skills in the unit. Have learners read the list of skills and discuss what they will learn in the unit.

FOLLOW-UP

Keeping Records: Have learners work in small groups. Ask each group to list documents that would be useful to save for their records, such as bank statements, bills, paycheck stubs, tax forms, etc. Have team reporters share their lists with the class

♦ Have teams think of situations in which it would be useful to have the documents listed above. Have team reporters share their ideas with the class.

WORKBOOK

Unit 7, Exercises 1A–1B

WORKFORCE SKILLS (page 76)

Understand a paycheck

★   ★   ★   ★   ★

Teaching Note

Use this page to introduce the new language in the unit. Whenever possible, encourage peer teaching. Supply any new language learners need.

SCANS Note

Encourage learners to organize a filing system at home for keeping track of financial documents such as paycheck stubs, canceled checks, and so on. If necessary, review filing systems, pages 22 and 23, with learners.

 **Getting Started**   Understanding a paycheck stub

TEAM WORK

Look at the paycheck stub. Put the words into the correct list.

| earnings | federal tax | gross pay | health insurance |
| life insurance | net pay | state tax | |

MERCY HOSPITAL

RATE	HOURS	EARNINGS	YEAR TO DATE
$9.40	80.00	$752.00	$12,784.00

DEDUCTIONS	
Federal tax	$90.24
State tax	60.16
FICA	36.00
Medicare	6.00
Health insurance	14.20
Life insurance	2.60

GROSS PAY	$752.00
PAY PERIOD BEGINNING	09/01/99
PAY PERIOD ENDING	09/15/99

TOTAL DEDUCTIONS	$209.20
NET PAY	$542.80

Pay	**Benefits**	**Taxes**
earnings	health insurance	federal tax
gross pay	life insurance	state tax
net pay		

PARTNER WORK

Student A asks questions about the paycheck. Student B answers.

A How much is the gross pay?

B It's $752.

 SURVEY

Talk to 5 classmates. How many have had a mistake on a paycheck? Was the mistake large? What did the company do about the mistake? Report your findings to the class.

     Unit 7

PREPARATION

Act out surprise at the amount of money deducted from a paycheck. Have learners ever felt this way? Do they understand why the money was taken out?

PRESENTATION

1. Have learners read and discuss the Purpose Statement. For more information, see "Purpose Statement" on page viii.

2. Encourage learners to say as much as they can about the paycheck stub. Have them read the word box and the list headings. Encourage learners to use peer teaching to clarify any unfamiliar vocabulary.

3. Have teams read the Team Work instructions. If necessary, model the first item. Remind the teams that they are responsible for making sure that each

member understands the new language. Then have teams complete the activity. If learners need help, encourage them to consult other teams. Have team reporters share their answers with the class.

4. Have partners read the Partner Work instructions. If necessary, model the activity. Then have pairs complete the activity. Have learners switch partners and repeat the activity. Supply any language needed. Have one or two partners present their dialogs to the class.

 5. Read the Survey instructions. Then have learners complete the activity. Have several learners share their findings with the class. For more information, see "Survey" on page viii.

FOLLOW-UP

What's Different? Ask learners to bring in their own paycheck stubs for this activity. (They will be working individually, but they can blacken out their earnings amounts if they wish.) Have them compare their stubs with the one in the book. What information is different? For example, some learners may not have deductions for state tax or life insurance. Have learners list the differences and share their lists with the class.

◆ Discuss learners' lists. Why are there differences between the paycheck stubs? Possible answers include that some states don't have income tax and not all employers offer life insurance.

WORKBOOK

Unit 7, Exercises 2A–2B

Talk About It ··········· **Talking about pay**

 PRACTICE THE DIALOG

A At Service Plastics, payday is every Friday, and your pay rate is $6.50 an hour.

B Excuse me. Could you repeat that?

A Of course. Payday is every Friday. Your pay rate is $6.50 an hour.

B Can I start soon?

A Sure, you can start today. Your shift starts at 5:00, so be here at least 10 minutes before 5:00.

> **Tip** When you get a new job, find out your pay rate, the start date, and time your shift starts.

PARTNER WORK

You're the boss. Tell your partner that payday is every Thursday. The rate of pay is $7 an hour and the shift starts at 3:00. Use the dialog above. Then switch roles. Talk about other pay rates and start times.

ASAP
PROJECT

As a team, gather important tax and payroll forms. Use them to create a class reference booklet. Include information on where to get the forms, how to fill them out, and when to file them.

Unit 7   **77**

Culture Note

Ensure learners understand that while it is important to discuss pay rate during a job interview, it is more appropriate to talk about pay later in the interview rather than early in the conversation.

ASAP
PROJECT

Have learners read the instructions. Discuss the project and its purpose with learners. Make sure that everyone understands. Help learners assign themselves to teams based upon their knowledge, skills, interests, or other personal strengths. Have each team select a leader, and have the team leaders or the whole class select an overall project leader. Throughout the rest of the unit, allow time for learners to work on the project. Have the teams agree on a deadline when the project will be finished. For more information, see "ASAP Project" on page vi.

PREPARATION

Preteach the new language on the page. Write **payday** on the board and ask learners what it means. Help them divide the word into **pay** and **day**, if necessary. To teach **pay rate**, write rates on the board such as **$8/hour, $100/day,** and **$350/week**. Say, *These are pay rates.*

PRESENTATION

1. Have learners read and discuss the Purpose Statement. For more information, see "Purpose Statement" on page viii.

 2. Focus attention on the picture. Encourage learners to say as much as they can about it. Have them imagine what the speakers are saying. Have them identify the place in the picture. Then present the dialog. See "Presenting a Dialog" on page ix.

3. Have partners read the Partner Work instructions. Make sure each pair knows what to do. If necessary, model the activity. Then have pairs complete the activity. Have learners switch partners and repeat the activity. Have one or two pairs present their dialogs to the class.

> **Tip** Have learners read the Tip independently. Have learners discuss how the advice will help them. For more information, see "Presenting a Tip" on page ix.

FOLLOW-UP

When is Payday? Have learners record in a table when their classmates get paid. They should title columns **Every Friday, Every Other Friday, the First**

and Fifteenth of the Month, etc. In each column, have learners write the names of their classmates who get paid on that schedule. Have learners share their tables with the class.

♦ Have learners use their table to make a bar graph. The horizontal scale should show the different pay schedules, while the vertical scale should show the number of learners who get paid on each schedule. Ask volunteers to share their bar graphs with the class.

WORKBOOK

Unit 7, Exercises 3A–3B

WORKFORCE SKILLS (page 78)

Report mistakes in your paycheck

★ ★ ★ ★ ★

Language Note

*Tell learners that polite expressions for introducing complaints and reports of mistakes include **I think . . . It seems that . . . It looks like . . .** and **There might be . . .** Write this vocabulary where learners can see and use it.*

Personal Dictionary

Have learners add the words in their Personal Dictionary to their *Workforce Writing Dictionary.* For more information, see "Workforce Writing Dictionary" on page v.

Keep Talking

Reporting mistakes in your paycheck

PRACTICE THE DIALOG

A Mr. Reynosa, I think there's a mistake in my paycheck.

B Can I see it?

A Here it is. Last week I worked 30 hours, but my paycheck is for only 24 hours.

B You're right. Let me check your timecard.

A OK.

B Hmm. It's because you worked 6 hours on Saturday. Those hours go on your next paycheck.

A Oh, I see. Thanks.

Tip If you think there's a mistake with your paycheck, talk to your boss or Human Resources right away.

ON YOUR JOB **PARTNER WORK**

You worked 40 hours last week, but your paycheck is for 30 hours. Tell your partner. Follow the dialog above.

Personal Dictionary Understanding Finances

Write the words and phrases that you need to know.

____

____

____

78 Unit 7

PREPARATION

Use realia to preteach or review **paycheck** and **timecard.** Then ask learners how the hours marked on a timecard relate to the hours noted on a paycheck stub and to pay received. Talk about possible discrepancies.

PRESENTATION

1. Have learners read the Purpose Statement. For more information, see "Purpose Statement" on page viii.

2. Focus attention on the picture. Encourage learners to say as much as they can about it. Have them imagine what the speakers are saying. Have them identify the place in the picture. Then present the dialog. See "Presenting a Dialog" on page ix.

ON YOUR JOB **3.** Have partners read the Partner Work instructions. Make sure each pair knows what to do. If necessary, model the activity with a volunteer. Then have pairs complete the activity. Have pairs write their dialogs and share them with the class.

4. Have learners read the Personal Dictionary instructions. Then use the Personal Dictionary procedures on page ix. Remind learners to continue to add words to their dictionaries throughout the unit.

Tip Have learners read the Tip independently. Have learners discuss how the advice will help them. For more information, see "Presenting a Tip" on page ix.

FOLLOW-UP

It Seems That . . . Have learners work in pairs to list other possible discrepancies in paychecks. Ask pairs to share their lists with the class.

◆ Have pairs use their lists to write dialogs. One learner should report a discrepancy and the other learner should respond. Have learners take turns presenting their dialogs to the class.

WORKBOOK

Unit 7, Exercise 4

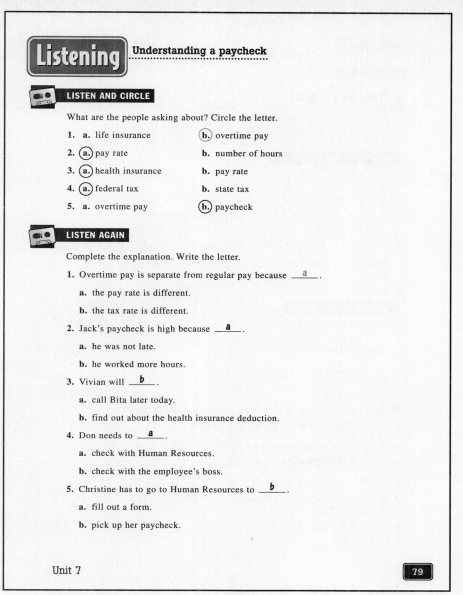

Listening — Understanding a paycheck

LISTEN AND CIRCLE

What are the people asking about? Circle the letter.

1. a. life insurance   **b.** overtime pay
2. **a.** pay rate   b. number of hours
3. **a.** health insurance   b. pay rate
4. **a.** federal tax   b. state tax
5. a. overtime pay   **b.** paycheck

LISTEN AGAIN

Complete the explanation. Write the letter.

1. Overtime pay is separate from regular pay because __a__ .

   a. the pay rate is different.

   b. the tax rate is different.

2. Jack's paycheck is high because __a__ .

   a. he was not late.

   b. he worked more hours.

3. Vivian will __b__ .

   a. call Bita later today.

   b. find out about the health insurance deduction.

4. Don needs to __a__ .

   a. check with Human Resources.

   b. check with the employee's boss.

5. Christine has to go to Human Resources to __b__ .

   a. fill out a form.

   b. pick up her paycheck.

Unit 7   79

WORKFORCE SKILLS (page 79)
Understand a paycheck
Report mistakes in your paycheck

★   ★   ★   ★   ★

PREPARATION

Use the sample paycheck and stub to preteach or review paycheck vocabulary: **insurance, federal tax, overtime,** and **deduction.** Encourage learners to use peer teaching to clarify vocabulary.

PRESENTATION

1. Have learners read and discuss the Purpose Statement. For more information, see "Purpose Statement" on page viii.

 2. Have learners read the Listen and Circle instructions. Make sure that everyone understands the instructions and the answer choices. If necessary, model the first item. Then play the tape or read the Listening Transcript aloud two or more times as learners complete the activity. Have learners check their work. For more information, see "Presenting a Listening Activity" on page ix.

3. Have learners read the Listen Again instructions. Then follow the procedures in 2.

FOLLOW-UP

Deductions: Have learners work in teams to think of as many types of paycheck deductions as they can. Ideas may include deductions for union dues, uniforms, and charities. Ask team reporters to share their teams' ideas with the class.

♦ Have teams divide their lists into two categories: optional deductions and required deductions. Why are some items required and some optional? Ask teams to discuss their lists.

WORKBOOK

Unit 7, Exercise 5

★　　★　　★　　★　　★

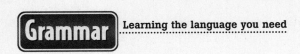

Grammar　· · · Learning the language you need

A. Study the Examples

Could you	look at my paycheck?
	answer a question?

COMPLETE THE QUESTIONS

Use the language in A.

1. _____ *Could you check* _____ (**check**) my W-4 form?

2. _____ *Could you change* _____ (**change**) the amount of my deduction?

3. _____ *Could you show* _____ (**show**) me my gross pay?

4. _____ *Could you tell* _____ (**tell**) me my net pay?

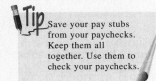

Tip: Save your pay stubs from your paychecks. Keep them all together. Use them to check your paychecks.

COMPLETE THE DIALOG

Use the language in A.

show	repeat	answer

A _____ *Could you answer* _____ a question about my paycheck?

B Sure. Go ahead.

A Well, I get paid $7.00 an hour, and I worked 25 hours last week.

B _____ *Could you repeat* _____ that? How many hours?

A 25. So my gross pay should be $175. But it's $200.

B OK. _____ *Could you show* _____ me your paycheck?

A Yes. Here it is.

B Let's see. Your pay went up because you sold a $250 camera. You got a $25 bonus.

A Oh, great! Thanks.

80

Unit 7

PREPARATION

Review the language in the grammar boxes with learners before they open their books, if necessary.

PRESENTATION

1. Have learners read and discuss the Purpose Statement. For more information, see "Purpose Statement" on page viii.

2. Have learners read the grammar box in A. Have learners use the language in the box to ask as many questions as possible. Tell learners that they can use the grammar boxes throughout the unit to review or check language patterns.

3. Have learners read the instructions for Complete the Questions. If necessary, model the first item. Allow learners to complete the activity. Have learners check each other's work in pairs. Ask several learners to read their questions aloud while the rest of the class checks their work.

4. Have learners read the instructions for Complete the Dialog. Have them read the word box. Use peer teaching to clarify any unfamiliar vocabulary. If necessary, model the first item. Allow learners to complete the activity. Have learners check each other's work in pairs. Ask several learners to read their answers aloud while the rest of the class checks their work.

Tip: Have learners read the Tip independently. Provide any clarification needed. Ask learners to give a few examples. For more information, see "Presenting a Tip" on page ix.

B. Study the Examples

> I need to talk to my supervisor because I want to go on vacation.
> I want to go on vacation, so I need to talk to my supervisor.

COMPLETE THE SENTENCES

Use *because* or *so*.

1. Eduardo always reads his paycheck ____because____ he wants to understand it.

2. Carmen, his wife, reads it too ____because____ she wants to make sure it's correct.

3. Once they found a mistake in Eduardo's paycheck, ____so____ Eduardo called Human Resources.

4. The employees in Human Resources thanked Eduardo for calling ____because____ there was a mistake on the check.

5. His paycheck was low, ____so____ Human Resources gave him a new check.

COMPLETE THE SENTENCES

Use *because* or *so*.

Tim had some questions about his paycheck, ____so____ he talked to his boss. She told him his pay went up ____because____ he was on time every day. But his taxes went up ____because____ he made more money. Also, he has new health insurance, ____so____ his pay went down a little. Tim is happy he talked to his boss ____because____ now he understands his paycheck.

PARTNER WORK

Take turns talking to your boss about the situations.
Use *because* and *so* to explain your reasons.

1. You want to go on vacation next month.

2. You need to arrive late tomorrow.

Unit 7   81

---

5. Focus attention on the grammar box in B. Follow the procedures in 2.

6. Have learners read the instructions for Complete the Sentences. If necessary, model the first item. Then have learners complete the activity independently. Have a different learner read each sentence aloud while the rest of the class checks their answers.

7. Have learners read the instructions for the second Complete the Sentences activity. Then follow the procedures in 6.

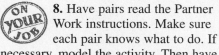 **8.** Have pairs read the Partner Work instructions. Make sure each pair knows what to do. If necessary, model the activity. Then have pairs complete the activity. Have several pairs share their dialogs with the class.

FOLLOW-UP

The So and Because Game: Make a statement such as *I bring my lunch to work.* Have learners work in teams to add to the statement using **because** or **so.** For example, *I bring my lunch to work because I don't like the food in the cafeteria* or *I bring my lunch to work so I can save money.* Have teams think of as many endings for the sentence as possible. Ask team reporters to share their teams' sentences with the class. The team with the most acceptable sentences wins.

♦ Have teams take turns making up a new sentence that can be completed using **because** or **so.** Use the statements to continue playing the game.

WORKBOOK

Unit 7, Exercises 6A–6D

BLACKLINE MASTERS

Blackline Master: Unit 7

★   ★   ★   ★   ★

Reading and Writing

Understanding Social Security

READ

Social Security Helps Millions of People

Social Security is a large government program that helps people who are not able to work. Social Security also helps some families after the husband or wife dies. Social Security pays cash benefits, usually in the form of a monthly check. Social Security is paid out of deductions from workers' paychecks. If you work in the United States, you have to pay Social Security taxes. Social Security helps millions of people. Right now over 49 million people get Social Security benefits.

SOCIAL SECURITY

000-74-9031

THIS NUMBER HAS BEEN ESTABLISHED FOR
MARIA GARCIA

Maria Garcia
SIGNATURE

WRITE YES OR NO

1. Social Security is a government program. ___YES___

2. Social Security helps only people who are older. _____

3. Taxes help pay for Social Security. _____

4. Very few people get Social Security benefits. _____

5. All workers in the United States pay Social Security taxes. _____

DISCUSSION

How do you feel about the taxes you pay? Do you think you pay too much in taxes? What services do your taxes pay for? Do you use any of these services?

82   Unit 7

PREPARATION

1. Clarify key language related to the topic of Social Security. Explain that a **government** consists of the people who rule a place, and **Social Security** is a government program that helps people who can't work. The help Social Security provides is called **benefits.**

2. Display the sample Social Security card. Ask, *What information is on a Social Security card? When can you use the card? What is its purpose?*

PRESENTATION

1. Have learners read and discuss the Purpose Statement. For more information, see "Purpose Statement" on page viii.

2. Have learners read the article's title and look at the illustration. Ask learners what the article might be about. Write their ideas on the board or restate them in acceptable English. Then have learners read the article independently.

3. Have learners read the instructions for Write *Yes* or *No*. Make sure everyone knows what to do. Then have learners complete the activity independently. Have learners review each other's work in pairs. Ask several learners to share their answers with the class while the rest of the class checks their work.

4. Have learners read the Discussion questions. Make sure everyone knows what to do. Then have learners work in teams to discuss their ideas. Have team reporters share their ideas with the class. Ask teams to compare ideas.

To work in the U.S., you need a Social Security card. To get a card, you have to fill out a form. Here is part of the form. Fill it out.

SOCIAL SECURITY ADMINISTRATION
Application for a Social Security Card

INSTRUCTIONS
- Please read "How To Complete This Form" on page 2.
- Print or type using black or blue ink. DO NOT USE PENCIL.
- After you complete this form, take or mail it along with the required documents to your nearest Social Security office.
- If you are completing this form for someone else, answer the questions as they apply to that person. Then, sign your name in question 16.

1 NAME
To Be Shown On Card
FIRST   FULL MIDDLE NAME   LAST

2 MAILING ADDRESS
STREET ADDRESS, APT. NO., PO BOX, RURAL ROUTE NO.

CITY   STATE   ZIP CODE

3 CITIZENSHIP
(Check One)
☐ U.S. Citizen ☐ Legal Alien Allowed To Work ☐ Legal Alien Not Allowed To Work ☐ Foreign Student ☐ Conditionally Legalized Alien ☐ Other

4 SEX
☐ Male ☐ Female

5 RACE/ETHNIC DESCRIPTION
(Check One Only–Voluntary)
☐ Asian, Asian-American Or Pacific Islander ☐ Hispanic ☐ Black (Not Hispanic) ☐ North American Indian Or Alaskan Native ☐ White (Not Hispanic)

6 DATE OF BIRTH
MONTH DAY YEAR

7 PLACE OF BIRTH
CITY   STATE OR FOREIGN COUNTRY   FCI

Office Use Only

8 MOTHER'S MAIDEN NAME
FIRST   FULL MIDDLE NAME   LAST NAME AT HER BIRTH

9 FATHER'S NAME
FIRST   FULL MIDDLE NAME   LAST

16 YOUR SIGNATURE

17 YOUR RELATIONSHIP TO THE PERSON IN ITEM 1 IS:
☐ Self ☐ Natural or Adoptive Parent ☐ Legal Guardian ☐ Other (Specify)

Unit 7   83

---

5. Have learners read the instructions for Complete the Form. Make sure everyone knows what to do. Then have learners complete the activity independently. Check learners' work.

FOLLOW-UP

Safekeeping: Have each learner copy onto a piece of paper his or her Social Security number and other important personal identification numbers. For example, learners may copy their driver's license number, their passport number, and/or their car license plate number. Explain to learners the importance of these numbers. Encourage learners to keep this copy of their identification numbers in a safe place, separate from the originals. For example, they may be stored in a file at home.

♦ As a class, talk about why it is useful to have copies of important identification numbers. In what situations would these copies be helpful?

WORKBOOK

Unit 7, Exercises 7A–7B

★　　★　　★　　★　　★

Extension · · · · · · · · · · **Understanding a W-2 form**

READ THE TAX FORM

A W-2 form tells you how much money you made last year. It also tells you the taxes you paid. Workers get these forms in January. Read the form and answer the questions.

Employer's identification number		Wages, tips, other compensation	Federal income tax withheld
06-33231687		$25,570.00	$3,068.40
Employer's name , address, and zip code		Social Security Wages	Social Security tax withheld
		$25,570.00	$1,534.20
Paco's Restaurant		Medicare wages and tips	Medicare tax withheld
1140 First Street		$25,570.00	$383.55
San Jose, CA 95128			

Employee's Social Security number	
000-01-8243	
Employee's name , address, and zip code	
Rosa Encida	
1245 Lane Street	
San Jose, CA 95128	

Name of State	State wages, tips, etc.	State income tax		
CA	$25,570.00	$2,045.60		

FORM W-2 **Wages and Tax Statement** **1999**

1. Who does the form belong to? ___Rosa Encida___
2. Where does she work? __Paco's Restaurant__
3. What year is this form for? _____1999_____
4. How much did she earn in 1999? ___$25,570.00___
5. How much was her state income tax in 1999? __$2,045.60__

 *Culture* Notes

At the end of each year, you get tax forms from your employer, your bank, and the government. What do you do if you don't receive a tax form?

84   Unit 7

PREPARATION

Review the large W-2 form. Ask, *Have you ever received a form like this? If so, who sent it?* Focus on key language in the form that learners need to know: **wages, tips, compensation, withhold,** and **income tax.**

PRESENTATION

1. Have learners read and discuss the Purpose Statement. For more information, see "Purpose Statement" on page viii.

2. Have learners preview the W-2 form on the page. Encourage them to say everything they can about it. Write their ideas on the board or restate them in acceptable English.

3. Have learners read the instructions for Read the Tax Form. Make sure everyone knows what to do. If necessary, model the first item. Then have learners complete the activity independently. Have learners review each other's work in pairs. Ask several learners to read their answers aloud while the rest of the class checks their work.

 4. Have learners read Culture Notes and talk over their responses in teams. Have team reporters share their ideas with the class. Ask the teams to compare each other's ideas.

FOLLOW-UP

U.S. Taxes: Provide learners with copies of a blank 1040EZ or 1040A tax form. Have them examine the form. Ask them to find the place on the form for recording their W-2 information.

♦ Provide learners with fictitious information about Rosa Encida, the character on the Student Book page. Have learners use this information and her W-2 to complete the 1040EZ or 1040A. Does everyone come up with the same amount of tax due?

WORKBOOK

Unit 7, Exercise 8

Performance Check — How well can you use the skills in this unit?
....

Complete the activities. Go over your work with a partner or your teacher.
Then complete the Performance Review on page 86.

SKILL 1   UNDERSTAND PAYCHECKS

Look at the paycheck. Circle the answer.

1. $70.20 is the: FICA   (federal tax)
2. $585 is the: (gross pay)   deductions
3. $500.80 is the: (net pay)   FICA

                                                    NO. 10000741

Albert Diego   111-22-3333

RATE	HOURS	EARNINGS	YEAR TO DATE	DEDUCTIONS
$9.00	65.00	$585.00	$11,115.00

Federal tax	$70.20
FICA	12.00
Medicare	2.00
Total deductions	$84.20

GROSS PAY $585.00
PAY PERIOD BEGINNING   08/15/99
PAY PERIOD ENDING   09/01/99   NET PAY $500.80

Park Auto Supply

Bank of Texas   NO. 10000741
Houston, Texas

PAY TO THE
ORDER OF   Albert Diego   DATE 09/01/99

FIVE HUNDRED DOLLARS AND EIGHTY CENTS

NOT GOOD AFTER 60 DAYS FROM DATE ISSUED   PAY THIS AMOUNT
MUST BE COUNTERSIGNED OVER $5000.00   ****500.80

⑈200005413⑈ ⑆0531079891⑆ 480026251⑈

SKILL 2   REPORT MISTAKES IN YOUR PAYCHECK

Usually you make $10 an hour, but this week your check is for $9 per hour.
Imagine that your partner or teacher is your boss. Report the mistake.

Unit 7   85

PRESENTATION

Use any of the procedures in
"Evaluation," page x, with pages 85
and 86. Record individuals' results
on the Unit 7 Individual Competency
Chart. Record the class's results on the
Class Cumulative Competency Chart.

Write *yes* or *no*.

1. Social Security helps only older people. __no__

2. Deductions from workers' paychecks help pay for Social Security. __yes__

3. To work in the United States, you must pay Social Security taxes. __yes__

SKILL 4   UNDERSTAND A W-2 FORM

How much federal tax did Martin pay? Circle the amount.

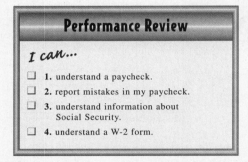

FORM W-2 Wages and Tax Statement 1999	Employee's Social Security number 000-64-7243	
Employer's name, address, and zip code Burger House 420 Forest Street Denver, Colorado 80223	Wages, tips, other compensation $21,300.00	Federal income tax withheld (circled) $2,556.00
		Social Security tax withheld $1,278.00
		Medicare tax withheld $319.50
Employer's name, address, and zip code Martin Schenk 3245 Elm Street Denver, Colorado 80224	State income tax $1,704.00	

Performance Review

I can...

☐ 1. understand a paycheck.

☐ 2. report mistakes in my paycheck.

☐ 3. understand information about Social Security.

☐ 4. understand a W-2 form.

DISCUSSION

Work with a team. How will your new skills help you? Make a list. Share your list with the class.

PRESENTATION

Follow the instructions on page 85.

INFORMAL WORKPLACE-SPECIFIC ASSESSMENT

Ask learners to think of a possible mistake on their paychecks. Have them role-play asking about the mistake.

WORKBOOK

Unit 7, Exercise 9

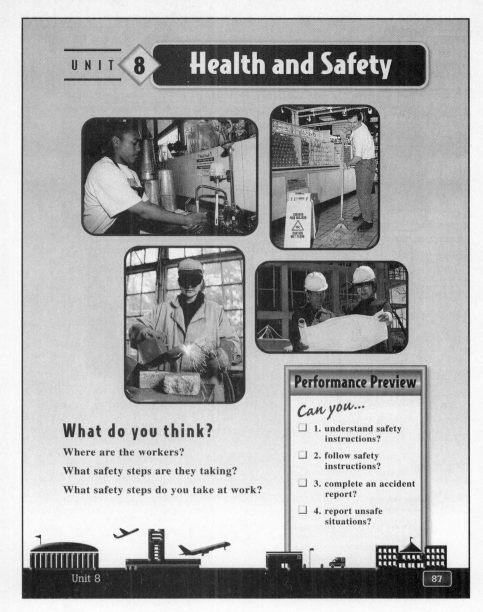

What do you think?

Where are the workers?

What safety steps are they taking?

What safety steps do you take at work?

Performance Preview

Can you...

☐ 1. understand safety instructions?

☐ 2. follow safety instructions?

☐ 3. complete an accident report?

☐ 4. report unsafe situations?

Unit 8   87

Unit 8 Overview
—SCANS Competencies—

★ Interpret information

★ Understand technological systems

★ Apply technology to specific tasks

★ Maintain and troubleshoot technologies

★ Work on teams

Workforce Skills

● Understand safety instructions

● Follow safety instructions

● Complete an accident report

● Report unsafe situations

Materials

● A common small appliance and its user's manual

● Examples of health and safety signs in this unit: **Wet Floor, Employees Must Wash Hands, Hard Hat Area, Do Not Block Door, No Smoking,** and **High Voltage**

● A picture or realia of a piece of safety equipment

● Blank index cards

Unit Warm-Up

To get learners thinking about the unit topic, display the small appliance. Act out reading its user's manual and following the safety instructions. Have learners talk about what you are doing.

★   ★   ★   ★   ★

WORKFORCE SKILLS (page 87)

Understand safety instructions

★   ★   ★   ★   ★

PREPARATION

1. Display the health and safety signs. Have learners identify them and talk about the health and safety practices that each sign encourages. Where have learners seen such signs or practices? Encourage learners to use peer teaching to clarify any unfamiliar vocabulary.

2. Ask learners to talk about safety signs at their workplace or school. Ask, *What do the signs look like? What do they tell workers to do? Where are the signs posted?*

PRESENTATION

1. Focus attention on the photographs. Ask learners what the unit might be about. Write their ideas on the board and/or restate them in acceptable English.

2. Have learners talk about the photographs. Ask learners to identify the health or safety practices in each one. Discuss reasons the safety practices are important. Where possible, help learners match the situations in the pictures to the health and safety signs you've displayed.

3. Help learners read the questions. Discuss the questions with the class.

4. You may want to use the Performance Preview to provide learners with an overview of the skills in the unit. Have learners read the list of skills and discuss what they will learn in the unit.

FOLLOW-UP

Our Safety: Have learners work in teams to act out a task. One member of the team should act out having an accident while completing the task. For example, team members could act out moving heavy boxes when one member drops a box on his/her foot. Have other teams say what the accident was: *He hurt his foot.*

♦ Have teams suggest ways to prevent the accident, such as by wearing safety shoes.

WORKBOOK

Unit 8, Exercises 1A–1B

★　　★　　★　　★　　★

Teaching Note

Use this page to introduce the new language in the unit. Whenever possible, encourage peer teaching. Supply any new language learners need.

| Getting Started | Wearing proper equipment |

TEAM WORK

Look at the pictures. What health and safety equipment are the people wearing? Where do you think they work?

PARTNER WORK

Student A names a piece of safety equipment. Student B says what it is used for. Use the dialog and Useful Language.

A Safety glasses.

B Safety glasses protect your eyes.

SURVEY

What health and safety equipment do you use at work? Ask your classmates. Make a chart. List the names of the equipment and why people use it.

> **Useful Language**
>
> safety glasses
> back support belt
> hard hat
> boots
> gloves
> hairnet
> dust mask
> ear protection

Unit 8

PREPARATION

Show learners a piece of safety equipment. Have they seen this item before? Ask them what it is used for. What can happen if workers don't use it?

PRESENTATION

1. Have learners read and discuss the Purpose Statement. For more information, see "Purpose Statement" on page viii.

2. Focus attention on the pictures. Encourage learners to say as much as they can about them. Write their ideas on the board and/or restate them in acceptable English.

3. Have teams read the Team Work instructions. Make sure each team knows what to do. If necessary, model the first item. Remind the teams that they are responsible for making sure that each member understands the new language. Then have teams complete the activity. If learners need help, encourage them to consult other teams. Have team reporters share their answers with the class.

4. Have partners read the Partner Work instructions. Make sure each pair knows what to do. If necessary, model the activity. Then have pairs complete the activity. Have learners switch partners and repeat the activity. Supply any language needed. Have one or two partners present their dialogs to the class.

5. Have partners read the Survey instructions. Make sure each person knows what to do. If necessary, model the activity. Then have the class complete the activity. Have learners share their answers with the class. For more information see "Survey" on page viii.

FOLLOW-UP

Bar Graph: Help teams use information from the Survey to make a bar graph showing the five most common pieces of safety equipment. The horizontal axis should show the names of the safety equipment, and the vertical axis should show the number of learners' workplaces where the equipment is used. For more information see "Survey" on page viii.

♦ Have learners think of additional safety equipment that they do not currently use, but that they might find useful. Ask volunteers to share their ideas with the class.

WORKBOOK

Unit 8, Exercises 2A–2B

Talk About It ..... Staying safe

PRACTICE THE DIALOG

A It's really hot in here.

B I agree. We should ask for a fan.

A That's a good idea.

PARTNER WORK

Talk about ways to stay safe and comfortable at work. Use the dialog and Useful Language above.

Useful Language

We should wear goggles.

We should sweep the floor.

We should put on gloves.

I think so, too.

I agree with you

TEAM WORK

Write some safety tips.

If you work in a hot area, you should use a fan.

ASAP PROJECT

Make a booklet of safety signs and rules. Include a list of the safety rules from everyone's workplace. Put in drawings of safety signs. Write what the signs mean. Complete this project as you work through this unit.

Unit 8

89

ASAP PROJECT

Have learners read the instructions. Discuss the project and its purpose with learners. Make sure that everyone understands. Help learners assign themselves to teams depending on their skills, knowledge, interests, or other individual strengths. Have each team select a leader. Throughout the rest of the unit, allow time for learners to work on the project. Have learners agree on a deadline when the project will be finished. For more information see "ASAP Project" on page vi.

PREPARATION

1. Present an unsafe situation in your classroom such as an electrical cord that someone could trip on. Ask learners to say what's the matter. Have learners talk about their own observations of potentially unsafe situations. Supply any language learners need.

2. Present new vocabulary from the dialog and the Useful Language box: **fan, goggles, sweep,** and **gloves.** Act out each one and use the word in a sentence.

PRESENTATION

1. Have learners read and discuss the Purpose Statement. For more information, see "Purpose Statement" on page viii.

2. Focus attention on the illustration. Encourage learners to say as much as they can about it. Have them identify the work location and speculate about how the speakers feel and what they are saying. Then present the dialog. See "Presenting a Dialog" on page ix.

 3. Have partners read the Partner Work instructions. Then focus attention on the Useful Language box. Help learners read the expressions. If necessary, model pronunciation. Then have learners complete the activity. Have learners switch partners and repeat several times. Have one or two pairs present their dialogs to the class.

4. Have partners read the Team Work instructions. Make sure each team knows what to do. If necessary, model the activity. Then have teams complete the activity. Ask teams to share their safety tips with the class.

FOLLOW-UP

We Should: Divide the class into teams. Name or show a picture of a situation which calls for work to be done, such as a kitchen that needs cleaning. Have teams think of suggestions using **should** to correct the problem, such as *We should wash the dishes. We should take out the trash.* The team with the most suggestions wins.

♦ Repeat the activity. Have teams take turns suggesting scenarios, while the other teams respond with appropriate sentences using **should.**

WORKBOOK

Unit 8, Exercises 3A–3B

Personal Dictionary

Have learners add the words in their Personal Dictionary to their *Workforce Writing Dictionary*. For more information, see "Workforce Writing Dictionary" on page v.

Keep Talking — Reporting unsafe situations

PARTNER WORK

Look at the picture. Talk about the unsafe situations.

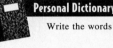

PRACTICE THE DIALOG

Warn the people in the picture about the unsafe situations. Use the dialog below.

A Excuse me. There's broken glass on the counter. You should clean it up.

B You're right. Thanks for telling me.

Useful Language

If you sit like that, you could fall.

A cord is across the door.

You should put up a wet floor sign.

Personal Dictionary ▸ Keeping Safe at Work

Write the words and phrases that you need to know.

_____

_____

_____

90   Unit 8

PREPARATION

Present the key language on the page: **across, broken, counter,** and **floor.** Use each word in several sample sentences and help learners figure out the meaning.

PRESENTATION

1. Have learners read and discuss the Purpose Statement. For more information, see "Purpose Statement" on page viii.

2. Have partners read the Partner Work instructions. Then focus attention on the illustration. Make sure each pair knows what to do. If necessary, model the activity with a volunteer. Then have pairs complete the activity. Ask pairs to share their ideas with the class.

3. Focus attention on Practice the Dialog and present the dialog. Follow the instructions on page ix. Then have learners follow the directions above the dialog and use the Useful Language to warn the people in the picture about the other hazards. Make sure each pair knows what to do. Model if necessary. Allow learners time to complete the activity. Then have learners change partners and repeat. Have several pairs present their dialogs to the class.

4. Have learners read the Personal Dictionary instructions. Then use the Personal Dictionary procedures on page ix. Remind learners to continue to add words to their dictionaries throughout the unit.

FOLLOW-UP

Safety Hazards: Have pairs list safety hazards such as water on the floor, sharp objects in the trash, or a cup of coffee on top of a computer. Have learners discuss why these items could be safety hazards. Ask several pairs to share their lists with the class.

◆ Have pairs talk about a specific unsafe situation that they have seen or heard of involving one of the hazardous items above. Have learners write how the situation was handled, and why. Have learners share their stories with the class.

WORKBOOK

Unit 8, Exercises 4A–4B

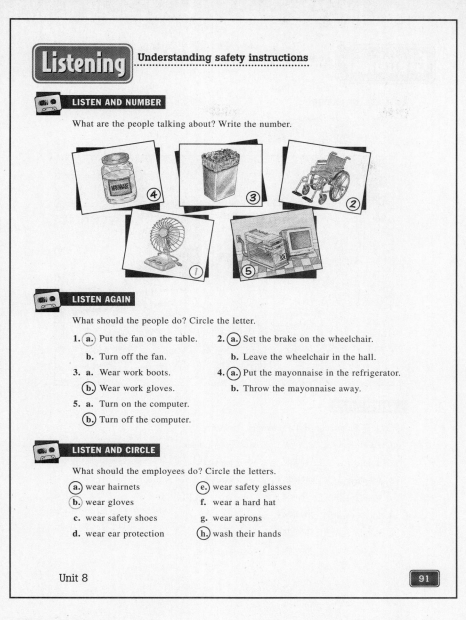

Listening ········ Understanding safety instructions

LISTEN AND NUMBER

What are the people talking about? Write the number.

LISTEN AGAIN

What should the people do? Circle the letter.

1. **a.** Put the fan on the table.　　2. **a.** Set the brake on the wheelchair.

   b. Turn off the fan.　　　　　　　**b.** Leave the wheelchair in the hall.

3. **a.** Wear work boots.　　　　　　4. **a.** Put the mayonnaise in the refrigerator.

   b. Wear work gloves.　　　　　　**b.** Throw the mayonnaise away.

5. **a.** Turn on the computer.

   b. Turn off the computer.

LISTEN AND CIRCLE

What should the employees do? Circle the letters.

a. wear hairnets　　　　　　**e.** wear safety glasses

b. wear gloves　　　　　　　**f.** wear a hard hat

c. wear safety shoes　　　　**g.** wear aprons

d. wear ear protection　　　**h.** wash their hands

Unit 8　　　　　　　　　　　　　91

PREPARATION

1. Use realia or pictures to preteach the new language **wheelchair** and **mayonnaise.** Explain to learners that a **brake** is what stops something, such as a car or wheelchair.

2. Talk about safety instructions. Ask, *When should you read safety instructions? Where do you keep safety instructions?*

PRESENTATION

1. Have learners read and discuss the Purpose Statement. For more information, see "Purpose Statement" on page viii.

 2. Have learners read the Listen and Number instructions. Then help learners identify the pictures. Make sure that

everyone understands the instructions. If necessary, model the first item. Then play the tape or read the Listening Transcript aloud two or more times as learners complete the activity. Have learners check their work. For more information see "Presenting a Listening Activity" on page ix.

 3. Have learners read the Listen Again instructions. Help learners read the answer choices. Then follow the procedures in 2.

 4. Have learners read the Listen and Circle instructions. Help learners read the answer choices. Then follow the procedures in 2.

FOLLOW-UP

Different Jobs, Different Safety Issues: Have teams list their jobs and/or

jobs of interest to them. Then have them list the types of safety issues relevant to those jobs. Have teams share their lists with the class.

♦ Have the class compile their lists into a master chart. Post the chart in your classroom.

WORKBOOK

Unit 8, Exercise 5

Understand safety instructions

Follow safety instructions

★   ★   ★   ★   ★

Language Note

*Help learners understand that the words **should/shouldn't** can have different degrees of necessity, from "must" to "Let's . . ." Give examples to illustrate the differences, such as **You should wear a hard hat** and **We should watch the news.** Then have volunteers provide sentences with **should/shouldn't,** write them on the board, and allow learners to determine the degree of necessity.*

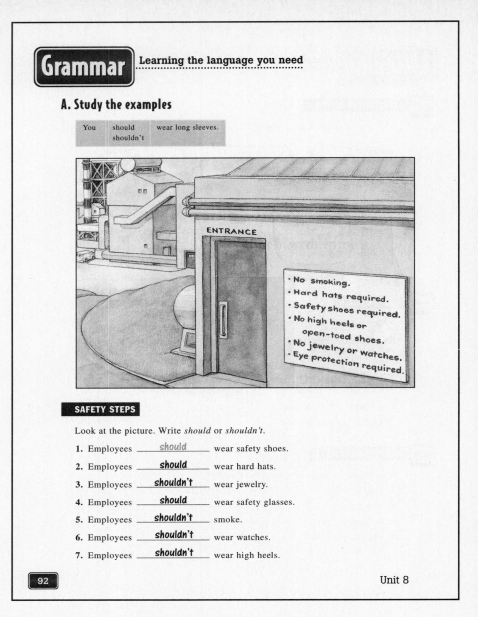

PREPARATION

Review the language in the grammar boxes with learners before they open their books, if necessary.

PRESENTATION

1. Have learners read and discuss the Purpose Statement. For more information, see "Purpose Statement" on page viii.

2. Have learners read the grammar box in A. Have learners use the language in the box to say as many sentences as possible. Tell learners that they can use the grammar boxes throughout the unit to review or check sentence structures.

3. Focus attention on the illustration. Help learners read the sign. Then have learners read the instructions for Safety Steps. If necessary, model the first item.

Allow learners to complete the activity. Have learners check each other's work in pairs. Ask several learners to read their sentences aloud while the rest of the class checks their work.

B. Study the Examples

> If she goes into the factory, she should wear a hard hat.
> She should wear a hard hat if she goes into the factory.

TEAM WORK

Look at the picture on page 92 and then look at the picture below. Talk about what the woman should and shouldn't do if she goes into the factory.

COMPLETE THE SENTENCES

Write the letter of the answer.

1. If you work around food, __*c*__ .
2. If you work on a construction site, __*a*__ .
3. If you lift heavy boxes, __*e*__ .
4. If you work at a gas station, __*b*__ .
5. If you work around loud machines, __*d*__ .

a. you should wear a hard hat

b. you shouldn't smoke

c. you should wash your hands often

d. you should wear ear protection

e. you shouldn't lift with straight knees

 TEAM WORK

What should you do at your workplace? Tell your team.

If you're a meat cutter, you should wear gloves.

Unit 8

93

---

4. Focus attention on the grammar box in B. Follow the procedures in 2.

5. Have teams read the Team Work instructions. Make sure each team knows what to do. If necessary, model the activity. Then have teams complete the activity. Ask team reporters to present their ideas to the class.

6. Have learners read the instructions for Complete the Sentences. If necessary, model the first item. Then have learners complete the activity independently. Have a different learner read each sentence aloud while the rest of the class checks their answers.

7. Have teams read the Team Work instructions. Make sure each team knows what to do. If necessary, model the activity. Then have teams complete the activity. Have team reporters share their sentences with the class.

FOLLOW-UP

Match: Write the first part of a safety tip on one index card and the last part on a second card. For example, on one card write **If there is water on the floor,** and on a second card write **you should put up a wet floor sign.** Distribute one card to each learner and have him or her find the learner whose card completes the sentence. Have pairs read their sentences to the class.

♦ Have learners make up their own **If . . . should** sentences and cards and repeat the activity.

WORKBOOK

Unit 8, Exercises 6A–6B

BLACKLINE MASTERS

Blackline Master: Unit 8

Understand safety instructions

Complete an accident report

★   ★   ★   ★   ★

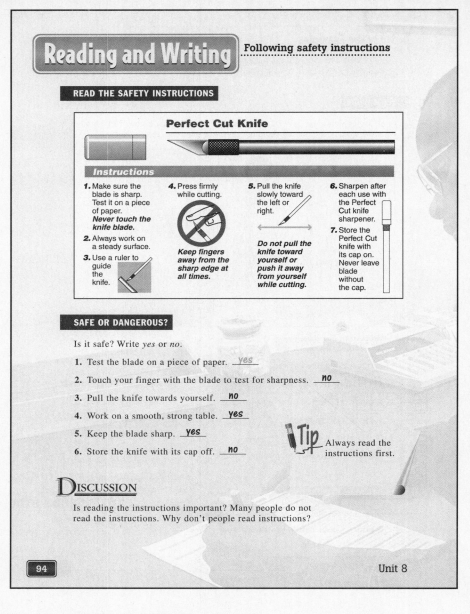

PREPARATION

Clarify the new language on the page: **steady, ruler,** and **sharpener.** To teach **steady,** vigorously shake a piece of paper. Say, *This is not steady.* Then firmly hold the paper still. Say, *This is steady.* Use realia or pictures to teach **ruler** and **sharpener.**

PRESENTATION

1. Have learners read and discuss the Purpose Statement. For more information, see "Purpose Statement" on page viii.

2. Have learners preview the safety instructions. Encourage learners to say everything they can about the instructions. Write their ideas on the board or restate them in acceptable English. Then have them read the instructions independently.

3. Have learners read the instructions for Safe or Dangerous? Make sure everyone knows what to do. Then have learners complete the activity independently. Have learners review each other's work in pairs. Ask several learners to share their answers with the class while the rest of the class checks their work.

4. Have teams read the Discussion instructions. Have learners work in teams to discuss their ideas. Have team reporters share their ideas with the class.

Have learners read the Tip independently. Have learners discuss how the advice will help them. For more information see "Presenting a Tip" on page ix.

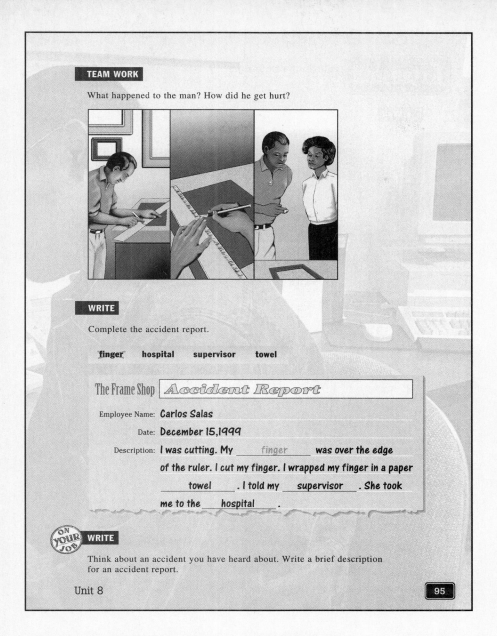

5. Have learners read the Team Work instructions. Make sure each team knows what to do. Then have teams complete the activity. Have team reporters share their ideas with the class. Ask teams to compare ideas.

6. Have learners read the instructions for Write. Model the activity if necessary by completing the first item. Have learners review the word list. Make sure that everyone understands what to do. Then have learners complete the activity. Have learners share their reports with the class.

7. Have learners read the instructions for the second Write activity. Model the activity if necessary. Make sure that everyone understands what to do. Then have learners complete the activity. Have learners share their reports with the class.

FOLLOW-UP

Accident Reports: Have learners work in teams. Have each team think of three possible purposes for a written accident report. Have teams write their list and share it with the class.

♦ Have learners discuss their workplaces' policies on filling out an accident report. How serious should an accident be to warrant a report? Why?

WORKBOOK

Unit 8, Exercises 7A–7C

Understand safety instructions

Report unsafe situations

★   ★   ★   ★   ★

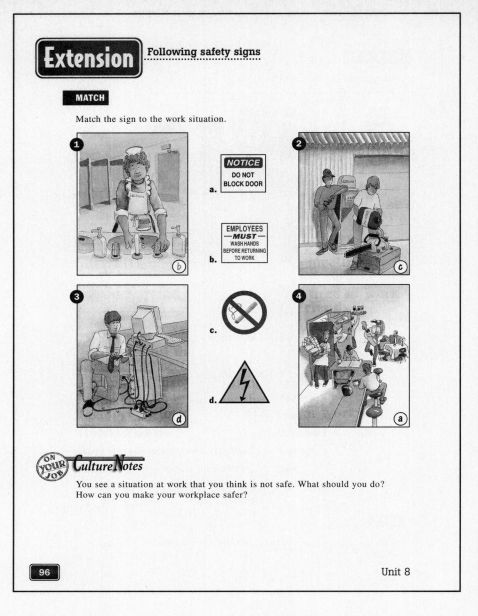

SCANS Note

The U.S. government requires that employers post standard signs in certain places. Encourage learners to discuss the advantages of using uniform signs.

PREPARATION

Display the safety signs and review their meanings with learners.

PRESENTATION

1. Have learners read and discuss the Purpose Statement. For more information, see "Purpose Statement" on page viii.

2. Have learners preview the signs and pictures on the page. Encourage them to say everything they can about them. Write their ideas on the board and/or restate them in acceptable English. Encourage peer teaching to clarify any unfamiliar vocabulary.

3. Have learners read the instructions for Match. Make sure each learner knows what to do. If necessary, model the first item. Allow learners to complete the

activity. Have learners review each other's work in pairs. Ask several learners to read their answers aloud while the rest of the class checks their work.

 4. Have learners read Culture Notes and talk over their responses in teams. Have team reporters share their ideas with the class. Ask the teams to compare each other's ideas.

FOLLOW-UP

Safety Signs in My Community:
Have teams make lists of safety signs or warnings that they see in their daily lives, such as pedestrian crossings or electrical shock hazard signs. Have team leaders share their lists with the class. Ask learners if they know the reasons for the signs.

♦ Have teams make simple safety signs for your classroom, such as **Open Door Slowly.**

WORKBOOK

Unit 8, Exercise 8

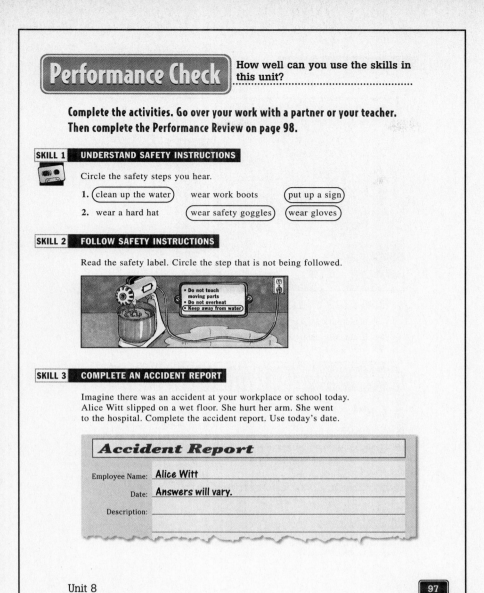

Performance Check
How well can you use the skills in this unit?

Complete the activities. Go over your work with a partner or your teacher. Then complete the Performance Review on page 98.

SKILL 1 — UNDERSTAND SAFETY INSTRUCTIONS

Circle the safety steps you hear.

1. (clean up the water)　　wear work boots　　(put up a sign)
2. wear a hard hat　　(wear safety goggles)　　(wear gloves)

SKILL 2 — FOLLOW SAFETY INSTRUCTIONS

Read the safety label. Circle the step that is not being followed.

- Do not touch moving parts
- Do not overheat
- Keep away from water

SKILL 3 — COMPLETE AN ACCIDENT REPORT

Imagine there was an accident at your workplace or school today. Alice Witt slipped on a wet floor. She hurt her arm. She went to the hospital. Complete the accident report. Use today's date.

Accident Report

Employee Name: **Alice Witt**

Date: **Answers will vary.**

Description: _____

Unit 8

97

PRESENTATION

Use any of the procedures in "Evaluation," page x, with pages 97 and 98. Record individuals' results on the Unit 8 Individual Competency Chart. Record the class's results on the Class Cumulative Competency Chart.

What safety step should he take? Tell him. Circle the letter.

a. You should put on a hard hat.

b. You should put up a wet floor sign.

c. You should wear safety glasses.

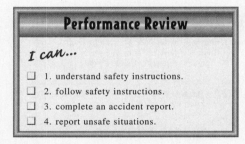

Performance Review

I can...

☐ 1. understand safety instructions.

☐ 2. follow safety instructions.

☐ 3. complete an accident report.

☐ 4. report unsafe situations.

Discussion

Work with a team. How will your new skills help you? Make a list. Share your list with the class.

98

Unit 8

PRESENTATION

Follow the instructions on page 97.

INFORMAL WORKPLACE-SPECIFIC ASSESSMENT

Ask learners to state one or two things they do to stay safe at work.

WORKBOOK

Unit 8, Exercise 9

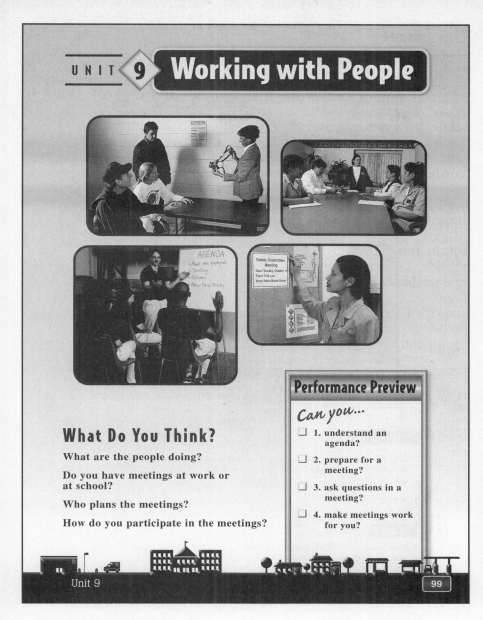

UNIT 9 Working with People

What Do You Think?

What are the people doing?

Do you have meetings at work or at school?

Who plans the meetings?

How do you participate in the meetings?

Performance Preview

Can you...

☐ 1. understand an agenda?

☐ 2. prepare for a meeting?

☐ 3. ask questions in a meeting?

☐ 4. make meetings work for you?

Unit 9

99

Unit 9 Overview
—SCANS Competencies—

★ Allocate time

★ Work on teams

★ Acquire and evaluate data

★ Interpret and communicate information

★ Understand social systems

★ Understand organizational systems

Workforce Skills

● Understand an agenda

● Prepare for a meeting

● Ask questions in a meeting

● Make meetings work for you

Materials

● A picture of people in a meeting

● A sign announcing a meeting with the time, date, place, and topic specified (use a time, date, and place relevant to learners)

● A large meeting agenda on a topic of relevance to all learners

Unit Warm-Up

To get learners thinking about the unit topic, show a picture of people in a meeting. Ask learners what is happening in the picture. Have learners been to meetings before?

★   ★   ★   ★   ★

WORKFORCE SKILLS (page 99)

Understand an agenda

Make meetings work for you

★   ★   ★   ★   ★

PREPARATION

Display the poster of a meeting announcement and help learners identify it. Have learners seen such an announcement before? What does it mean? Encourage learners to use peer teaching to clarify any unfamiliar vocabulary.

PRESENTATION

1. Focus attention on the photographs. Ask learners what the unit might be about. Write their ideas on the board and/or restate them in acceptable English.

2. Have learners talk about the pictures. Have them identify the situations. Ask learners, *Which meetings look like ones you've attended? What is different about the meetings in the pictures compared to those you've attended? Are they more or less formal? Are they a similar size?*

3. Help learners read the questions. Discuss the questions with the class.

4. You may want to use the Performance Preview to provide learners with an overview of the skills in the unit. Have learners read the list of skills and discuss what they will learn in the unit.

FOLLOW-UP

Lots of Meetings: Have the class make a list of all the different types of meetings they can think of, such as workplace meetings, club meetings, school

meetings, church meetings, community meetings, or any other type of meeting that they have heard of or attended. Have teams share their lists with the class.

◆ Have teams discuss the different types of meetings. What are the meetings about? Do people find out information or make decisions? Have teams share their ideas with the class.

WORKBOOK

Unit 9, Exercises 1A–1B

WORKFORCE SKILLS (page 100)

Understand an agenda

★   ★   ★   ★   ★

 **Understanding an agenda**

TEAM WORK

Look at the agendas. What information is usually in an agenda?

Data Input Department

Department Meeting Agenda

Topic: New Computers and Training
Date: 9/12
Time: 10:30 a.m. to 11:30 a.m.
Place: Meeting Room A
Purpose: To talk about problems with the new computers and set up a training schedule

10:30 – 10:35 Greetings and Introductions

10:35 – 10:45 Explain common problems with new computers

10:45 – 11:15 Discussion of our problems with the computers

11:15 – 11:30 Discuss needs for training

ALL EMPLOYEE MEETING

Tuesday
7:00 a.m.—8:00 a.m.
in the break room

Meet new employees — (5 minutes)
Stocking shelves — New procedure (15 minutes)
Pricing machines — Demonstration (15 minutes)
New food carts — (15 minutes)
Questions — (10 minutes)

PARTNER WORK

Look at the agendas. Ask and answer questions about the time, the place, and the topic of the meetings.

A What's the topic of the first meeting?
B New computers.

 SURVEY

How many students have been to a meeting at work? List the students' names. What were the meetings about? Make another list.

100   Unit 9

Teaching Note

Use this page to introduce the new language in the unit. Whenever possible, encourage peer teaching. Supply any new language learners need.

PREPARATION

Display the sample agenda and identify it. Tell learners that an **agenda** is a list of items to discuss at a meeting. Explain that each item is called a **topic.** Ask teams to list two or three meeting topics for their workplace. Have team leaders share their topics with the class.

PRESENTATION

1. Have learners read and discuss the Purpose Statement. For more information, see "Purpose Statement" on page viii.

2. Focus attention on the meeting agendas. Encourage learners to say as much as they can about them. Write their ideas on the board and/or restate them in acceptable English.

3. Have teams read the Team Work instructions. Make sure each team knows what to do. Remind the teams that they are responsible for making sure that each member understands the new language. Then have teams talk about the agendas. If learners need help, encourage them to consult other teams. Have team reporters share their answers with the class.

4. Have partners read the Partner Work instructions. If necessary, model the activity with a volunteer. Then have pairs complete the activity. Have learners switch partners and repeat the activity. Supply any language needed. Have one or two pairs present their dialogs to the class.

 5. Have learners read the Survey instructions. Then have the class complete the activity. For more information, see "Survey" on page viii.

FOLLOW-UP

Tracking Numbers: Have learners figure out the percentage of learners in the class who have attended a meeting at work. Then help them use this percentage to create a pie chart. Have learners talk about the pie chart. For more information, see "Survey" on page viii.

◆ Have learners make a second pie chart representing class members who have been to meetings. Was an agenda used at the most recent meeting they've been to? Show on a pie chart the percentage of these meetings that used an agenda and the percentage that didn't use an agenda.

WORKBOOK

Unit 9, Exercises 2A–2C

 **Talk About It** .... Preparing for a meeting

 PRACTICE THE DIALOG

A Excuse me, Ms. Chen. Can we talk about Monday's meeting?

B Of course.

A Well, several people have questions about the new vacation policy.

B OK, I'll add it to the agenda. Thanks, Rhonda.

Useful Language

Could we discuss . . .

I'd like to talk about . . .

Could you give us more information about . . . ?

 PARTNER WORK

Your department is having a meeting next Tuesday. Your partner is the boss. You have questions about benefits, uniforms, or safety equipment. Suggest a meeting topic. Use the dialog and Useful Language above.

ASAP
PROJECT

In teams, plan a meeting. Choose a topic you think is important. Decide who should be at the meeting. Choose a time and place for the meeting. Check that the place is open. Write an agenda for the meeting.

Unit 9

101

WORKFORCE SKILLS (page 101)

Prepare for a meeting

 ★   ★   ★   ★   ★

Language Note

If learners are uncomfortable speaking at meetings, encourage them to write down in advance questions they would like to ask. Then, they can simply read their questions aloud at meetings.

ASAP
PROJECT

Have learners read the instructions. Discuss the project and its purpose with learners. Make sure that everyone understands. Help learners assign themselves to teams depending upon their skills, knowledge, interests, or other individual strengths. Have each team select a leader. Throughout the rest of the unit, allow time for learners to work on the project. Have the teams agree on a deadline when the project will be finished. For more information, see "ASAP Project" on page vi.

PREPARATION

Preteach or review the new language on the page. Explain that a company's **vacation policy** is a set of rules about how and when workers can take their vacation time. **Uniforms** are the clothes that some workplaces require employees to wear. **Benefits** are things such as health insurance that companies provide for workers in addition to their pay.

PRESENTATION

1. Have learners read and discuss the Purpose Statement. For more information, see "Purpose Statement" on page viii.

 2. Focus attention on the illustration. Encourage learners to say as much as they can about it. Write their ideas on the board and/or restate them in acceptable English. Then present the dialog. See "Presenting a Dialog" on page ix.

 3. Have partners read the Partner Work instructions. Focus attention on the Useful Language box. Help learners read the expressions. If necessary, model pronunciation. Then have learners complete the activity. Have learners switch partners and repeat the activity. Have one or two pairs present their dialogs to the class.

FOLLOW-UP

Meeting Topics: Have teams make a list of topics appropriate for discussing at a meeting, and a list of topics appropriate for discussing one-on-one with a supervisor, such as an individual's pay or job performance. Have teams share their lists with the class.

♦ Discuss with learners why these topics are different. Do they involve privacy issues? Are legal issues involved?

WORKBOOK

Unit 9, Exercises 3A–3B

★　　★　　★　　★　　★

Teaching Note

Always model good listening habits during class. Look at learners when they ask a question. Rephrase learners' questions or thoughts to make sure that you've understood, to help other learners understand, and to model language for the learner.

Personal Dictionary

Have learners add the words in their Personal Dictionary to their *Workforce Writing Dictionary*. For more information, see "Workforce Writing Dictionary" on page v.

Keep Talking — Participating in a meeting

 PRACTICE THE DIALOG

A Excuse me. I'd like to ask a question.

B Go ahead.

A I have a question about our new dress code. Do we have to wear our company shirts every day?

B Yes, you have to wear the shirt and the pants every day.

Useful Language

I have a question.

Can I ask a question?

Is there time for a question?

 TEAM WORK

You're at a meeting. You have questions about the dress code, the attendance policy, or the benefits. Take turns asking your questions. Use the dialog and Useful Language above.

 Personal Dictionary ▸ Meetings

Write the words and phrases that you need to know.

_____

_____

_____

102   Unit 9

PREPARATION

1. Help learners think of ways to enter a group discussion, such as raising one's hand, saying *Excuse me*, or clearing one's throat. Then model the expressions in the Useful Language box.

2. Clarify that a workplace's **dress code** is a set of rules about the clothes employees can wear to work. Do learners have dress codes at their workplaces? Explain that a company's **attendance policy** consists of its rules about employees being present at work.

PRESENTATION

1. Have learners read the Purpose Statement. For more information, see "Purpose Statement" on page viii.

 2. Focus attention on the illustration. Encourage learners to say as much as they can about it. Have learners identify the location and event. Then present the dialog. See "Presenting a Dialog" on page ix.

3. Have teams read the Team Work instructions. Make sure each team knows what to do. If necessary, model the activity. Focus attention on the Useful Language box. Help learners read the expressions. If necessary, model pronunciation. Then have teams complete the activity. Have learners switch teams and repeat the activity. Ask several teams to present their conversations to the class.

4. Have learners read the Personal Dictionary instructions. Then use the Personal Dictionary procedures on page ix. Remind learners to continue to add words to their dictionaries throughout the unit.

FOLLOW-UP

Asking Questions: Have learners think of topics they have questions about regarding their workplace or class. Have them write their questions and present them to the class.

♦ Have teams role-play asking and answering their questions (the answers may be fictitious). Have teams present their role plays to the class.

WORKBOOK

Unit 9, Exercise 4

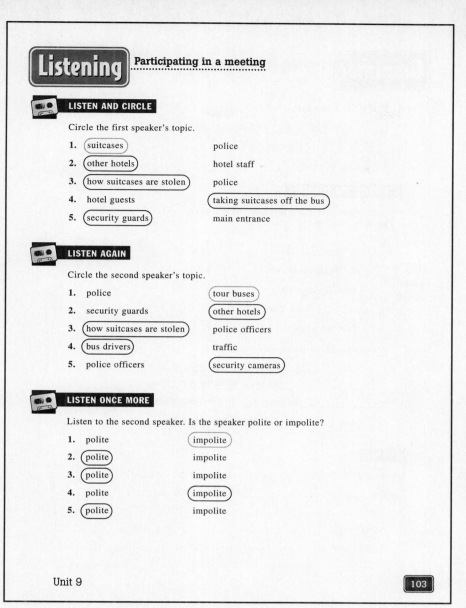

Listening · Participating in a meeting

LISTEN AND CIRCLE

Circle the first speaker's topic.

1. (suitcases)   police
2. (other hotels)   hotel staff
3. (how suitcases are stolen)   police
4. hotel guests   (taking suitcases off the bus)
5. (security guards)   main entrance

LISTEN AGAIN

Circle the second speaker's topic.

1. police   (tour buses)
2. security guards   (other hotels)
3. (how suitcases are stolen)   police officers
4. (bus drivers)   traffic
5. police officers   (security cameras)

LISTEN ONCE MORE

Listen to the second speaker. Is the speaker polite or impolite?

1. polite   (impolite)
2. (polite)   impolite
3. (polite)   impolite
4. polite   (impolite)
5. (polite)   impolite

Unit 9

103

SCANS Note

Explain what a meeting leader does. Help learners understand that this person may call on people who want to speak, and is responsible for keeping the meeting on schedule and on topic. He or she may also help people make decisions that are needed.

PREPARATION

1. Use pictures and examples to clarify **suitcases, security guards,** and **security cameras.**

2. Explain the difference between **polite** and **impolite.** Review the polite ways to enter a discussion presented on page 102. Ask learners if they can think of ways it would be impolite to enter the conversation during a meeting. You may want to act out inappropriate behavior, such as interrupting, with a volunteer and have learners say what you're doing wrong.

PRESENTATION

1. Have learners read and discuss the Purpose Statement. For more information, see "Purpose Statement" on page viii.

 2. Have learners read the Listen and Circle instructions. Make sure that everyone understands the instructions and the answer choices. If necessary, model the first item. Then play the tape or read the Listening Transcript aloud two or more times as learners complete the activity. Have learners check their work. For more information, see "Presenting a Listening Activity" on page ix.

 3. Have learners read the Listen Again instructions. Then follow the procedures in 2.

 4. Have learners read the Listen Once More instructions. Then follow the procedures in 2.

FOLLOW-UP

Manners: Have partners list good manners in meetings, such as listening carefully and not interrupting. Have pairs share their lists with the class.

♦ Have learners compile their lists into a booklet on good meeting manners.

WORKBOOK

Unit 9, Exercise 5

Make meetings work for you

★   ★   ★   ★   ★

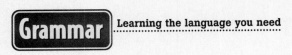 **Grammar** Learning the language you need

A. Study the Examples

| I
We
You
They | have to go to a meeting. | He
She | has to go to a meeting. |

ANSWER THE QUESTION

Look at the supervisor's to-do list. What does the supervisor have to do? Write sentences using *has to*.

TO DO

Call the plant supervisors.

Go to the main office.

Call Mary in Human Resources.

Send the package.

1. _He has to call the plant supervisors._
2. _He has to go to the main office._
3. _He has to call Mary in Human Resources._
4. _He has to send the package._

 WRITE

What do the people have to do tomorrow? Write five sentences.

1. I _____ Answers will vary. _____.
2. I _____.
3. My boss _____.
4. My coworkers _____.
5. _____

104   Unit 9

PREPARATION

Review the language in the grammar boxes with learners before they open their books, if necessary.

PRESENTATION

1. Have learners read and discuss the Purpose Statement. For more information, see "Purpose Statement" on page viii.

2. Have learners read the grammar boxes in A. Have learners use the language in the boxes to say as many sentences as possible. Tell learners that they can use the grammar boxes throughout the unit to review or check sentence structures.

3. Have learners read the instructions for Answer the Question. Help learners read the to-do list. If necessary, model the first item. Allow learners to complete the activity. Have learners check each other's work in pairs. Ask several learners to read their sentences aloud while the rest of the class checks their work.

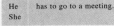 **4.** Have learners read the instructions for Write. If necessary, model the first item. Allow learners to complete the activity. Check learners' work. Ask several learners to read their sentences aloud.

PARTNER WORK

Ask your partner what he or she has to do tomorrow.

B. Study the Examples

I'd	like to ask about our vacation time.
He'd	
She'd	
We'd	
You'd	
They'd	

 TEAM WORK

Talk about something you'd like to discuss in a meeting at your workplace or school.

A What would you like to discuss?

B I'd like to discuss the schedule.

A Good idea.

C. Study the Examples

We need to work faster because our customers want good service.
Our customers want good service, so we need to work faster.

MATCH

Match the need and the reason. Write the letter

1. We are having a meeting at work ___b___.

2. I talked to my boss after the meeting ___c___.

3. I want to get a good seat, ___a___.

4. I'll take notes ___d___.

a. so I'll arrive at the meeting early

b. because the company has a new uniform policy

c. because I had several questions

d. so I'll remember everything

Unit 9

105

---

5. Have partners read the Partner Work instructions. Make sure each pair knows what to do. If necessary, model the activity. Then have learners complete the activity. Have learners switch partners and repeat the activity. Ask several learners to report their partners' plans to the class.

6. Focus attention on the grammar box in B. Follow the procedures in 2.

7. Have teams read the Team Work instructions. Make sure each team knows what to do. If necessary, model the activity. Then have teams complete the activity. Have learners switch teams and repeat the activity. Ask several teams to present their conversations to the class.

8. Focus attention on the grammar box in C. Follow the procedures in 2.

9. Have learners read the instructions for Match. If necessary, model the first item. Allow learners to complete the activity. Have learners check each other's work in pairs. Ask several learners to read their sentences aloud while the rest of the class checks their work.

FOLLOW-UP

The Remember-It Game: Play a game. Have learners sit in a circle. Have the first learner make a work-related request using *I'd like to*, or state a work responsibility using *I have to*. Have the next learner repeat the first learner's statement and add his or her own: *She'd like to change her work shift, and I have to deliver these flowers.* Have learners continue around the circle until each

learner has added a sentence using *I'd like to* or *I have to*. If someone cannot remember the whole list or cannot add a sentence, he or she has to drop out. The learner who can remember the longest list wins.

◆ Have learners write a list of several requests using *I'd like to* or several responsibilities using *I have to*. Have learners present their lists.

WORKBOOK

Unit 9, Exercises 6A–6E

BLACKLINE MASTERS

Blackline Master: Unit 9

WORKFORCE SKILLS (pages 106–107)

Understand an agenda

Prepare for a meeting

★   ★   ★   ★   ★

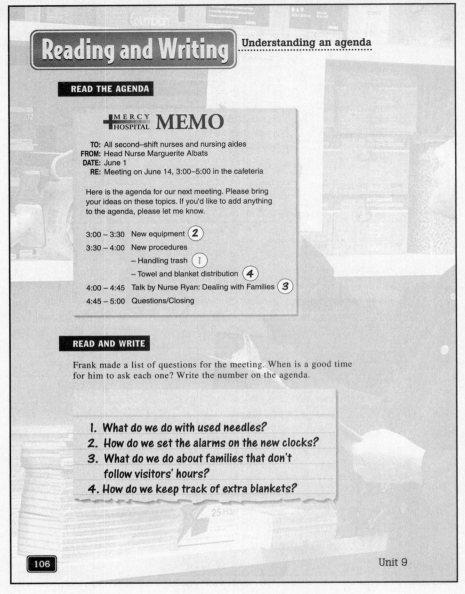

Reading and Writing — Understanding an agenda

READ THE AGENDA

MERCY HOSPITAL MEMO

TO: All second–shift nurses and nursing aides
FROM: Head Nurse Marguerite Albats
DATE: June 1
RE: Meeting on June 14, 3:00–5:00 in the cafeteria

Here is the agenda for our next meeting. Please bring your ideas on these topics. If you'd like to add anything to the agenda, please let me know.

3:00 – 3:30 New equipment ②
3:30 – 4:00 New procedures
            – Handling trash ①
            – Towel and blanket distribution ④
4:00 – 4:45 Talk by Nurse Ryan: Dealing with Families ③
4:45 – 5:00 Questions/Closing

READ AND WRITE

Frank made a list of questions for the meeting. When is a good time for him to ask each one? Write the number on the agenda.

1. What do we do with used needles?
2. How do we set the alarms on the new clocks?
3. What do we do about families that don't follow visitors' hours?
4. How do we keep track of extra blankets?

106   Unit 9

PREPARATION

Preteach or review the language on the pages. Use realia or pictures to clarify **towel, blanket,** and **planner.** Remind learners that **equipment** means the tools used for a task. Explain that **procedures** are the ways tasks are completed.

PRESENTATION

1. Have learners read and discuss the Purpose Statement. For more information, see "Purpose Statement" on page viii.

2. Have learners preview the memo. Encourage learners to say everything they can about it. Write their ideas on the board or restate them in acceptable English. Then have them read the memo independently.

3. Have learners read the instructions for Read and Write. Make sure everyone knows what to do. Then have learners complete the activity independently. Have learners review each other's work in pairs. Ask several learners to share their answers with the class while the rest of the class checks their work.

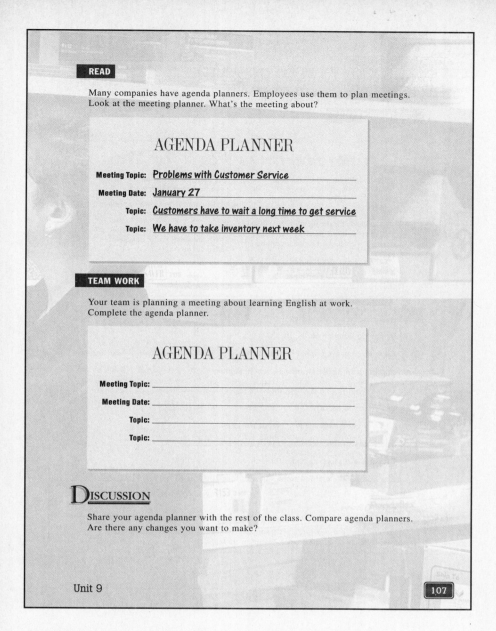

READ

Many companies have agenda planners. Employees use them to plan meetings.
Look at the meeting planner. What's the meeting about?

AGENDA PLANNER

Meeting Topic: _Problems with Customer Service_

Meeting Date: _January 27_

Topic: _Customers have to wait a long time to get service_

Topic: _We have to take inventory next week_

TEAM WORK

Your team is planning a meeting about learning English at work.
Complete the agenda planner.

AGENDA PLANNER

Meeting Topic: _____

Meeting Date: _____

Topic: _____

Topic: _____

Discussion

Share your agenda planner with the rest of the class. Compare agenda planners.
Are there any changes you want to make?

Unit 9

107

4. Have learners read the instructions for Read. Make sure everybody understands what to do. Then have learners complete the activity independently. Have several learners share their answers with the class.

5. Have learners read the Team Work instructions. Make sure each team knows what to do. If necessary, model the activity. Then have teams complete the activity.

6. Have teams read the Discussion instructions. Make sure everyone knows what to do. Then have learners complete the activity.

FOLLOW-UP

Does It Belong? Supply the class with a large meeting agenda on a topic of relevance to all learners. Then, have

each learner write one or two questions or comments about the meeting topic. Have learners share their questions or comments with the class. Have the class decide if the question or comment belongs at the meeting.

♦ Have learners say when they would make their questions or comments during the meeting. Have learners discuss whether that time is appropriate.

WORKBOOK

Unit 9, Exercises 7A–7B

★   ★   ★   ★   ★

 **Extension** Making meetings work for you

READ THE ARTICLE

Make Meetings Work for You

Most employees attend meetings from time to time. Follow these tips. See how you can make meetings work for you.

◆ Get ready for the meeting. Find out the topic of the meeting, if possible. Read the agenda. Prepare questions.

◆ Bring things you will need, such as a pencil, paper, and the agenda.

◆ Be there on time or early. Sit where you can see and hear clearly.

◆ Take notes. Write down important information.

◆ Ask questions. If there isn't time, talk to the meeting leader or your boss after the meeting.

WHAT SHOULD THEY DO?

Write the tip number on the line.

1. Ed is at a meeting about quality assurance. There's a lot of important information he wants to remember. __4__

2. Doris is going to a training meeting on new cash registers. She wants to be sure she can see the cash registers. __3__

3. Clara is going to a meeting about benefits. She wants to find out about the dental plan. __1__

4. Elena is at a meeting about the new attendance policy. She doesn't understand some of the information. __5__

 **Culture Notes**

When you are in a meeting, it's important to show that you are listening. For example, look at the leader. Name more ways to show you are listening.

108   Unit 9

PREPARATION

1. Share your own personal experiences at meetings. What have you done to help make meetings successful for you? Have learners talk about their personal experiences at meetings.

2. Preteach or review the key language on the page. Explain that to **attend** a meeting means to be at the meeting. **Quality assurance** is making sure products are in good condition. Show a picture to clarify **cash register.** A **dental plan** is a health insurance policy for taking care of a person's teeth.

PRESENTATION

1. Have learners read and discuss the Purpose Statement. For more information, see "Purpose Statement" on page viii.

2. Have learners preview the article. Encourage them to say everything they can about it. Write their ideas on the board or restate them in acceptable English. Then have learners read the article.

3. Have learners read the instructions for What Should They Do? If necessary, model the first item. Allow learners to complete the activity. Have learners review each other's work in pairs. Ask several learners to read their answers aloud while the rest of the class checks their work.

 4. Have learners read the Culture Notes and talk over their responses in teams. Have team reporters share their ideas with the class. Ask the teams to compare each other's ideas.

FOLLOW-UP

Are We Listening? Announce a meeting on a topic of interest to most learners, such as improving the food in the company cafeteria. Hold the meeting. Have learners grade themselves using the participation checklist on page 108. After the meeting, have learners share and discuss their observations with each other.

◆ Have learners write about ways that they can improve their meeting participation skills. Have them discuss how their new behaviors will help make meetings successful.

WORKBOOK

Unit 9, Exercise 8

**Performance Check** | How well can you use the skills in this unit?

Complete the activities. Go over your work with a partner or your teacher. Then complete the Performance Review on page 110.

SKILL 1 | **UNDERSTAND AN AGENDA**

Read the agenda. Write *yes* or *no*.

1. The meeting is about customer service. __*yes*__

2. The company is changing the telephone greeting. __*yes*__

3. The meeting is February 17. __*no*__

> ## CUSTOMER SERVICE DEPARTMENT
> ### Employee Meeting
>
> Agenda
>
> **Topic:** Improving Customer Service
> **Date:** February 16
> **Time:** 3:00 p.m.
> **Place:** Conference Room B
>
> 1. New telephone greeting
> 2. Expanded customer service hours
> 3. Responding to complaints

SKILL 2 | **PREPARE FOR A MEETING**

What should you do to prepare for a meeting? Circle the numbers.

(1.) Read the agenda.

2. Tell everyone you don't like meetings.

(3.) Prepare questions.

4. Think of a reason to avoid the meeting.

(5.) Suggest topics to your boss.

Unit 9

109

PRESENTATION

Use any of the procedures in "Evaluation," page x, with pages 109 and 110. Record individuals' results on the Unit 9 Individual Competency Chart. Record the class's results on the Class Cumulative Competency Chart.

| SKILL 3 | ASK QUESTIONS IN A MEETING |

You and your partner or teacher are having a meeting.
You have a question about uniforms, the schedule, or benefits.
Take turns asking a question politely.

| SKILL 4 | MAKE MEETINGS WORK FOR YOU |

What should you do in a meeting? Write *yes* or *no*.

1. You should listen carefully. __yes__

2. You should finish other work during the meeting. __no__

3. You should be on time. __yes__

Performance Review

I can...

☐ 1. understand an agenda.
☐ 2. prepare for a meeting.
☐ 3. ask questions in a meeting.
☐ 4. make meetings work for me.

DISCUSSION

Work with a team. How will the skills help you? Make a list.
Share your list with the class.

Unit 9

PRESENTATION

Follow the instructions on page 109.

INFORMAL WORKPLACE-SPECIFIC ASSESSMENT

Have each learner mention one way he or she plans to participate in upcoming meetings.

WORKBOOK

Unit 9, Exercise 9

UNIT 10 ▶ Career Development

What do you think?

Look at the pictures.

What are the people doing?

How did you find your job?

How did you apply?

Performance Preview

Can you...

☐ 1. look for a job?

☐ 2. interview for a job?

☐ 3. understand hiring decisions?

☐ 4. complete a job application?

Unit 10

111

Unit 10 Overview
—SCANS Competencies—

★ Organize and maintain information

★ Interpret and communicate information

★ Understand social systems

★ Understand organizational systems

★ Monitor and correct performance

Workforce Skills

● Look for a job

● Interview for a job

● Understand hiring decisions

● Complete a job application

Materials

● A sample job application

● A sample resume

● An enlarged copy of the job announcements in the newspaper classified ads

Unit Warm-Up

To get the learners thinking about the unit topic, talk about job applications. Show the sample job application. Have learners brainstorm about the information needed to fill out a job application.

★   ★   ★   ★   ★

WORKFORCE SKILLS (page 111)

Look for a job

Interview for a job

★   ★   ★   ★   ★

PREPARATION

Display the sample job application and resume. Have learners discuss them. Where have learners seen these items? Encourage learners to use peer teaching to clarify any unfamiliar vocabulary.

PRESENTATION

1. Focus attention on the photographs. Ask learners what the unit might be about. Write their ideas on the board and/or restate them in acceptable English.

2. Have learners talk about the pictures. Have them identify the situations. How does each situation show people making an effort to find a job? Why does it require time and preparation to find a job? Why is it important to prepare for an interview? Help learners relate the situations in the pictures to the sample job application and resume.

3. Help learners read the questions. Discuss the questions with the class.

4. You may want to use the Performance Preview to provide learners with an overview of the skills in the unit. Have learners read the list of skills and discuss what they will learn in the unit.

FOLLOW-UP

A Job Poll: Have learners take a job poll and tally answers on the board. Have learners find out answers to questions such as *How many people are looking for jobs? How many people like/dislike the jobs they have?* Discuss the results with learners.

◆ Have each learner write a few sentences about a previous job and a job they have or want. Have volunteers share their sentences.

WORKBOOK

Unit 10, Exercises 1A–1B

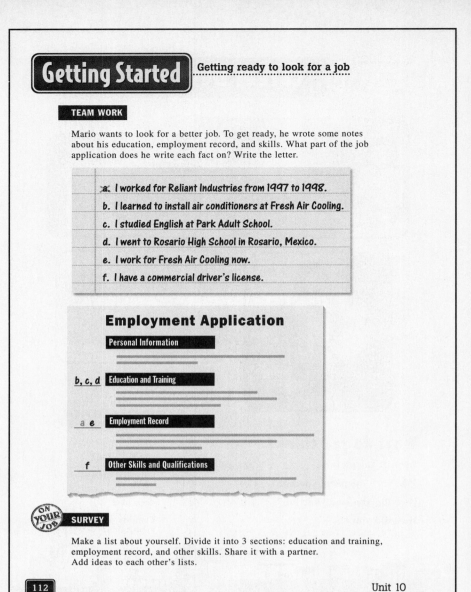

Getting Started · Getting ready to look for a job

TEAM WORK

Mario wants to look for a better job. To get ready, he wrote some notes about his education, employment record, and skills. What part of the job application does he write each fact on? Write the letter.

> a. I worked for Reliant Industries from 1997 to 1998.
> b. I learned to install air conditioners at Fresh Air Cooling.
> c. I studied English at Park Adult School.
> d. I went to Rosario High School in Rosario, Mexico.
> e. I work for Fresh Air Cooling now.
> f. I have a commercial driver's license.

Employment Application

Personal Information

b, c, d **Education and Training**

a e **Employment Record**

f **Other Skills and Qualifications**

SURVEY

Make a list about yourself. Divide it into 3 sections: education and training, employment record, and other skills. Share it with a partner. Add ideas to each other's lists.

112

Unit 10

Teaching Note

Use this page to introduce the new language in the unit. Whenever possible, encourage peer teaching. Supply any new language learners need.

PREPARATION

Ask teams to list two or three things that they do to prepare for a job search. Have team leaders share their lists with the class.

PRESENTATION

1. Have learners read and discuss the Purpose Statement. For more information, see "Purpose Statement" on page viii.

2. Focus attention on the information Mario wrote. Have learners talk about his background and the employment application. If necessary, clarify that before beginning a job search, people may list all of their training, skills, and interests in order to figure out jobs they can get. Encourage learners to use peer teaching to clarify any unfamiliar vocabulary.

3. Have teams read the Team Work instructions. Make sure each team knows what to do. If necessary, model the first item. Remind the teams that they are responsible for making sure that each member understands the new language. Then have teams complete the activity. If learners need help, encourage them to consult other teams. Have team reporters share their answers with the class.

4. Have partners read the Survey instructions. Make sure everyone knows what to do. If necessary, model the activity. Then have learners complete the activity. Have learners share their answers with other class members. For more information, see "Survey" on page viii.

FOLLOW-UP

Jobs You Can Get: Help the class use the information from the Survey to create a table showing each learner's name and his or her most important job skills.

♦ Have partners look at the job announcements in the newspaper classifieds. Have them find jobs that match their job skills. Have pairs report their findings to the class.

WORKBOOK

Unit 10, Exercises 2A–2B

Talk About It
Talking about work experience

 PRACTICE THE DIALOG

A Did you drive a van on your last job?

B Yes, I did. I drove a van part time for a florist.

A How long were you at that job?

B For three years.

A Why did you leave?

B I wanted full time work.

Useful Language

I was laid off.

I found a better job.

I wanted more responsibility.

 PARTNER WORK

Student A asks about work experience. Student B tells about his or her work experience. Use the dialog and the Useful Language above.

ASAP
PROJECT

Work in teams. Think of different questions that interviewers ask. Make a list of questions about education and training, experience, work habits, and reasons for leaving a job. Copy the list and answer the questions. Use the questions and answers to prepare for job interviews.

Unit 10

113

 WORKFORCE SKILLS (page 113)

Look for a job

Interview for a job

★　　★　　★　　★　　★

Language Note

Encourage learners to be positive at job interviews. When asked why they left a job, they shouldn't say, "I hated my boss." Rather, they should say, "I wanted more opportunities for growth." Talk about other positive words and phrases.

ASAP
PROJECT

Have learners read the instructions. Discuss the project and its purpose with learners. Make sure that everyone understands. Help learners assign themselves to teams based upon their skills, knowledge, interests, or other individual strengths. Have each team select a leader, and have the team leaders or the whole class select an overall project leader. Throughout the rest of the unit, allow time for learners to work on the project. Have the teams agree on a deadline when the project will be finished. For more information, see "ASAP Project" on page vi.

PREPARATION

1. Use the sample job application and resume to have learners talk about work experience. Have learners share their personal experiences.

2. Present key language in the dialog and in the Useful Language box: **van, florist, responsibility,** and **laid off.** Use a picture to preteach **van.** Explain that a **florist** sells flowers. See page 60 to review **responsibility.** Explain that being **laid off** means losing your job, usually because your employer eliminated the position.

PRESENTATION

1. Have learners read and discuss the Purpose Statement. For more information, see "Purpose Statement" on page viii.

 2. Focus attention on the picture. Encourage learners to say as much as they can about it. Have them imagine what the speakers are saying. Have them identify where they are. Then present the dialog. See "Presenting a Dialog" on page ix.

3. Have partners read the Partner Work instructions. Focus attention on the Useful Language box. Help learners read the expressions. If necessary, model pronunciation. Then have learners complete the activity. Have learners switch partners and repeat the activity. Have one or two pairs present their dialogs to the class.

FOLLOW-UP

Changing Jobs: Have teams of learners brainstorm reasons why people leave jobs. Then have the teams share their ideas.

◆ Have the class discuss their ideas. What are good reasons for leaving a job? Why? What may not be good reasons? Why not?

WORKBOOK

Unit 10, Exercises 3A–3B

WORKFORCE SKILLS (page 114)

Interview for a job

★   ★   ★   ★   ★

Keep Talking — Expressing confidence

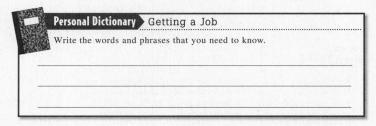

Tip
If you don't have specific job experience, talk about a related experience. If you don't have any related experience, say "I think I can learn that quickly" or "I'm a fast learner."

PRACTICE THE DIALOG

A Can you replace floor tiles?

B Yes, I have a lot of experience replacing floor tiles.

A Where did you learn?

B At Village Floor Company.

A Can you put down carpet?

B No, but I can learn quickly.

Useful Language

I went to City Technical School.

I got training on my last job.

My father taught me to put down carpet.

 PARTNER WORK

Take turns interviewing each other for different jobs. Use the dialog and the Useful Language above.

Personal Dictionary ▶ Getting a Job

Write the words and phrases that you need to know.

_____

_____

_____

114   Unit 10

 Personal Dictionary

Have learners add the words in their Personal Dictionary to their *Workforce Writing Dictionary*. For more information, see "Workforce Writing Dictionary" on page v.

PREPARATION

Preteach or review the language on the page. Ensure learners understand that **work experience** refers to jobs a person has held and the period of time the jobs were held. Use your classroom's floor or a picture to clarify **floor tiles.**

PRESENTATION

1. Have learners read the Purpose Statement. For more information, see "Purpose Statement" on page viii.

2. Focus attention on the photograph. Encourage learners to say as much as they can about it. Then present the dialog. For more information, see "Presenting a Dialog" on page ix.

3. Have partners read the instructions for Partner Work. Then focus attention on the Useful Language box. Help learners read the expressions. Then have pairs complete the activity. Have learners switch teams and repeat the activity. Ask several pairs to present their conversations to the class.

4. Have learners read the Personal Dictionary instructions. Then use the Personal Dictionary procedures on page ix. Remind learners to continue to add words to their dictionaries throughout the unit.

Tip Have learners read the Tip independently. Have learners discuss how the advice will help them. For more information, see "Presenting a Tip" on page ix.

FOLLOW-UP

Related Skills: Have learners work in pairs or teams. Have learners think of a skill, such as hanging wallpaper. Then, have learners think of related skills. For example, measuring and cutting are important skills for hanging wallpaper. Encourage learners to share their ideas with the class.

♦ Have pairs of learners create dialogs in which an interviewer asks about the candidate's main skills and related skills. Have pairs present their dialogs to the class.

WORKBOOK

Unit 10, Exercise 4

 **Understanding why you did or did not get a job**

LISTEN AND CIRCLE

Did they get the jobs? Circle *yes* or *no*.

1. (yes)　no　2. (yes)　no　3. yes　(no)
4. (yes)　no　5. yes　(no)

LISTEN AGAIN

Answer the questions. Circle the correct answer.

1. When can Ms. Binh start?
   (in two weeks)　immediately
2. What are Eduardo's questions about?
   hours and vacation time　(pay and benefits)
3. How did Sunja get the news about the job?
   (a letter)　a telephone call
4. Who did Marta talk to?
   (Diego's teacher)　Diego's boss
5. What position did Hermenia apply for?
   (secretary)　marketing director

 LISTEN ONCE MORE

Why did they get the job or not get the job? Circle the letter.

1. a.　She needs more computer skills.
   (b.) Her skills are right for this job.
2. (a.) He has experience managing people.
   b.　He can use a computer.
3. a.　The company hired a person from inside the company.
   (b.) The company decided not to hire for this position now.
4. a.　His math skills are strong.
   (b.) He got along well with others and was on time.
5. (a.) The company hired someone who had more experience.
   b.　The company hired a person who speaks English and Spanish.

Unit 10　　　　　115

SCANS Note

Tell learners that if they don't get a job they've applied for, they should ask interviewers why. Encourage them to express a desire to improve their skills. Tell them to ask for interviewers' advice and suggestions on how to become a better job applicant.

PREPARATION

1. Clarify the vocabulary on this page. Explain that **position** is another word for **job,** and to **hire** someone is to give a job to that person. Ensure learners understand that **managing** people means being their boss.

2. Talk about factors that influence hiring decisions. Ask learners questions about why they were hired for a job.

PRESENTATION

1. Have learners read and discuss the Purpose Statement. For more information, see "Purpose Statement" on page viii.

 2. Have learners read the Listen and Circle instructions. Make sure that everyone understands the instructions. If necessary, model the first item. Then play the tape or read the

Listening Transcript aloud two or more times as learners complete the activity. Have learners check their work. For more information, see "Presenting a Listening Activity" on page ix.

 3. Have learners read the Listen Again instructions. Make sure that everyone understands the instructions. Ask learners to read the questions and answer choices independently. Then play the tape or read the Listening Transcript aloud one or more times as learners complete the activity. Have learners check their work. For more information, see "Presenting a Listening Activity" on page ix.

4. Have learners read the Listen Once More instructions. Then follow the procedures in 3.

FOLLOW-UP

Mock Interview: Have learners work in teams of four. Assign each team a job. Have teams list three or four hiring criteria for this job. Have teams share their lists with the class.

◆ Have the teams write several specific questions that a job applicant might be asked to show that he or she meets a particular hiring criterion. Then have the teams create a list of appropriate responses and use the questions and answers to create job interview dialogs. Have several pairs present their team's dialogs to the class.

WORKBOOK

Unit 10, Exercises 5A–5B

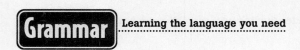

Learning the language you need

A. Study the Examples

Did	you	work in a factory?		Yes	I	did.
	they			No		didn't.

COMPLETE THE DIALOG

A _____Did_____ you _____work_____ (**work**) in a repair shop?

B Yes, I _____did_____ . I _____worked_____ (**work**) in a repair shop
for five years.

A Did you _____repair_____ (**repair**) cars?

B No, I _____didn't_____ . I _____repaired_____ (**repair**) trucks.

A _____Did_____ you _____study_____ (**study**) truck repair?

B Yes, I _____did_____ . I _____studied_____ (**study**) for one year
at City Technical School.

A _____Did_____ you _____show_____ (**show**) other workers how
to repair trucks?

B Yes, I _____did_____ . I _____helped_____ (**help**) them with their work.

PREPARATION

Review the language in the grammar boxes with learners before they open their books, if necessary.

PRESENTATION

1. Have learners read and discuss the Purpose Statement. For more information, see "Purpose Statement" on page viii.

2. Have learners read the grammar boxes in A. Have learners use the language in the boxes to say as many sentences as possible. Tell learners that they can use the grammar boxes throughout the unit to review or check sentence structures.

3. Have learners answer Complete the Dialog. If necessary, model the first item. Allow learners to complete the activity.

Have learners check each other's work in pairs. Ask several pairs of learners to read the dialog aloud while the rest of the class checks their work.

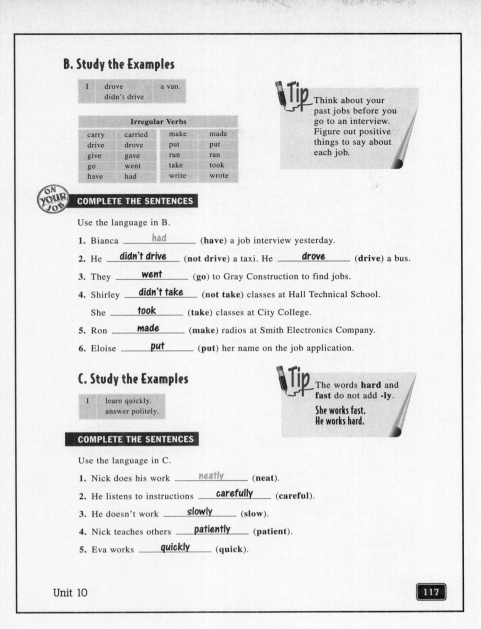

B. Study the Examples

I	drove	a van.
	didn't drive	

Irregular Verbs

carry	carried	make	made
drive	drove	put	put
give	gave	run	ran
go	went	take	took
have	had	write	wrote

Tip Think about your past jobs before you go to an interview. Figure out positive things to say about each job.

COMPLETE THE SENTENCES

Use the language in B.

1. Bianca _____had_____ (**have**) a job interview yesterday.

2. He ___didn't drive___ (**not drive**) a taxi. He ___drove___ (**drive**) a bus.

3. They ___went___ (**go**) to Gray Construction to find jobs.

4. Shirley ___didn't take___ (**not take**) classes at Hall Technical School.

   She ___took___ (**take**) classes at City College.

5. Ron ___made___ (**make**) radios at Smith Electronics Company.

6. Eloise ___put___ (**put**) her name on the job application.

C. Study the Examples

I	learn quickly.
	answer politely.

Tip The words **hard** and **fast** do not add **-ly**.

She works fast.
He works hard.

COMPLETE THE SENTENCES

Use the language in C.

1. Nick does his work ___neatly___ (**neat**).

2. He listens to instructions ___carefully___ (**careful**).

3. He doesn't work ___slowly___ (**slow**).

4. Nick teaches others ___patiently___ (**patient**).

5. Eva works ___quickly___ (**quick**).

Unit 10   **117**

---

4. Focus attention on the grammar boxes in B. Follow the procedures in 2.

 5. Have learners read the instructions for Complete the Sentences. If necessary, model the first item. Then have learners complete the activity independently. Have learners check each other's work in pairs. Have a different learner read each sentence aloud while the rest of the class checks their work.

6. Focus attention on the grammar box in C. Follow the procedures in 2.

7. Have learners read the instructions for Complete the Sentences. If necessary, model the first item. Allow learners to complete the activity. Have learners check each other's work in pairs. Ask volunteers to read their sentences aloud while the rest of the class checks their work.

Tip Have learners read the Tips independently. Provide any clarification needed. For more information, see "Presenting a Tip" on page ix.

FOLLOW-UP

What Job? Have learners work in groups of four. Have each learner think of a past job that he or she has held. Have the learner say things that he or she did or didn't do on the job. Have the other learners listen until they can figure out what the job was.

♦ Have learners list their daily duties in past jobs. Have them share their lists.

WORKBOOK

Unit 10, Exercises 6A–6D

BLACKLINE MASTERS

Blackline Master: Unit 10

★   ★   ★   ★   ★

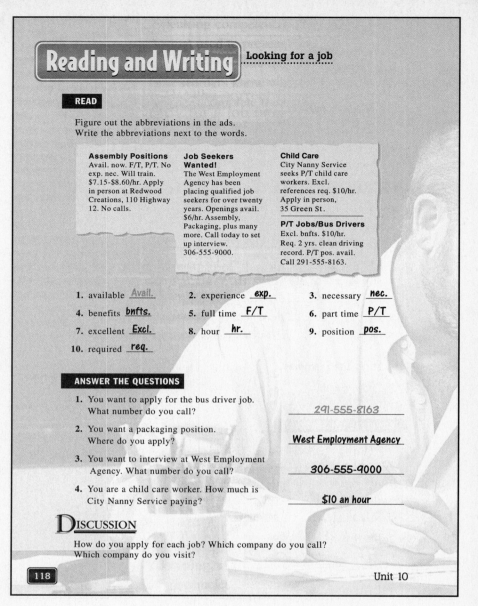

Reading and Writing — Looking for a job

READ

Figure out the abbreviations in the ads.
Write the abbreviations next to the words.

Assembly Positions
Avail. now. F/T, P/T. No exp. nec. Will train. $7.15-$8.60/hr. Apply in person at Redwood Creations, 110 Highway 12. No calls.

Job Seekers Wanted!
The West Employment Agency has been placing qualified job seekers for over twenty years. Openings avail. $6/hr. Assembly, Packaging, plus many more. Call today to set up interview. 306-555-9000.

Child Care
City Nanny Service seeks P/T child care workers. Excl. references req. $10/hr. Apply in person, 35 Green St.

P/T Jobs/Bus Drivers
Excl. bnfts. $10/hr. Req. 2 yrs. clean driving record. P/T pos. avail. Call 291-555-8163.

1. available _Avail._
2. experience _exp._
3. necessary _nec._
4. benefits _bnfts._
5. full time _F/T_
6. part time _P/T_
7. excellent _Excl._
8. hour _hr._
9. position _pos._
10. required _req._

ANSWER THE QUESTIONS

1. You want to apply for the bus driver job. What number do you call? _291-555-8163_

2. You want a packaging position. Where do you apply? _West Employment Agency_

3. You want to interview at West Employment Agency. What number do you call? _306-555-9000_

4. You are a child care worker. How much is City Nanny Service paying? _$10 an hour_

Discussion

How do you apply for each job? Which company do you call? Which company do you visit?

118   Unit 10

Teaching Note

Explain to learners that employers get a better impression of an applicant whose application is neat and legible. Encourage learners to fill out job applications in black or blue pen, not in pencil. Encourage them to print rather than use handwriting. You might encourage learners to carry a list of their job experience with them to help them complete applications quickly, neatly, and accurately.

PREPARATION

Preteach or review the language in items 1–10 of Read. Clarify **abbreviation** by giving the following example. Write **St.** on the board and say, *This is an abbreviation for **Street**.*

PRESENTATION

1. Have learners read and discuss the Purpose Statement. For more information, see "Purpose Statement" on page viii.

2. Have learners preview the help-wanted ads. Encourage learners to say everything they can about them. Write their ideas on the board or restate them in acceptable English.

3. Have learners read the instructions for Read. Make sure everyone knows what to do. Then have learners complete the activity independently. Have learners review each other's work in pairs. Ask several learners to share their answers with the class while the rest of the class checks their work.

4. Have learners read the statements and questions for Answer the Questions. Make sure everyone knows what to do. Then have learners complete the activity independently. Have learners review each other's work in pairs. Ask several learners to share their answers with the class while the rest of the class checks their work.

5. Have learners read the Discussion questions. Make sure everyone knows what to do. Tell teams to discuss their ideas. Have team reporters share their ideas with the class. Ask the teams to compare each other's ideas.

Choose a job you'd like. Complete the job application.

APPLICATION FOR EMPLOYMENT

• PERSONAL INFORMATION

Name ___**Answers will vary.**_____

Address _____

_____

Telephone _____ Social Security Number _____

Job Applied for _____

• WORK RECORD

Job Title _____ Company _____

Address _____

Telephone _____ How long were you at this job? _____

Job Title _____ Company _____

Address _____

Telephone _____ How long were you at this job? _____

• READ AND SIGN

The above information is true and correct.

Signature _____ Date _____

PARTNER WORK

Use your partner's application to interview your partner.

Unit 10

119

6. Have learners read the instructions for Write. Make sure everyone knows what to do. Model the activity if necessary by filling out the first line of the application. Then have learners complete the activity. Have several learners share their applications with the class.

7. Have learners read the Partner Work instructions. Make sure each pair knows what to do. If necessary, model the activity. Then have pairs complete the activity. Have several pairs share their interviews with the class.

FOLLOW-UP

Help Wanted: Distribute copies of job announcements in the classifieds of your local newspaper. Have teams make a list of all the abbreviations they find in the ads. Encourage them to figure out what the abbreviations mean. Have team reporters present their lists to the class.

♦ Have learners find ads for jobs for which they might be qualified. Have individuals share their ads with the class and tell why they are qualified for the jobs.

WORKBOOK

Unit 10, Exercises 7A–7B

★ ★ ★ ★ ★

Extension Interviewing successfully

READ THE ARTICLE

Get the Job You Want!

Usually, the first time an employer sees you is at an interview. What can you do to look and sound right for the job? Here are some tips.

- Look your best. Make sure your clothes are clean and neat.
- Arrive 5 or 10 minutes early so the employer knows you can be on time.
- Bring a pen or a pencil with you so you can complete the application.
- Answer the employer's questions clearly. Talk about your experience. If you have no experience, say that you want to learn.
- Ask a few polite questions about the job.
- Don't smoke, chew gum, or drink coffee during the interview.

Remember, if you don't get the job, you are getting practice for your next interview. If you know how to interview, you can get the job you want.

WRITE

Write *yes* or *no*.

1. Look clean and neat for an interview. _yes_
2. It's OK to be late for an interview. _no_
3. Drink coffee during an interview. _no_
4. Don't ask any questions about the job. _no_
5. Bring a pen or pencil with you. _yes_

 ***Culture*Notes**

How can you find out about job openings? Who can you talk to? Where can you look? Which ways are the most useful?

120   Unit 10

PREPARATION

1. Preteach or review the vocabulary on the page. Remind learners that an **interview** is a conversation between an employer and a job-seeker to see if the job-seeker can do the job and if he or she wants the job. A **successful** interview is one that goes well and results in a job offer. Getting **practice** means getting experience doing something so you can do it better in the future.

2. Discuss with learners their experiences with interviews. Share your own experiences. What have you done to make interviews successful for you?

PRESENTATION

1. Have learners read and discuss the Purpose Statement. For more information, see "Purpose Statement" on page viii.

2. Have learners look over the article before they read. Have them examine the title and look at the illustration. Encourage them to say as much as they can about the article. Then have learners read the article independently.

3. Have learners read the instructions for Write. Make sure everyone knows what to do. Then have learners complete the activity independently. Have learners review each other's work in pairs. Ask several learners to share their answers with the class while the rest of the class checks their work.

 4. Have learners read Culture Notes and talk over their responses in teams. Have team reporters share their ideas with the class. Ask the teams to compare each other's ideas.

FOLLOW-UP

Polish Your Interview: Divide learners into teams of three. The first learner interviews the second learner for a job. The third learner observes the interview and takes notes. Have the observer report why the interview was successful or not based on the advice in the article on the page. Have learners switch roles so that everyone gets a turn at each role. Have pairs revise their interviews based on the feedback and perform them for the class.

◆ Have two teams join together and make a list of good interview behaviors. Post the lists in the classroom.

WORKBOOK

Unit 10, Exercise 8

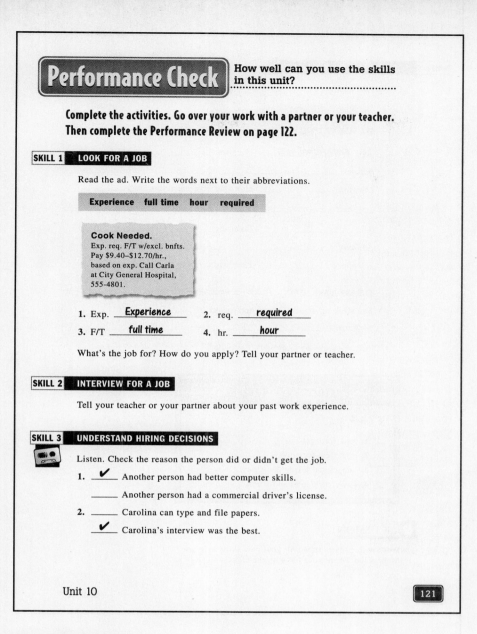

Performance Check

How well can you use the skills in this unit?

Complete the activities. Go over your work with a partner or your teacher. Then complete the Performance Review on page 122.

SKILL 1   LOOK FOR A JOB

Read the ad. Write the words next to their abbreviations.

| Experience   full time   hour   required |

Cook Needed.
Exp. req. F/T w/excl. bnfts.
Pay $9.40–$12.70/hr.,
based on exp. Call Carla
at City General Hospital,
555-4801.

1. Exp. ___Experience___   2. req. ___required___

3. F/T ___full time___   4. hr. ___hour___

What's the job for? How do you apply? Tell your partner or teacher.

SKILL 2   INTERVIEW FOR A JOB

Tell your teacher or your partner about your past work experience.

SKILL 3   UNDERSTAND HIRING DECISIONS

Listen. Check the reason the person did or didn't get the job.

1. __✔__ Another person had better computer skills.

   _____ Another person had a commercial driver's license.

2. _____ Carolina can type and file papers.

   __✔__ Carolina's interview was the best.

Unit 10   121

PRESENTATION

Use any of the procedures in "Evaluation," page x, with pages 121 and 122. Record individuals' results on the Unit 10 Individual Competency Chart. Record the class's results on the Class Cumulative Competency Chart.

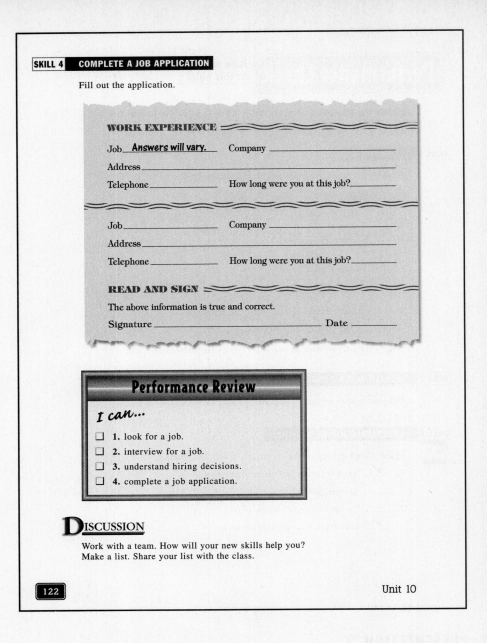

SKILL 4   COMPLETE A JOB APPLICATION

Fill out the application.

WORK EXPERIENCE

Job __Answers will vary.__   Company _____

Address _____

Telephone _____   How long were you at this job? _____

Job _____   Company _____

Address _____

Telephone _____   How long were you at this job? _____

READ AND SIGN

The above information is true and correct.

Signature _____   Date _____

Performance Review

I can...

☐ **1.** look for a job.
☐ **2.** interview for a job.
☐ **3.** understand hiring decisions.
☐ **4.** complete a job application.

DISCUSSION

Work with a team. How will your new skills help you?
Make a list. Share your list with the class.

122   Unit 10

PRESENTATION

Follow the instructions on page 121.

INFORMAL WORKPLACE-SPECIFIC ASSESSMENT

Have learners interview with you (or with another learner) for a new or better job. Make the interview as realistic as possible. For example, set up appointments with learners and ask them to come dressed as they would for a real interview.

WORKBOOK

Unit 10, Exercise 9

Listening Transcript

UNIT ◇ 1

Listening (page 7)

LISTEN AND CIRCLE

Circle the name of the caller.

1.

A: This is Janie in the supply room. I can't answer the phone, but if you leave a message, I'll call you back.

B: Janie, this is Shelly in Accounting. I need two staplers. Please call me at extension 3317 and let me know if I can have them today.

2.

A: Big Mountain Skis. How may I help you?

B: I'm trying to reach Yolanda Marcos.

A: Yolanda's in a meeting. May I take a message?

B: Yes, will you please tell her that Mark at Computer Express called. The office computer is fixed and ready to be picked up.

A: Oh, good. She'll be glad to hear that the computer's fixed and ready. What's your number, Mark?

B: 555-9000.

A: 555-9000. Thank you.

3.

A: Spaghetti City.

B: Hello, is Sandra Lee in?

A: Sandra doesn't work on Thursdays, but she will be in tomorrow. Can I take a message?

B: Yes, please. My name is Young Kim. I'm calling about the waiter job.

A: Is there a telephone number where she can reach you, Mr. Kim?

B: Yes, it's 555-0191.

A: OK, then. I'll have Sandra call you when she gets back.

4.

A: Bright Industries.

B: I'd like to speak to Alice Wilson.

A: One moment. I'll transfer you.

C: Accounting.

B: Is Alice there?

C: Alice is away from her desk right now. Can I take a message?

B Yes, please. This is Winston Smith from Baker Office Furniture. Please tell Alice we will pay our invoice by Friday.

C: OK, Mr. Smith. I'll tell her that you will pay the invoice for Baker Office Furniture by Friday. Is there a phone number where she can reach you if she has any questions?

B: Yes, the number is 555-3200.

LISTEN AGAIN

Write the caller's telephone number or extension. *(Play the tape or read the transcript of Listen and Circle aloud again.)*

LISTEN ONCE MORE

Circle the reason for each call. *(Play the tape or read the transcript of Listen and Circle aloud again.)*

Performance Check (page 13)

SKILL 1   TAKE TELEPHONE MESSAGES

Listen to the telephone calls. Who's calling? Circle the letter.

1.

A: Sinclair Manufacturing. This is Isabel.

B: Good morning, Isabel. This is John Drummond.

A: Good morning, Mr. Drummond. How can I help you today?

B: I'd like to speak with Martin Valdez. Is he in?

A: I'm sorry, he's in a meeting all morning. May I take a message?

B: Tell him I called . . . and ask him to call back.

A: I'll give him the message.

Listening Transcript

123

2.

A: Good morning, Atlas Auto Parts.

B: This is Cindy Grey. May I speak to Ms. Mars?

A: Ms. Mars isn't available right now. Would you like to leave a message?

B: Yes, please. I have a 4:00 meeting with Ms. Mars today, but I'm afraid I need to cancel it.

A: All right, Ms. Grey. I will cancel that meeting for you. Would you like to reschedule?

B: Thank you, I would.

LISTEN AGAIN

What's the message? Circle the letter. *(Play the tape or read the transcript for Skill 1 aloud again.)*

UNIT 2

Listening (page 19)

LISTEN AND MATCH

Match the item with its location.

1.

A: Welcome to the hotel, Lance.

B: Thanks.

A: You're going to need a uniform. Let's see . . . . What size shirt do you wear?

B: I usually wear a size medium shirt.

A: OK, let's go to the supply room and see if there are shirts your size in the closet. Otherwise we'll have to order them.

2.

A: I need Mrs. Anderson's file. She was here last in 1995.

B: After three years we put files in storage.

A: Can I still get to them?

B: Oh, yes. Old files are in boxes in the storage room. They're arranged by letter of the alphabet. They should be in a box marked A.

3.

A: What's the policy for people who forget or lose their room keys?

B: If they've got ID and sign this form with their name and room number, you can give them a spare key. We keep spare keys in a box in the security room. The keys are organized by room number, so they're easy to find. I'll show you the box when we go back to the security room.

4.

A: I'd like to touch up the paint around the new door in the maintenance barn. Where can I find the paint around here?

B: We keep paint in the storage room along with the cleaning supplies, extra furniture, and old computers. The paint is organized by date, so use the cans in the front first.

A: By date? What do you mean?

B: The cans of paint in the front of the storage room are older, and they're already open. We generally try to use them before we open new cans.

LISTEN AGAIN

Write the way the next item is organized. *(Play the tape or read the transcript of Listen and Match aloud again.)*

UNIT 3

Listening (page 31)

LISTEN AND WRITE

Write the name of the machine on the maintenance report.

1.

A: Have you had a chance to check the microwave oven in the nurses' lounge yet?

B: Yes, I did. I changed the electrical cord. It was really worn.

2.

A: The lawn mower could use new blades, Ernesto.

B: I know, but there isn't any money in the budget to do that this month.

A: Well, I wouldn't worry too much. I just sharpened the blades. They should be fine for now.

3.

A: Hi, Morris. I saw you working on the van. What was the matter?

B: Nothing, really. I changed the oil. Otherwise everything looked OK.

4.

A: This cash register needed a key. What did you do?

B: I made a new key. I used the master key in the front office.

LISTEN AGAIN

On the maintenance report, write what each person did. *(Play the tape or read the transcript of Listen and Write aloud again.)*

U N I T 4

Listening (page 43)

LISTEN AND MATCH

What needs to be done in each meeting room? Write the letter next to the room.

1.

A: All right everybody, listen up. We have a busy day tomorrow and a lot to go over. First up, the Lake Room. Skill Seminars has an all-day meeting scheduled there tomorrow and they want 300 chairs set up. Chris, Manuel, Sandy, if the three of you work in the Lake Room, you should have no problem getting 300 chairs in there by 9:00.

2.

A: Next, Meeting Room 1. The Downtown Real Estate Association is having its monthly meeting in Meeting Room 1. They'll need the usual meeting table and ten chairs. Laura, can you take care of that by 8:30?

B: That was Meeting Room 1? They need a table and . . .

A: Ten chairs. By 8:30.

B: Got it.

3.

A: National Video Company is in Meeting Room 2 tomorrow. They need two long tables, 20 chairs, and a VCR. That room needs to be ready at 8:30, also. John, I'd like you to be responsible for Meeting Room 2.

B: Sorry, Tim. What was in Meeting Room 2?

A: Two tables, 20 chairs, and a VCR ready by 8:30. All right?

B: Sure thing.

4.

A: Finally, the Citywide Boy Scouts dinner is planned for the Grand Ballroom tomorrow night. They want us to set up for 600 people, so we're looking at 50 of the large round tables and 600 chairs. That all needs to be ready by 5:00, so I want all of you to move to the Grand Ballroom and start setting up in there as soon you're done with the other rooms. If we all work together on this, we can have those 50 tables and 600 chairs up in no time at all.

LISTEN AGAIN

Write the deadline for each task. *(Play the tape or read the transcript of Listen and Match aloud again.)*

LISTEN AND WRITE

When are the customers' appointments? Write the names on the schedule.

1.

A: Good morning. Lewis's Beauty Shop. This is Monica. How can I help you?

B: Monica, this is Ellen North. I'm calling to confirm my appointment with Lewis at 10:00 on Saturday.

A: I've got it right here, Ellen. Saturday at 10:00.

B: Thanks.

2.

A: Lewis's Beauty Shop. Lewis speaking.
B: Hi, Lewis. It's Hong. I was wondering if I could come in on Saturday for a haircut. I'm going on vacation and I could really use a cut.
A: Hi, Hong. I've got an opening at 11:00 on Saturday. Does 11:00 work for you?
B: That's great, Lewis. Thanks.

3.

A: Hello?
B: Hello, Mrs. Matesa. This is Monica from Lewis's Beauty Shop returning your call about your appointment with Lewis for Saturday at 9:00.
A: Hi, Monica. Thanks for calling back. I was wondering if you could change my appointment to some time later in the day.
B: I'm sorry, Mrs. Matesa. Lewis is booked all day. 9:00 is the only time he has open.
A: Well, OK. I'll see you then.

4.

Donna, this is Monica calling from Lewis's Beauty Shop. I'm calling to remind you about your appointment with Lewis for Saturday at 12:00. If you can't make it, please call and let me know. Our phone number is 555-3264. Otherwise, we look forward to seeing you Saturday at 12:00.

U N I T 5

Listening (page 55)

LISTEN AND CIRCLE

Where are the speakers?

1.

A: What's the special today?
B: That'd be the cheeseburger deluxe. It comes with fries and coleslaw.
A: Can I replace the coleslaw with a salad?
B: I'm sorry, but there are no substitutions on the special.

2.

A: May I help you?
B: Yes, I was wondering if I could get a refund on these clothes. I bought them here last month.
A: Last month? That could be a problem.
B: Why? I've got the receipt.
A: You see, we don't give refunds after ten days. But let me talk to my manager. She decides these things.
B: Thank you. Tell your manager I'd appreciate it if she could help.

3.

A: Is there a Speedy Mail store near the Town Hall?
B: Yes, sir. There's a Speedy Mail right on this bus route. It's one stop before the Town Hall. This bus stops right in front of the store. I'll let you know when we get there.
A: That would really help me out.
Thank you.

4.

A: When will the tables be ready?
B: It should probably take us about a week to paint and assemble your tables. But don't worry. I know you need your furniture delivered on Saturday. We'll get it there in plenty of time. In fact, we'll make yours our first delivery on Saturday morning.
A: Thanks. I really need those tables no later than Saturday morning.

5.

A: Mr. Carlisle called to say he's coming back today to buy that stereo. He said he's looked at a lot of electronics stores and that we have the best prices in town.
B: Good, could you go down to storage and bring one up?
A: I already brought up the stereo he wants from storage. I put it behind the cash register.

LISTEN AGAIN

Match the request and the response. *(Play the tape or read the transcript of Listen and Circle aloud again.)*

Listening (page 67)

LISTEN AND CIRCLE

Listen and circle what the boss says during the performance review in column A.

1.

A: Dottie?

B: Yes, come in, Mary. You're here for your performance review, aren't you?

A: Yes, I am. Am I too early?

B: No, this is fine. It's always a pleasure to do your performance review. You're one of our best cashiers.

A: I like my job. I enjoy all the people.

B: It shows. You have such a good attitude. Your coworkers and managers all have nice things to say about you.

A: Well, it's easy to have a good attitude around here.

B: We've also noticed that you're very responsible. Your work area is always clean, and you're polite and helpful to your customers. And so, I'm pleased to tell you that you'll be getting a very nice raise this quarter. It will show up in your next paycheck.

2.

A: Lester, you're a careful worker, and that's important in your job. Your work is neat and well-organized.

B: Thank you, Lily. It's nice of you to say that.

A: There is one problem, however. You and I have talked about how important it is to get to work on time. But I notice that you're often late.

B: I know I'm late too much. Sometimes I'm late because I have to take my kids to school. But starting next week, my wife is going to take care of that.

A: That's good, Lester. I'm glad you're working on it. You really need to be here on time.

B: I will be.

A: In general, it's been a good year for you, Lester. But you have some things to learn and you need to work on your lateness, so I'm afraid there's no promotion this time around.

B: I understand why I'm not getting a promotion this year. But is there anything I should be doing so I can get one next year? Should I take classes or . . .

LISTEN AGAIN

What happens? Circle the answer in column B. *(Play the tape or read the transcript of Listen and Circle aloud again.)*

LISTEN AND CIRCLE

Circle all the reasons Sergio is Employee of the Year.

May I have your attention, please? As you know, every year at our annual picnic, I have the pleasure of announcing the Metro Bus Line Employee of the Year. This year's Employee of the Year award goes to the first assistant in our machine shop, Sergio Garcia.

Sergio's manager tells me that Sergio shows his commitment to his job in many ways. For example, he's never absent. Not absent once in five years. That's amazing. And his manager says that Sergio works hard and that he does good work. There's nothing more important than that in this or any other business.

To me, one of Sergio's best qualities is that he's a team player. He helps others whenever he can. His coworkers all know that if they have a problem, Sergio will help. And he'll help them in a friendly way, always with a smile on his face.

Many of you might not know this, but to be a good assistant, you have to think about the details. And Sergio thinks about the details a lot—he repairs and maintains our buses as if they were his own. And as president of Metro Bus Lines, that means a lot to me.

Sergio, would you please come up here and accept your award?

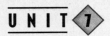

UNIT 7

Listening (page 79)

LISTEN AND CIRCLE

What are the people asking about? Circle the letter.

1.
A: Stephanie, do you have a minute to answer a question about my paycheck?
B: Sure, let me take a look at it.
A: My paycheck shows my regular pay as $437.65.
B: Yes, I see that.
A: But I worked overtime last week.
B: Oh, overtime pay is added in separately because the pay rate is different. Here it is . . . your overtime pay for the paycheck is $92.50.
A: Thanks.

2.
A: My pay rate is $6.50 an hour, but on this week's paycheck it's $7.00. Do you know why?
B: I have a pretty good idea. Were you late any day this week?
A: No, I wasn't late at all.
B: Well then, that's why your pay rate is $7.00. It's company policy. If you're on time every day, your pay rate goes up $.50 an hour for the week.
A: I didn't know that. From now on I'll always be on time.

3.
A: Human Resources. This is Vivian.
B: Hi, Vivian. This is Bîta Rami. I have a question about my paycheck.
A: Yes, Bita. How can I help you?
B: It looks as if the health insurance deduction wasn't taken out of my paycheck.
A: Was the deduction taken out of your last paycheck?
B: Yes, it was.
A: OK, tell you what. Bring your paycheck down to HR and I'll find out what happened to your health insurance deduction.
B: That'd be great. Thanks.

4.
A: Don, do you have a minute?
B: Sure, what's up?
A: Well, I think there's a mistake on my paycheck. Usually my federal tax is $48.50, but this week it's $78.00. Any idea why my federal tax would have gone up?
B: I can't imagine why that would have happened. I'll have to check with Human Resources on that one. I'll get right back to you.
A: Thanks, Don.

5.
A: Human Resources. This is Patty.
B: Hi, Patty. It's Christine.
A: Hi, Christine. What's up?
B: Well, I was out on Friday, so I didn't get my paycheck. Is it in your office?
A: Right. Your paycheck's here in Human Resources. When can you pick it up?
B: I can pick it up during my break.
A: See you then.

LISTEN AGAIN

Complete the explanation. Write the letter.
(Play the tape or read the transcript of Listen and Circle aloud again.)

UNIT 8

Listening (page 91)

LISTEN AND NUMBER

What are the people talking about? Write the number of the conversation.

1.
A: Jake, that fan shouldn't be up there. Put the fan on the table.
B: It's not in anybody's way.
A: Last year a cook had her radio up there. It fell and splashed hot grease on her. She got burned.
B: Wow, I didn't think of that.

2. Set the brake on the wheelchair when you're not using it. It could roll away. Someone could get hurt.

Listening Transcript

3.

A: Mack, here's a pair of work gloves for you. Always wear them when you handle garbage.

B: How come?

A: Sometimes there are sharp things in the trash.

B: Will gloves really help?

A: These gloves will. They're pretty thick, and they have a special lining.

B: Thanks, I'll wear them.

4.

A: You should put the mayonnaise in the refrigerator after you use it.

B: But I'm going to use it again later.

A: Even so, it should go back in the refrigerator. If mayonnaise gets warm and spoils, it can make people sick.

B: Really? I didn't know that. I'll put it in the refrigerator.

5.

A: I finally figured out what's wrong with this computer. I just need to open it and fix one thing.

B: You really should turn the computer off before you open it.

A: I'm just going to do one thing.

B: It doesn't matter. When you work on the inside of a computer, you should turn it off first. You could easily get an electric shock.

LISTEN AGAIN

What should the people do? Circle the letter. *(Play the tape or read the transcript of Listen and Number aloud again.)*

LISTEN AND CIRCLE

What should the employees do? Circle the letters.

Commercial Meat Cutting Company places great importance on employee safety. In fact, we have had over 1,000 operating days without a serious accident or injury. In order to keep up this record and stay safe, we follow these simple precautions.

First, we require everyone to wear gloves, safety glasses, and a hairnet. There are no exceptions. Managers and crew, employees, and visitors—everyone must wear gloves, safety glasses, and a hairnet. In addition, employees are expected to wash their hands regularly. They wash their hands before they begin work, before and after all breaks, and when they leave the plant at the end of their shift.

Performance Check (page 97)

SKILL 1   UNDERSTAND SAFETY INSTRUCTIONS

Circle the safety steps you hear.

1.

A: There's a lot of water on the floor by the door.

B: Yes, it's because of all that rain.

A: We'd better call maintenance. They can clean up the water and put up a sign.

B: Good idea. I'll ask for them to clean up the water and put up a sign as soon as possible.

2.

A: The new saw is really powerful.

B: Yes, you should wear safety goggles.

A: I've got goggles, but I think I need some gloves, too.

B: You're right. Make sure the gloves have a good grip.

U N I T ◆9◆

Listening (page 103)

LISTEN AND CIRCLE

Circle the first speaker's topic.

1.

A: As you all know, two suitcases were stolen from outside the hotel last Thursday . . . .

B: It's not our fault. We're really busy when the tour buses get to the hotel.

A: Please let me finish. We'll have time for discussion later. But you're right. When a tour bus parks in front of the hotel, there are many suitcases and many people on the sidewalk. However, it is still our job to be sure the suitcases are not stolen.

2.
A: Someone is taking suitcases from in front of other hotels, too.
B: Excuse me, James. May I add something here?
A: Yes, of course. You all know Morris Wright, manager of the bell staff.
B: Thank you. The other hotels do the same thing we do. The bus drivers take the suitcases from the bus and put them on the sidewalk. The suitcases are stolen from the sidewalk.

3.
A: We think that the person who is taking the suitcases works alone. He or she takes only one or two suitcases at a time.
B: Excuse me. Are you saying that a person just walks by, picks up a suitcase from the sidewalk, and walks away?
A: Yes, that's what we think happens.

4.
A: Here's an idea. Let's not leave the suitcases on the sidewalk. The bell staff could take the suitcases off the bus and carry them directly into the hotel.
B: What about the bus drivers? Couldn't they carry the suitcases into the hotel?
A: No, I don't think that would work. That's really not their job.

5.
A: We need to look at what the other hotels are doing. The Campbell Hotel hired security guards. The security guards stand on the sidewalk. They watch the buses, the people, and the suitcases.
B: James?
A: Yes, Natalie.
B: I heard that the Owens Inn uses security cameras to watch the tour buses. Are you thinking about installing cameras also?

LISTEN AGAIN

Circle the second speaker's topic. *(Play the tape or read the transcript of Listen and Circle aloud again.)*

LISTEN ONCE MORE

Listen to the second speaker. Is the speaker polite or impolite? *(Play the tape or read the transcript of Listen and Circle aloud again.)*

U N I T 10

Listening (page 115)

LISTEN AND CIRCLE

Did they get the jobs? Circle *yes* or *no*.

1.
A: Hello, Ms. Binh. This is Joyce from West Trucking.
B: Hi, Joyce. It's nice to hear from you.
A: We were very pleased with your application and would like to make you a job offer. The training you got at the Career and Technical Institute is excellent. Your skills are just right for the job.
B: I got the job? That's wonderful. Thank you.
A: You're welcome. We're very pleased, too. So tell me, when can you start?
B: How's two weeks from now?
A: Two weeks will be fine.

2.
A: Congratulations, Eduardo. With all your experience managing people, I think this will be a good job for you.
B: I think my experience managing people will be a help, too. That's one of the reasons I'm so pleased I got the job.
A: And you're ready to move to an office job?
B: Well, of course I'll miss being on the floor, but I think I can make a difference.

A: We do, too. Now let me take you down to Human Resources. They need you to sign some papers before you can get started.

B: Good. I'd also like to talk to someone there about benefits and pay. I have some questions.

A: I'm sure someone there can help you.

3.

A: Sunja, are you OK? You look a little sad.

B: I am a little. I just got this letter from Blue Star Industries.

A: Is it about the welder's job?

B: Yes, it is, and I didn't get the job.

A: Does the letter say why?

B: Let me read it to you. It says, "Thank you for coming to Blue Star to interview for the position of apprentice welder. However, we are not hiring for that position at this time."

A: So no one got the job?

B: I guess not.

4.

A: Hello, Diego. This is Marta Corona from Big Sam's Grocery. I'm calling to talk to you about the job as stock boy.

B: Yes?

A: Well, I talked to your teacher. She says you're a good student and a hard worker.

B: Thank you, Ms. Corona.

A: She also said that you got along well with your classmates and that you were always on time for class. So I think you'll fit in just fine at Big Sam's and I'd like to offer you the job. Congratulations.

B: I got the job! That's great.

5.

A: Marketing. This is Avis. How may I help you?

B: Avis, this is Hermenia Salvador. I interviewed for the secretary's job last week. I was wondering if I got the job.

A: I'm sorry, Hermenia. I was going to call you this afternoon. I'm afraid you didn't get the job. We hired someone who had more experience than you have.

B: I'm sorry, too. I really like your company a lot.

A: Look, after you finish your secretarial classes and have a little more experience, give me a call. Maybe we can work something out then.

B: Thank you. I'll do that.

LISTEN AGAIN

Answer the questions. Circle the correct answer. *(Play the tape or read the transcript of Listen and Circle aloud again.)*

LISTEN ONCE MORE

Why did they get the job or not get the job? Circle the letter. *(Play the tape or read the transcript of Listen and Circle aloud again.)*

Performance Check (page 121)

SKILL 3   **UNDERSTAND HIRING DECISIONS**

Listen. Check the reason the person did or didn't get the job.

1.

A: I'm sorry, Ted, but you didn't get the job. We hired someone who has better computer skills than you do. You have a lot of good experience, but you need to improve your skills on the computer.

B: I know I need to have better computer skills. That's why I've started taking classes at Norton Technical College.

A: That sounds like a good idea.

2.

A: Carolina, I've got some good news for you.

B: About the job?

A: Yes, that's right. You got the job. Congratulations.

B: Thank you.

A: I want you to know that we spoke with many people about the manager's job and that your interview was the best one. You spoke carefully and intelligently about your experience selling shoes and working with people. I think this is a great opportunity for you.

Vocabulary

 **UNIT 1**

extension
message
Rolodex
telephone number
telephone roster

 **UNIT 2**

bulletin board
cart
file cabinet
file folder
glue
hammer
hand truck
ladder
paper clip
pen
rubber bands
scissors
stapler

top shelf
middle shelf
bottom shelf

box of
roll of

 **UNIT 3**

cash register
lawn mower
microwave oven
vacuum cleaner
van

cash register tape
gas
oil
sponge
tire

change
make
sharpen

break
leak
spill

maintenance department
maintenance request

out of order

 UNIT 4

first shift
second shift

appointment
calendar
holiday schedule
schedule

first
second
then

 **UNIT 5**

refund
return
store credit

request
suggestion

of course
no problem
sure

 **UNIT 6**

compromise
get along
goal
mission statement
rule

 **UNIT 7**

earnings
federal tax
gross pay
health insurance

life insurance
net pay
state tax

Social Security

paycheck
payday
pay rate

 **UNIT 8**

back support belt
boots
dust mask
ear protection
gloves
hairnet
hard hat
safety glasses

 **UNIT 9**

agenda
meeting

date
time
place
topic

UNIT 10

education
employment record
interview
personal information
training

part time
full time

available
benefits
excellent
experience
hour
necessary
position
required

Vocabulary

Irregular Verbs

am, are, is	was, were	have	had
begin	began	keep	kept
break	broke	make	made
bring	brought	pay	paid
build	built	put	put
buy	bought	read	read
come	came	ride	rode
cut	cut	see	saw
do	did	sell	sold
drive	drove	send	sent
eat	ate	speak	spoke
feed	fed	spend	spent
feel	felt	sweep	swept
find	found	take	took
forget	forgot	tell	told
get	got	think	thought
give	gave	wear	wore
go	went	write	wrote

Name _____

A. Complete the sentences. Follow the example. Use contractions for **be.**

1. Marina ___*manages*___ (manage) the mail room. She _'s_____ (be)
   the supervisor.

2. Rico _____ (talk) with his workers every day.

   He _____ (be) a good manager.

3. Karen and Eva _____ (answer) the phones, and they _____

   (greet) people. They _____ (be) receptionists.

4. I _____ (be) a tailor. I _____ (sew) clothes.

5. We _____ (help) customers. We _____ (be) sales clerks.

6. My department _____ (have) a new photocopier.

   It _____ (be) fast.

7. Marilyn _____ (drive) children to school.

   She _____ (be) a school bus driver.

B. Complete the sentences. Follow the example.

1. **A** Do you know Elena?

   B Yes, I know ___*her*___ (her/it).

2. **A** Are you working with Park and Lou this week?

   B Yes, I'm helping _____ (them/him).

3. **A** Do you have Petra's phone number?

   B Yes, I have _____ (it/them).

4. **A** Is that package for you?

   B Yes, it's for _____ (me/her).

5. **A** Do you know Mr. Robinson?

   B No, I don't know _____ (him/me).

6. **A** Is that message for me?

   B Yes, it's for _____ (me/you).

Blackline Masters

Name_____

A. Look at the picture. Complete the questions and answers. Follow the example.

1. **A** I need a place for my lunch. _____**Is there**_____ a refrigerator in the

   break room?

   B Yes, _____**there is**_____. All employees can use it.

2. **A** And _____ vending machines?

   B Yes, _____. The machines have soda and snacks.

3. **A** _____ coffee in the break room?

   B Yes, _____. The company pays for it.

4. **A** _____ a phone in the break room?

   B No, _____. You can make personal calls on the phone in the hall.

B. Look at the picture again. Complete the sentences.
Use **against, behind, inside, on top of, over,** and **under.**

1. The coffee machine is _____**on top of**_____ the counter.

2. The dishes are _____ the cabinet.

3. The shelf is _____ the sink.

4. The glasses are _____ the cups.

5. The vending machines are _____ the wall.

6. The sink is _____ the shelf.

Name _____

A. Complete the sentences. Follow the examples.

1. The cleaners _____**emptied**_____ (**empty**) your wastebasket, but they
_____**didn't empty**_____ (**not empty**) my wastebasket.

2. The cleaners _____ (**clean**) the sink, but they
_____ (**not clean**) the coffee maker.

3. The custodian _____ (**fix**) the window, but he
_____ (**not fix**) the door.

4. The factory workers _____ (**work**) overtime last week, but
the office workers _____ (**not work**) overtime.

5. I _____ (**apply**) for the job as a waiter, but I
_____ (**not apply**) for the job as a cook.

6. Sunja _____ (**change**) jobs, but she _____
(**not change**) companies.

7. We _____ (**ask**) Human Resources our questions about
insurance. We _____ (**not ask**) our manager.

B. Complete the questions and answers. Follow the example.

1. A _____**Did**_____ the mail clerks _____**deliver**_____ (**deliver**)
the mail already?
B Yes, _____**they did**_____ .

2. A _____ you _____ (**call**) maintenance about
the broken desk?
B No, _____ . Ellen called maintenance about it.

3. A _____ Margie _____ (**clock**) in late today?
B No, _____ . She was on time.

4. A _____ the repairer _____ (**fix**) the photocopier?
B Yes, _____ . He repaired it this morning.

C. Complete the sentences. Follow the example.

1. Ricardo ____*didn't send*____ (**not send**) the package overnight.

   He _____*sent*_____ (**send**) it by regular mail.

2. Lisbeth _____ (**not bring**) sandwiches for lunch.

   She _____ (**bring**) a salad.

3. I _____ (**not buy**) soda from the vending machine.

   I _____ (**buy**) some juice.

4. We _____ (**not have**) our morning break, but we _____

   (**have**) our afternoon break.

5. I _____ (**not go**) to a restaurant for lunch.

   I _____ (**go**) to the cafeteria.

D. Read the list of Sylvia's tasks. She completed the tasks that have checks (✔).
Finish the report about Sylvia's work. Use **didn't** when Sylvia didn't do a task.

✔ type the report	✔ take the report to the copy room
buy supplies	✔ call the maintenance department about the broken chair
send faxes	✔ clean the empty office

Dear Mr. Johnson:

   Yesterday was a busy day. I _____*typed*_____ (**type**) your report. Then I

_____ (**take**) it to the copy room. The copies will be ready tomorrow.

I _____ (**send**) the faxes. The fax machine is broken. I sent the

information to the people by overnight mail.

   I _____ (**call**) the maintenance department. Someone is going to fix

the chair on Friday. I _____ (**clean**) the empty office. It is ready for the

new employee. I _____ (**buy**) the supplies. I _____ (**not have**)

the time. I'll order them tomorrow.

Sylvia

Name _____

A. Complete the sentences. Use **has to, have to, doesn't have to,** or **don't have to.**

1. Maria wants a job as a bus driver. She _____ *has to get* _____ (get) a special driver's license.

2. Construction workers _____ (wear) hard hats. The hats are required for safety.

3. We _____ (not work) on Monday. It's a holiday.

4. Chang _____ (be) at work early today. There's a meeting at 8:00.

B. Complete the questions. Follow the example.

1. A _____ *Do* _____ the workers _____ *have to punch* _____ (punch) timecards?
   B Yes, they do.

2. A _____ you _____ (wear) a uniform for your job?
   B Yes, I do.

3. A _____ Martha _____ (use) a computer on the job?
   B Yes, she does.

4. A _____ James _____ (complete) a daily time report?
   B No, he doesn't.

C. What do you have to do at work? Use the words in the box.
Use **have to** or **don't have to.**

use computers for my job	work on Saturdays
wear a uniform for my job	punch in on a time clock

1. I _____ .

2. I _____ .

3. I _____ .

4. I _____ .

Blackline Masters

D. Complete the sentences. Follow the example.

1. Tomorrow we __'re going to move__ (move) to a new site.

2. Ali _____ (take) inventory next week.

3. I _____ (read) the new employee manual during my break.

4. The fire drill _____ (be) this afternoon.

5. She _____ (clean) the tables. Then she _____ (mop) the floor.

6. They _____ (cut) the grass today.

7. The telephone repair person _____ (install) new phones this afternoon.

8. We _____ (work) the second shift next week.

9. The package _____ (arrive) before noon.

10. The chef _____ (make) a special dish today.

E. Complete the dialog. Follow the example.

1. **A** What ___are___ we ___going to do___ (do) tomorrow?

   B We __'re going to deliver__ (deliver) some furniture.

2. **A** Where _____ we _____ (make) the delivery?

   B We _____ (deliver) the furniture to a hotel in the suburbs.

3. **A** How long _____ the trip _____ (take)?

   B I think the trip _____ (take) about one hour.

4. **A** So, when _____ we _____ (load) the truck?

   B We _____ (load) it at 8:00. We'll be ready to leave here by 9:00.

5. **A** And when _____ we _____ (be) back here at the warehouse?

   B I'll think we _____ (be) back before 1:00.

A. Write about Vassily's day yesterday. Use the correct forms of the verbs in the box.

1.

~~go~~	take	wear

He _____**went**_____ to work at 8:00.

He _____ his coveralls.

He _____ his lunch with him.

2.

find	replace	work

He _____ on a car in the morning.

He _____ the problem with the car.

He _____ the spark plugs.

3.

buy	go	pay

At noon, he _____ to a supermarket.

He _____ a soda to drink with his lunch.

He _____ $1.00 for the soda.

4.

get	talk	tell

In the afternoon, he _____ to his boss.

He _____ his boss about his day.

He _____ his paycheck.

Blackline Masters

B. Complete the questions in the dialog. Write **where, when,** or **how.**

1. **A** _____**Where**_____ did you work before your current job?

    B I worked in a cafeteria. I made sandwiches and salads.

2. **A** _____ did you start your current job?

    B I got it two years ago. I'm a cook.

3. **A** _____ did you find out about this job?

    B An employee of the company told me about the opening in the cafeteria.

4. **A** _____ did you learn how to cook?

    B I learned in my country. I worked in a restaurant.

5. **A** _____ can you start work?

    B I can start any time.

C. Complete the sentences. Follow the example.

1. The boss _____**didn't tell**_____ (**not tell**) the employees about the fire drill.

    The secretary _____**told**_____ (**tell**) us about it.

2. I _____ (**not pay**) with cash. I _____ (**pay**) with a credit card.

3. We _____ (**not see**) the pictures of the picnic. But we _____

    (**see**) pictures of the new employees on the bulletin board.

4. Edward _____ (**not find**) the tool in the toolbox. He

    _____ (**find**) it on a shelf.

5. Hans _____ (**not get**) a job as a carpenter. But he _____

    (**get**) a job as a carpenter's assistant.

6. Jane _____ (**not buy**) her uniforms downtown. She

    _____ (**buy**) them in a store near here.

7. Kay and Rosa _____ (**not make**) radios in the factory. They

    _____ (**make**) cellular phones.

8. The mechanics _____ (**not wear**) jeans. They _____

    (**wear**) coveralls.

Name _____

A. Complete the sentences. Follow the example.

1. My new computer is _____**faster than**_____ (fast) my old one.

2. The employee cafeteria is _____ (cheap) most restaurants.

3. The copier in the mail room is _____ (big) the copier down the hall.

4. I like working at Norco. The people are _____ (friendly) the people at Alexander's.

5. The electric stapler is _____ (large) the manual one.

   It's also _____ (light) the manual one.

   But it's _____ (noisy) the manual one.

6. Moya has to take care of her mother in the evening, so the first shift is _____ (good) the second shift for her.

B. Complete the sentences. Follow the example.

1. Hai is _____**more reliable than**_____ (reliable) Kim.

   I think Hai will get the job.

2. Driving to work is _____ (expensive) taking the bus.

3. Betty wants to work in the sales department. She thinks it's _____ (interesting) the customer service department.

4. The lounge chairs are _____ (comfortable) the office chairs.

5. The blue coveralls are _____ (practical) the brown ones. They'll last longer.

6. The phone instructions are _____ (difficult) the copy machine instructions.

Blackline Masters

A. Complete the questions. Use the words in the box. Follow the example.

deliver	repeat	help ~~get~~
answer	fix	give

1. I can't reach the top shelf. _____**Could you get**_____ that box for me?

2. We didn't understand what you said. _____ that, please?

3. The lawn mower isn't working. _____ it for me?

4. I can't find the mail room. _____ me directions to it?

5. _____ a question about my paycheck?
   I don't understand something in it.

6. Kim is new in the kitchen. _____ him use the dishwasher?

7. _____ the tables to the south side?
   I have to make deliveries on the north side.

B. Complete the sentences. Use **because** or **so**. Follow the example.

1. Construction workers wear hard hats _____**because**_____ their jobs are dangerous.

2. Tony is studying English _____ he wants to be a manager.

3. Hoan needed some pencils, _____ he went to the supply room.

4. The copier isn't working _____ it's out of paper.

5. The restaurant is going to be very busy tonight, _____ we need to make extra soup and salads.

6. We washed the dishes by hand _____ the dishwasher broke down.

7. It rained today, _____ the children at the daycare center stayed inside.

8. Elaine and Marge need new jobs, _____ they're reading the help-wanted ads.

Name _____

A. Complete the sentences. Use **should** or **shouldn't.**

1. You _____should dress_____ (dress) neatly for a job interview.

2. You _____ (chew) gum at a job interview.

3. You _____ (learn) your coworkers' names quickly.

4. In case of fire, you _____ (use) the elevator. Use the stairs.

5. You _____ (speak) politely to customers.

6. You _____ (read) the newspaper during a meeting.

7. You _____ (stay) up too late, or you'll be tired at work the next day.

8. You _____ (follow) all the safety rules. It's best for you.

9. You _____ (report) unsafe situations.

10. You _____ (make) a lot of personal calls at work.

B. Complete the sentences. Use the words in the box. Use **should.** Follow the example.

arrive early	be careful around machines	be polite to customers
bring the receipt	complete an accident report	obey traffic rules
report it	~~take classes at night~~	wash your hands often

1. If you want a better job, __you should take classes at night__.

2. If you have a job interview, _____.

3. If you work in a factory, _____.

4. If you work as a driver, _____.

5. If you work as a sales clerk, _____.

6. If you work with food, _____.

7. If you find a mistake in your paycheck, _____.

8. If you return merchandise, _____.

9. If you cut yourself at work, _____.

_____.

Name _____

A. Write sentences. Use **have to** or **has to.** Use the words in the box. Follow the example.

fix it	move a lot of boxes	park in the back lot
read the instructions again	~~wash the walls first~~	wear a hard hat

1. The workers are going to paint the walls.

   They _____ *have to wash the walls first* _____ .

2. I can't remember how to use this mixer.

   I _____ .

3. Phil is getting a large cart from the warehouse.

   He _____ .

4. Sara works on a construction site.

   She _____ .

5. The workers are going to paint stripes on the front parking lot today.

   Employees _____ .

6. The copier is broken.

   Mr. Gomez _____ .

B. Complete the sentences. Use **'d like to.** Follow the example.

1. We _*'d like to take*_____ **(take)** a vacation day tomorrow. The weather is going to be nice.

2. Roger and Carl are taking night classes. They _____ **(get)** jobs as mechanics.

3. Marta doesn't like to work during the day. She _____ **(work)** the second shift.

4. There's an opening for a press operator. I _____ **(apply)** for the job.

5. Toshi wants a full time job. He _____ **(have)** health insurance.

6. Mario and Rick work as busboys. They _____ **(be)** waiters.

Name _____

RESUME
Gerardo Monte

Work History

Job	Years	Company
Taxi Driver	1994–1997	City Cab Company
Electrician's Apprentice/Assistant	1997–1998	Pauley & Son, Electricians

Education

School	Years
Lincoln High School	Completed high school in 1994
Citywide Technical School	1995–1997, Electrical repair classes
	Received a certificate in electrical repairs

A. Read Gerardo's resume. Complete the sentences about Gerardo. Follow the example.

1. Gerardo ___didn't drive___ (drive) a bus. He ___drove___ (drive) a taxi.

2. Gerardo _____ (finish) high school.

3. Gerardo _____ (go) to Citywide Technical School.

4. Gerardo _____ (study) computer programming.

5. Gerardo _____ (take) classes in electrical repair.

6. Gerardo _____ (work) for a plumbing company.

B. Complete the dialog. Use the information for Gerardo.

1. A ___Did___ you ___work___ (work) as an

   electrician before?

   B No, I _____. I _____ (work) as an electrician's

   apprentice. I _____ (help) the electricians.

2. A _____ you _____ (study) electrical repair

   at school?

   B Yes, I _____. I _____ (go) to Citywide Technical

   School. I _____ (study) electrical repair for two years.

3. A _____ you _____ (do) any other kinds of jobs?

   B Yes, I _____. I _____ (drive) a taxi for two years.

   I _____ (learn) how to work with customers on that job.

C. Complete the sentences. Follow the example.

1. Martina _____**didn't have**_____ (**not have**) a job interview yesterday.

   She _____**had**_____ (**have**) one last week.

2. Jan _____ (**not run**) the meat-cutting machine.

   He _____ (**run**) the meat-wrapping machine in his last job.

3. Ona and Paula _____ (**not make**) men's clothes.

   They _____ (**make**) children's clothes at that factory.

4. Mike _____ (**not take**) TV repair classes.

   He _____ (**take**) computer programming classes.

5. Ellen _____ (**not put**) the letter in the "Out" box.

   She _____ (**put**) it in the "In" box.

6. The boss _____ (**not give**) Ted the award.

   He _____ (**give**) the Employee of the Month Award to me!

7. I _____ (**not write**) down the name of the company.

   But I _____ (**write**) down the company's phone number.

8. Sasha _____ (**not take**) her car to work yesterday.

   She _____ (**take**) the subway.

9. The warehouse workers _____ (**not carry**) the packages.

   I _____ (**carry**) the packages to the warehouse by myself.

10. The new employees _____ (**not go**) to their departments. They

    _____ (**go**) to an orientation meeting in Human Resources first.

D. Complete the sentences. Follow the example.

1. All workers should follow instructions _____**carefully**_____ (**careful**).

2. Sales clerks have to treat customers _____ (**patient**).

3. Receptionists have to write messages _____ (**neat**).

4. Customer service workers have to talk to customers _____ (**polite**).

5. Firefighters have to move _____ (**quick**).

UNIT 1

A.
1. manages, 's
2. talks, 's
3. answer, greet, 're
4. 'm, sew
5. help, 're
6. has, 's
7. drives, 's

B.
1. her
2. them
3. it
4. me
5. him
6. you

UNIT 2

A.
1. **A** Is there, **B** there is
2. **A** are there, **B** there are
3. **A** Is there, **B** there is
4. **A** Is there, **B** there isn't

B.
1. on top of
2. inside
3. over
4. behind
5. against
6. under

UNIT 3

A.
1. emptied, didn't empty
2. cleaned, didn't clean
3. fixed, didn't fix
4. worked, didn't work
5. applied, didn't apply
6. changed, didn't change
7. asked, didn't ask

B.
1. **A** Did, deliver, **B** they did
2. **A** Did, call, **B** I didn't
3. **A** Did, clock, **B** she didn't
4. **A** Did, fix, **B** he did

C.
1. didn't send, sent
2. didn't bring, brought
3. didn't buy, bought
4. didn't have, had
5. didn't go, went

D. typed, took
   didn't send

called
cleaned
didn't buy, didn't have

UNIT 4

A.
1. has to get
2. have to wear
3. don't have to work
4. has to be

B.
1. Do, have to punch
2. Do, have to wear
3. Does, have to use
4. Does, have to complete

C. Answers will vary.

D.
1. 're going to move
2. 's going to take
3. 'm going to read
4. 's going to be
5. 's going to clean, 's going to mop
6. 're going to cut
7. 's going to install
8. 're going to work
9. 's going to arrive
10. 's going to make

E.
1. **A** are, going to do, **B** 're going to deliver
2. **A** are, going to make, **B** 're going to deliver
3. **A** is, going to take, **B** 's going to take
4. **A** are, going to load, **B** 're going to load
5. **A** are, going to be, **B** 're going to be

UNIT 5

A.
1. went, wore, took
2. worked, found, replaced
3. went, bought, paid
4. talked, told, got

B.
1. Where
2. When
3. How (or Where)
4. Where (or How)
5. When

C.
1. didn't tell, told
2. didn't pay, paid
3. didn't see, saw
4. didn't find, found

5. didn't get, got
6. didn't buy, bought
7. didn't make, made
8. didn't wear, wore

U N I T 6

A. 1. faster than
   2. cheaper than
   3. bigger than
   4. friendlier than
   5. larger than, lighter than, noisier than
   6. better than
B. 1. more reliable than
   2. more expensive than
   3. more interesting than
   4. more comfortable than
   5. more practical than
   6. more difficult than

U N I T 7

A. 1. Could you get
   2. Could you repeat
   3. Could you fix
   4. Could you give
   5. Could you answer
   6. Could you help
   7. Could you deliver
B. 1. because
   2. because
   3. so
   4. because
   5. so
   6. because
   7. so
   8. so

U N I T 8

A. 1. should dress
   2. shouldn't chew
   3. should learn
   4. shouldn't use
   5. should speak
   6. shouldn't read
   7. shouldn't stay
   8. should follow
   9. should report
   10. shouldn't make

B. 1. you should take classes at night
   2. you should arrive early
   3. you should be careful around machines
   4. you should obey traffic rules
   5. you should be polite to customers
   6. you should wash your hands often
   7. you should report it
   8. you should bring the receipt
   9. you should complete an accident report

U N I T 9

A. 1. have to wash the walls first
   2. have to read the instructions again
   3. has to move a lot of boxes
   4. has to wear a hard hat
   5. have to park in the back lot
   6. has to fix it
B. 1. 'd like to take
   2. 'd like to get
   3. 'd like to work
   4. 'd like to apply
   5. 'd like to have
   6. 'd like to be

U N I T 10

A. 1. didn't drive, drove
   2. finished
   3. went
   4. didn't study
   5. took
   6 didn't work
B. 1. **A** Did, work, **B** didn't, worked, helped
   2. **A** Did, study, **B** did, went, studied
   3. **A** Did, do, **B** did, drove, learned
C. 1. didn't have, had
   2. didn't run, ran
   3. didn't make, made
   4. didn't take, took
   5. didn't put, put
   6. didn't give, gave
   7. didn't write, wrote
   8. didn't take, took
   9. didn't carry, carried
   10. didn't go, went
D. 1. carefully
   2. patiently
   3. neatly
   4. politely
   5. quickly

 **Level 2**

Individual Competency Chart

Learner _____

Class _____

Teacher _____

Unit 1

	Date Presented	Date Checked	Result (✔)	Comments
1. Take telephone messages				
2. Answer the telephone at work				
3. Make telephone calls				
4. Find telephone numbers				

Unit 2

	Date Presented	Date Checked	Result (✔)	Comments
1. Get supplies				
2. Organize materials				
3. Maintain supplies and equipment				
4. Use filing systems				

Individual Competency Chart

 **Level 2**

Individual Competency Chart

Learner _____

Class _____

Teacher _____

Unit 3

	Date Presented	Date Checked	Result (✔)	Comments
1. Complete a maintenance report				
2. Talk about problems with machines				
3. Read a user's manual				

Unit 4

	Date Presented	Date Checked	Result (✔)	Comments
1. Understand schedules				
2. Interpret a holiday schedule				
3. Use calendars and planners				

 **Level 2**

Individual Competency Chart

Learner _____

Class _____

Teacher _____

Unit 5

	Date Presented	Date Checked	Result (✔)	Comments
1. Respond to requests				
2. Handle special requests				
3. Offer suggestions				
4. Understand customer service policies				

Unit 6

	Date Presented	Date Checked	Result (✔)	Comments
1. Follow rules				
2. Make compromises				
3. Understand company goals				
4. Get along with others				

Individual Competency Chart

Level 2

Individual Competency Chart

Learner _____

Class _____

Teacher _____

Unit 7

	Date Presented	Date Checked	Result (✔)	Comments
1. Understand a paycheck				
2. Report mistakes in your paycheck				
3. Understand Social Security				
4. Understand a W-2 form				

Unit 8

	Date Presented	Date Checked	Result (✔)	Comments
1. Understand safety instructions				
2. Follow safety instructions				
3. Complete an accident report				
4. Report unsafe situations				

Individual Competency Chart

Learner _____

Class _____

Teacher _____

Unit 9

	Date Presented	Date Checked	Result (✔)	Comments
1. Understand an agenda				
2. Prepare for a meeting				
3. Ask questions in a meeting				
4. Make meetings work for you				

Unit 10

	Date Presented	Date Checked	Result (✔)	Comments
1. Look for a job				
2. Interview for a job				
3. Understand hiring decisions				
4. Complete a job application				

Individual Competency Chart

Class Cumulative Competency Chart

Unit _____

Class _____

Teacher _____

Workforce Skills

Name | | | | | | | | | **Comments**

Name									Comments

English ASAP:
Connecting English to the Workplace
Certificate of Completion

This is to certify that

_____

has successfully completed Level 2 of
Steck-Vaughn's English ASAP series

Instructor _____

Organization or Program _____

City and State _____   Date _____

STECK-VAUGHN®
COMPANY

A Division of Harcourt Brace & Company